JN044066

学ぶ人は、
変えて
ゆく人だ。

目の前にある問題はもちろん、

人生の問いや、

社会の課題を自ら見つけ、

挑み続けるために、人は学ぶ。

「学び」で、

少しずつ世界は変えてゆける。

いつでも、どこでも、誰でも、

学ぶことができる世の中へ。

旺文社

7日間完成

文部科学省後援

英検®準1級 予想問題ドリル

[6訂版]

英検®は，公益財団法人 日本英語検定協会の登録商標です。

はじめに

　もうすぐ試験本番─そんなときに一番大事な英検対策は，試験形式に慣れることです。

　『7日間完成 英検 予想問題ドリル』シリーズは，7日間で試験本番に向けて，直前の総仕上げができる問題集です。目安として1日1セットずつ学習することで，最新の試験形式に慣れることができ，合格への実力が養成されるように構成されています。

　本書には以下のような特長があります。

本番に限りなく近い予想問題！
過去問分析を基にした本番に近い予想問題を収録しています。
学習スタイルに合わせて音声が聞ける！
リスニングアプリ「英語の友」を使ってスマホでの音声再生が可能です。また，PCからの音声ファイルダウンロードにも対応しています。
面接（スピーキングテスト）にも対応！
本書1冊で面接対策までカバーしています。
採点・見直しが簡単にできる！
各Dayの筆記試験・リスニングテストは採点・見直し学習アプリ「学びの友」対応。
解答をオンラインマークシートに入力するだけで簡単に採点ができます。

　本書を活用し，合格に向かってラストスパートをかけてください！

　皆さんの英検準1級合格を心より願っています。

　最後に，本書を刊行するにあたり，多大なご尽力をいただきました入江泉先生に深く感謝の意を表します。

※本書の内容は，2024年2月時点の情報に基づいています。実際の試験とは異なる場合があります。受験の際は，英検ウェブサイト等で最新情報をご確認ください。
※本書は旧版である5訂版の収録問題を，2024年度以降の試験形式に合わせて問題追加・再編集したものです。
※このコンテンツは，公益財団法人 日本英語検定協会の承認や推奨，その他の検討を受けたものではありません。

Contents

執筆：入江泉

編集協力：株式会社シー・レップス，鹿島由紀子，Richard Knobbs，内藤香，株式会社友人社，Elizabeth Nishitateno，Peter Vincent，Nadia McKechnie，Jason A. Chau

デザイン：相馬敬徳（Rafters）

装丁イラスト：根津あやぼ　**本文イラスト**：有限会社アート・ワーク

録音：ユニバ合同会社

ナレーション：Ann Slater，Jack Merluzzi，Rachel Walzer，Michael Rhys，Emma Howard，大武芙由美

本書の使い方

本書を以下のような流れに沿って使うことで，7日間で対策をすることができます。

┌───┐
│ **❶試験について知る** │
│ 本冊p.5「英検準1級の試験形式と攻略法」をよく読んで内容を把握しましょう。 │
└───┘

─── **Day 1～7に7日間取り組む** ───

┌───┐
│ **❷問題を解く** │
│ 模試 に挑戦しましょう。 │
│ ●制限時間内に解きましょう。 │
│ ●付属のマークシートもしくは自動採点サービス(詳しくはp.4)で解答しま │
│ しょう。 │
└───┘

┌───┐
│ **❸答え合わせをする** │
│ 別冊の「解答と解説」で答え合わせをしましょう。 │
│ ●どの技能も7割以上正解していれば，合格の可能性は高いでしょう。 │
└───┘

音声について

本書の音声は，以下の2通りでご利用いただけます。

音声ファイルで再生

詳しくはp.4をご覧ください。収録箇所は 🔊 **001** などで示しています。

アプリ「英語の友」(iOS/Android) で再生

❶「英語の友」公式サイトより，アプリをインストール

　（右の二次元コードから読み込めます）

　https://eigonotomo.com/　　英語の友　　検索

❷ライブラリより本書を選び，「追加」ボタンをタップ

※本アプリの機能の一部は有料ですが，本書の音声は無料でお聞きいただけます。アプリの詳しいご利用方法は「英語の
　友」公式サイト，あるいはアプリ内のヘルプをご参照ください。
※本サービスは予告なく終了することがあります。

Web特典について ※本サービスは予告なく終了することがあります。

アクセス方法

❶以下のURLにアクセス（右の二次元コードから読み込めます）

https://eiken.obunsha.co.jp/yosoudrill/

❷「準1級」を選択し，以下の利用コードを入力

gtbecr ※すべて半角アルファベット小文字

特典内容

音声ファイルダウンロード

「音声データダウンロード」からファイルをダウンロードし，展開してからオーディオプレーヤーで再生してください。音声ファイルはzip形式にまとめられた形でダウンロードされます。展開後，デジタルオーディオプレーヤーなどで再生してください。

※音声の再生にはMP3を再生できる機器等が必要です。
※ご利用機器，音声再生ソフト等に関する技術的なご質問は，ハードメーカーまたはソフトメーカーにお願いいたします。

スピーキングテスト対策

スピーキングテストの予想問題が体験できます。画面と音声の指示に従い，受験者になったつもりで音読したり，面接委員の質問に答えたりしましょう。問題は巻末に収録されている面接問題で，巻末の二次元コードを読み込むことでもアクセスできます。

自動採点サービスについて

本書収録の筆記試験・リスニングテストを，採点・見直し学習アプリ「学びの友」で簡単に自動採点することができます。（ライティングは自己採点です）

□ 便利な自動採点機能で学習結果がすぐにわかる

□ 学習履歴から間違えた問題を抽出して解き直しができる

□ 学習記録カレンダーで自分のがんばりを可視化

❶「学びの友」公式サイトへアクセス(右の二次元コードから読み込めます)

https://manatomo.obunsha.co.jp/ 　学びの友　｜検索

❷アプリを起動後，「旺文社まなびID」に会員登録（無料）

❸アプリ内のライブラリより本書を選び，「追加」ボタンをタップ

※iOS／Android端末，Webブラウザよりご利用いただけます。アプリの動作環境については「学びの友」公式サイトをご参照ください。なお，本アプリは無料でご利用いただけます。
※詳しいご利用方法は「学びの友」公式サイト，あるいはアプリ内ヘルプをご参照ください。
※本サービスは予告なく終了することがあります。

英検準1級の試験形式と攻略法

筆記試験（**90**分）

1 短文の語句空所補充　　目標時間**10**分　｜　**18**問

短文または短い会話文の空所に入る適切な語句を4つの選択肢から選ぶ問題です。18問中最後の4問の選択肢は，2〜3語から成る句動詞が出題されます。

攻略法　攻略には幅広い分野に関する豊富な語彙を必要とします。解く際は，次の2つのステップを踏むとよいでしょう。

①　与えられた文の状況をつかみ，文脈や構文から空所内に入る語句の意味を推測する。
1問当たり30〜40秒程度を目安に解く必要がありますので，英文を読むときは後戻りせずに，頭から内容をつかむようにし，空所に入る語句の意味を推測します。
②　意味や用法などの面から，選択肢を慎重に検討し，正解を絞り込む。
意味はもちろん，用法やコロケーションも考えて，最適な語句を絞り込みましょう。

2 長文の語句空所補充　　目標時間**15**分　｜　**6**問

250語前後の長文2つにそれぞれ空所が3カ所ずつ（計6カ所）あり，空所に入る適切な語句を4つの選択肢から選び，英文を完成させる問題です。

攻略法　時事問題，社会問題，文化，科学技術などさまざまなジャンルの長文が出題されます。空所に入る選択肢としては，述部（動詞を中心としたまとまり）・接続表現・名詞句などがあります。効率的に解答するために，次の2つのステップを踏むとよいでしょう。

①　各段落における論旨の展開を確認しながら，全体の大きな流れや主張を捉える。
空所の前後のみを検討しても，入るべき語句の判断がつかない場合もあるので，段落全体の論旨の展開を読み取りましょう。
②　各空所の前後を精読し，空所に入る語句を推測した上で，選択肢を絞り込む。
空所の前後で文脈がどのように流れるのかを把握し，空所に入る語句を考えましょう。空所に入る語としても，それ以外の部分にある語としても，以下のような接続表現を押さえることが大切です。
　　順接：accordingly, consequently, hence, therefore, that's why
　　逆接：however, nevertheless
　　例示：for example, for instance
　　追加：further, furthermore, moreover

3 長文の内容一致選択 | 目標時間**25分** | **7問**

それぞれ約400語，500語の2つの長文に対して，内容を問う設問が計7問出題され，4つの選択肢の中から長文の内容と合うものを選ぶ問題です。速読と緻密な読みの両方が要求されます。

攻略法　長文の内容は，時事問題，社会，文化，国際，生物，歴史，科学技術など多岐にわたりますが，専門的な知識がないと解けない問題が出題されることはありません。時間内に解答するには，次の3つのステップを手際よく進める必要があるでしょう。

① **全体にざっと目を通して，論理展開の流れや筆者の主張の大筋をつかむ。**
速読が求められます。内容がすべてがわからなくても，論理展開が把握できれば構いません。文全体を把握する上ではタイトルが役立つこともあります。
② **設問に目を移し，何が問われているのかを押さえた後，本文から該当箇所を探す。**
設問中の重要表現やキーワードに着目し，本文の該当箇所を探します。たいていの場合，段落の順序どおりに設問が設けられています。常に全体を視野に入れ，読み直すべき箇所を探すようにしましょう。
③ **該当箇所を精読し，選択肢を慎重に検討して正解を絞り込む。**
正解の選択肢は通常，本文の表現をそのまま使用せず別の表現に言い換えられています。また逆に本文の表現を使用した誤答選択肢もあります。検討は慎重に行いましょう。

4 英作文（要約問題） | 目標時間**20分** | **1問**

200語程度の英文を読み，その要約文を60〜70語で書きます。専門的な予備知識は必要ないですが，英文を読む力が必要です。

攻略法　英文は3段落構成で，〈第1段落：導入（話題提起），第2段落：肯定的側面，第3段落：否定的側面〉の展開がよくあるパターンです。以下のステップに沿って，準備から見直しまで含めて20分程度で解答が作成できるように練習しましょう。

① **英文を読み，話題・要点を押さえる。**
② **各段落の要点を短くまとめ，解答を作成する。**
　解答では英文の論理展開を維持することが大事です。第2段落と第3段落が対照的な内容であれば，On the other handやHoweverなどを使ってつなげます。
　〈要点のまとめ方〉
　・重要な情報を見極める。細かい数字や，such asやincludingに続く具体的な例，冗長な補足情報などは省く。
　・具体的な内容は抽象化する。〈主語＋動詞〉を含む文を「句」で表す練習が効果的。
③ **全体を読み返し，文法や語彙，スペルミスをチェックする。**
　要約文は，英文を読んでいない人，予備知識がない人にも伝わるような内容でなければなりません。見直しの際は，この観点を意識して読みましょう。

英作文（要約問題）では**内容・構成・語彙・文法**の4つの観点から採点されます。上で挙げたような要点のまとめ方（内容）や論理展開（構成）のほか，指示文に「できるだ

け自分自身の言葉で」とあることから，意味を変えずに文章を短く表したり，別の表現に言い換えたりする力（語彙・文法）が評価されます。

---

5 英作文（意見論述問題）　｜　目標時間**20分**　｜　1問

TOPIC に関するエッセイを120〜150語で書きます。自分の立場（賛成・反対など）を支持する論拠として，与えられた4つのPOINTS のうち，2つを使用する必要があります。

攻略法　以下のステップに沿って，20分程度で解答が作成できるよう練習しましょう。

① **TOPIC を注意深く読む。**
② **自分の立場・主張を述べるのに使用するPOINTS を2つ決める。**
③ **解答を作成する。**（基本は4段落構成・本論の段落が2つ）
　　1）序論（introduction）：自身の立場を明確にする。
　　2）本論（main body）：論拠1（POINT 1）/ 論拠2（POINT 2）
　　3）結論（conclusion）：自身の立場を再度確認し，提示する。
④ **全体を読み返し，文法や語彙，スペルミスをチェックする。**

英作文（意見論述問題）でも，内容・構成・語彙・文法の4つの観点から採点されます。③で挙げたような論理的な内容と構成，適切な語彙・文法の使用が求められます。無理に難しい単語を使うよりも，誤りが少なく全体的に読みやすい文章であることが重要です。また，立場や使用するPOINTSを決める際には，自分の考えと同じかどうかや社会的・道徳的に優れているかといった観点だけで選ぶのではなく，英語で説得力ある内容が書けるものを選ぶのも重要です。

リスニングテスト（約**30分**）

Part 1 会話の内容一致選択　｜　放送回数1回　｜　12問

100 語前後のやり取りから成る男女の会話とそれに関する質問を聞き，問題冊子にある4つの選択肢の中から答えを選ぶ形式です。

攻略法　会話の内容は，家族や友人との日常会話，職場や学校での雑談，公共施設や店舗でのやり取り，電話での会話など，多岐にわたります。それほど専門的な話は出題されません。質問は会話の後に放送されるので最後までしっかりと会話全体の内容を聞き取りましょう。

　会話文の聞き取りでは，会話をしている男性と女性の関係や場面を推測し，どちらが何を言ったか最後までしっかり押さえることがポイントです。

　質問の聞き取りでは，誰/何について，いつのことを問う質問かを正しく聞き取りましょう。質問は，内容と合っているものを問うもの，話者の意図や今後の行動を問うもの，理由や問題点を問うものなど，多岐にわたります。

Part 2 文の内容一致選択　　　放送回数1回　　12問

150 語前後の英文とそれに関する2つの質問を放送で聞き，質問に対する答えを問題冊子にある4つの選択肢から選ぶ形式です。英文は6つ（計12問）あります。

攻略法　放送される英文のトピックは科学上の発見，新技術，動物の生態，新しいスポーツ，歴史的な事件，海外の風習，芸術家の話など，多岐にわたります。その中には聞き慣れない人名や地名，専門用語，新しい概念などがよく登場しますが，それを気にしていると大事なところを聞き逃してしまいます。わからない語が出てきても気にせず聞き取りを続けましょう。

　　質問は，ほとんどがWhatで始まる疑問文で，WhyとHowで始まる疑問文が出題されることもあります。すなわち聞き取るポイントは「何が話題となっているのか」「何が起きたのか」「何をすることになったのか」や，「なぜ」「どのようにして」です。

Part 3 Real-Life 形式の内容一致選択　　　放送回数1回　　5問

問題冊子の「状況」「質問」「選択肢」を10 秒間で読んだ後，アナウンスなどの日常生活で耳にする100語前後の英文を放送で聞き，4つの選択肢から質問に対する答えを選ぶ形式です。

攻略法　留守番電話のメッセージ，自動音声案内，館内放送，ガイドの説明，大学職員のアドバイス，交通情報など，日常生活に根差した素材が放送されます。臨場感あふれる効果音を伴う場合もあります。このパートのポイントは，問題冊子にある「状況」「質問」「選択肢」に事前に目を通し，聞き取るべき情報を把握した上で，放送を聞くという点です。

　　「状況」は必ず主語がYouです。その状況に自分が置かれたことを想像して，自分にとって必要な情報のみを聞き取ることがポイントとなります。「質問」は，与えられた「状況」の中で「何をするべきか」や「何を選ぶべきか」を問うものがほとんどです。

リスニングテストの指示文

準1級のリスニングテストで放送される英語の指示文は以下のとおりです。

The listening test for the Grade Pre-1 examination is about to begin. Listen carefully to the directions. You will not be permitted to ask questions during the test. This test has three parts. All of the questions in these three parts are multiple-choice questions. For each question, choose the best answer from among the four choices written in your test booklet. On your answer sheet, find the number of the question and mark your answer. You are permitted to take notes for every part of this listening test.

Part 1 Now, here are the directions for Part 1. In this part, you will hear 12 dialogues, No. 1 through No. 12. Each dialogue will be followed by one question. For each question, you will have 10 seconds to choose the best answer and mark your answer on your answer sheet. The dialogue and the question will be given only once. Now, we will begin the Grade Pre-1 listening test.

Part 2 Here are the directions for Part 2. In this part, you will hear six passages, (A) through (F). Each passage will be followed by two questions, No. 13 through No. 24. For each question, you will have 10 seconds to choose the best answer and mark your answer on your answer sheet. The passage and the questions will be given only once. Now, let's begin.

Part 3 Finally, here are the directions for Part 3. In this part, you will hear five passages, (G) through (K). The passages represent real-life situations and may contain sound effects. Each passage will have one question, No. 25 through No. 29. Before each passage, you will have 10 seconds to read the situation and question written in your test booklet. After you hear the passage, you will have 10 seconds to choose the best answer and mark your answer on your answer sheet. The passage will be given only once. Now, let's begin.

Your time is up. Stop writing and wait quietly until the answer sheets have been collected.

面接（スピーキングテスト）（約8分）

簡単な日常会話の後, 4コマのイラストの付いた問題カードが渡されます。1分間の準備時間に続いて2分間でナレーションをします。それから, 4つの質問をされます。

問題	形式・課題詳細
自由会話	面接委員と簡単な日常会話を行う。
ナレーション	4コマのイラストの展開を説明する。
No. 1	イラストに関連した質問に答える。
No. 2／No. 3	カードのトピックに関連した内容についての質問に答える。
No. 4	カードのトピックにやや関連した, 社会性のある内容についての質問に答える。

面接（スピーキングテスト）については, 本冊p.102「準1級の面接（スピーキングテスト）はどんなテスト？」でより詳しく説明しています。

筆記試験

試験時間 **筆記90分**

1　*To complete each item, choose the best word or phrase from among the four choices. Then, on your answer sheet, find the number of the question and mark your answer.*

---

(1)　**A:** Welcome to the Houston Health Clinic and Gym. What exactly is your (　　　)?

B: I want to lose 30 pounds by summer.

1 observation　　**2** reflection　　**3** reaction　　**4** objective

(2)　The congresswoman has an excellent record in (　　　). She often proposes and supports regulations for environmental protection.

1 conservation　**2** corruption　**3** exploration　**4** extension

(3)　The history professor (　　　) a lecture about George Washington, the first American president.

1 besieged　　**2** congregated　　**3** delivered　　**4** indented

(4)　At the time when she boarded the boat, little did Karen know that she was (　　　) on the adventure of a lifetime.

1 filtering　　**2** portraying　　**3** embarking　　**4** intervening

(5)　Doctors believe one reason for the rising (　　　) of back problems among young people is the heavy backpacks they carry to school.

1 intolerance　　**2** inheritance　　**3** incidence　　**4** insertion

(6)　She gave (　　　) love to her husband. She trusted and supported him even when he was having hard times.

1 unconditional　**2** unauthorized　**3** exaggerated　**4** expedient

(7)　After weeks of intense debate, the Diet finally (　　　) the administration's annual budget proposal.

1 approximated　**2** embezzled　**3** endorsed　　**4** admonished

(8) The police fired tear gas to (　　　) the riot and stop the demonstrators from rampaging through the streets.

1 quell　　　　**2** rouse　　　　**3** stir　　　　**4** incite

(9) You must take your knee problem seriously. If you do not get proper medical treatment, it will become (　　　).

1 chronic　　　**2** reckless　　　**3** neutral　　　**4** expectant

(10) According to club regulations, wearing a tie and jacket in the dining hall is (　　　). You really have no choice.

1 collective　　**2** nomadic　　　**3** protective　　**4** compulsory

(11) *A:* Why are you in such a hurry to get a new job?
B: As a foreigner, I want to get a full-time job before my work visa (　　　).

1 asserts　　　**2** expires　　　**3** inserts　　　**4** inspires

(12) *A:* My parents pushed me into studying economics at university. I really wanted to be a musician.
B: So, that's why you're so (　　　) to your studies.

1 vigorous　　**2** indifferent　　**3** enduring　　**4** meager

(13) In order to inspect the home of the suspected thief, the police had to get a search (　　　) from the court.

1 citation　　　**2** grant　　　**3** deed　　　**4** warrant

(14) Trains in Tokyo are sometimes so (　　　) packed with commuters that those waiting on a platform find it impossible to board their train.

1 sparsely　　**2** densely　　　**3** clumsily　　**4** devoutly

(15) After some early defeats, the team (　　　) to win the championship.

1 passed down　**2** dropped in　**3** mixed up　**4** bounced back

(16) I kept raising my hand in class, but the teacher never (　　　) me. I talked to the teacher after class, who explained that he wanted to give shyer students more chances to speak.

1 told off　　　　　　　　**2** spoke out
3 talked through　　　　　**4** called on

Day 1
Day 2
Day 3
Day 4
Day 5
Day 6
Day 7

(17) Megan had a bad headache and took a pain reliever. However, the effects of the medicine (   ) after a few hours, so she had to take another one.

    1 dropped out   **2** wore off   **3** took off   **4** fell out

(18) While hiking along the trail, please (   ) for falling rocks, especially in places where you walk below the cliff.

    1 make out   **2** look out   **3** catch up   **4** see off

（筆記試験の問題は次のページに続きます。）

Day
1

Day
2

Day
3

Day
4

Day
5

Day
6

Day
7

Read each passage and choose the best word or phrase from among the four choices for each blank. Then, on your answer sheet, find the number of the question and mark your answer.

A Changing World

One of the biggest challenges for businesses these days is keeping up with change—in technology, laws, and trends, for example. In order to do this successfully, businesses need flexible thinkers who are not afraid to embrace non-traditional methods. However, people who fit into these roles are difficult to find. Therefore, (**19**) searching for the perfect match in a new employee, businesses are using improvisation to develop the skill set of their current employees.

Improvisation, also known as improv, is a type of theater performance that is created spontaneously, or without a script, by the actors. Contrary to popular belief, improv requires planning and practice to cultivate the ability to act and react in the moment. The most important rule in improv is to answer every statement with "yes, and." Saying "yes" shows openness and acceptance of the speaker's idea and creates a positive stage for communication. Adding "and" followed by a statement builds on what the person has said. This (**20**). The "yes, and" rule in business fosters cooperation and encourages employees to bring their ideas to the table for brainstorming and problem solving.

Improv techniques are expected to be especially useful in developing future leaders from the current generation of college students. Not only is this generation more open emotionally than previous generations, but they also learn well by doing, are excellent collaborators, and enjoy social interaction—characteristics that (**21**). As more business schools in the U.S. integrate improv courses into their curriculums, we can expect the idea to become more mainstream.

---

(19) **1** instead of **2** similar to **3** thanks to **4** except for

(20) **1** helps co-workers get to know each other
   2 highlights which employees should be promoted
   3 can transform work into fun
   4 is the basis for teamwork and collaboration

(21) **1** are generally developed on the job
   2 people generally possess in their youth
   3 reflect those necessary in improv
   4 require great effort to master

Senegal's Pink Lake

Senegal's Lake Retba is famous around the world for its pink water. The color comes from algae called *Dunaliella salina*, which has high concentrations of β-carotene. The reason *Dunaliella salina* flourishes in Lake Retba is because of (**22**). Severe droughts in the 1970s had transformed the fishing lake into one for salt harvesting.

Responding to these environmental changes, companies sprang up nearby to collect and sell salt from the lake. Men broke up the salt at the bottom of the lake with sticks and dove to collect it. Besides this being intense labor, the corrosive nature of the salty water (**23**). To avoid this, salt diggers rubbed shea butter on their bodies before entering the lake. With boats full of salt, the men returned to shore where women unloaded it and created huge mounds along the lake. The salt was mixed with amounts of the element, called iodine, bagged, and sold mostly to fishermen for preserving fish.

Unfortunately, problems quickly emerged. Dishonest companies failed to pay wages and constantly violated workers' rights. Construction around Lake Retba interfered with water runoff. Salt was being collected from the whole lake without letting areas recover. (**24**), in 1994, the community took responsibility into their own hands. The five villages surrounding Lake Retba elected representatives and formed the Management Committee. Thanks to the committee, both workers and the environment now have an advocate. While there are still issues to be addressed, the community's decision to take action was a powerful step in the right direction.

---

(22)
1 a change in the locals' regular diet
2 a decrease in recreational sports on the lake
3 the introduction of new fish to the lake
4 the high salt content of the water

(23)
1 led to the creation of a new industry
2 caused a high turnover of workers
3 brought about skin problems
4 drove workers to invent new tools

(24)
1 Moreover
3 Nonetheless
2 Consequently
4 Likewise

Day 1 Day 2 Day 3 Day 4 Day 5 Day 6 Day 7

Read each passage and choose the best answer from among the four choices for each question. Then, on your answer sheet, find the number of the question and mark your answer.

Health and the Hard Sell

The differences in product advertising on the Internet highlight disparities between American and British health cultures. Tap into the Internet and the user will find a vast range of health experts advertising their services and proclaiming forth upon every syndrome, illness, or disorder imaginable. Pick up any American magazine, especially of the lifestyle variety, and there is an abundance of advertisements for doctors, medical services, and prescription-only drugs. These drug advertisements are of the type only found in medical journals in Britain. Turn on the television and one is exposed to yet more drug companies' advertisements, or talk shows presenting celebrity physicians discussing their latest book. From the British point of view, it would seem that Americans are being bombarded with so much health information that their health-care decisions become overly complex.

Many conscientious American doctors think that this form of advertising is unethical and that it is putting doctors in the position of having to defend their prescription choices to patients who are only superficially informed about the drugs they've been persuaded to want and may well not need. The problem becomes one of half-informed patient against professional doctor. Other doctors believe that it is a good thing for patients to be as informed as possible, and if the Internet, and advertising in general, can promote this, then it is not a bad thing.

This portrait of the American health consumer or patient is very different from the British counterpart—lining up, waiting for appointments at a National Health Service surgery, and worrying about wasting the doctor's time. Also very different is the still-present attitude in Britain of doctor knows best, which often halts questioning or discussion between patient and doctor regarding new developments in the medical field.

Although Britain's General Medical Council has recently changed its guidelines to allow doctors to advertise, the conservative medical profession generally holds the strong view that such self-promotion is improper. However, advertisements provide a means through which much needed information may be passed on to people, so some regard this fear of being associated with commercialism as a form of snobbery. Change is also gradually happening in Britain with the increased use of the Internet to access medical websites, television dramas bringing medical terminology into the home, and a raised awareness of what is available in health services.

(25) According to the passage, which of the following is true?
1 There is greater focus on advertising to patients in the U.S.
2 Medical information in the media is more readily available in Britain.
3 The majority of American doctors agree that drug and doctor promotions benefit patients.
4 Americans are much more suspicious of information in the media than British people.

(26) How do many British people see Americans?
1 They believe Americans are so overwhelmed with medical information that choices become unnecessarily difficult.
2 They think Americans are fortunate to have so much medical information at their disposal, and are better off than British patients.
3 They think that the information Americans gain from the Internet gives them a false sense of expertise, when they should rely on the doctor instead.
4 They see Americans as too nonchalant about their health care, and believe Americans should be more skeptical of advertisements.

(27) What changes are occurring in British health care?
1 Doctors are pushing their patients to ask more questions and become more informed.
2 The majority of physicians are beginning to advertise in the media.
3 More people are becoming informed about medicine and health care.
4 Conservative doctors have pushed for new laws to block medical advertising.

A New Look at Anne Hathaway

Journalists and scholarly critics of William Shakespeare have not been kind to Shakespeare's wife, Anne Hathaway. They paint her as a plain woman who, at 26 years of age, seduced 18-year-old William and, through her pregnancy, forced him to marry her. Shakespeare was said to have escaped his unhappy home life in Stratford-upon-Avon for the more exciting and freer life of London, where he gained success as a playwright. They cite Shakespeare's omission of Anne from his will as evidence of marital estrangement.

However, biographer and feminist Germaine Greer disagrees with this portrait. Citing documentary evidence from Elizabethan times, Greer argues in *Shakespeare's Wife* that Hathaway was actually loved by Shakespeare. In fact, she may have been the model for the solid women in Shakespeare's plays who were faithful in their love despite long periods of separation. So why the negative perception of Hathaway by Shakespeare scholars? Greer says, "The possibility that a wife may be closer to their idol than they could ever be, understood him better than they ever could, could not be entertained." She believes that the younger William really did fall in love with the older Anne, but for her, the marriage was far from an ideal pairing. She was a wealthy landowner who would benefit little from seducing a teenager who had nothing more than pennies and a primary school education. She was likely not so desperate to find a mate at 26 as so often portrayed, for the average age for an Elizabethan woman to marry was a very mature 27. Furthermore, if she had truly seduced a teenager against his will, she would surely have been in trouble with legal officials in her village: there is no record or mention of such an event.

Though Shakespeare and Hathaway lived separately for the majority of their married life, she never denounced him, nor did he denounce her. Hathaway faithfully raised Shakespeare's three children through harsh times and she made her success independently as a producer of malt as well as a moneylender. Hathaway was the one to purchase and prepare New Place, the large and elegant home which Shakespeare would return to and retire in.

Greer is careful not to overplay her hand by showing Hathaway as free of faults. She concedes that Hathaway was most likely lonely from the years of separation from her husband and she probably feared that he was not always loyal to her, for villagers and others who had visited London reported that Shakespeare had other girlfriends—and even boyfriends. Moreover, after the publication of Shakespeare's *Venus and Adonis*, an erotic poem about a desirous older woman, Hathaway was likely open to ridicule.

Greer's book is a real researched work that is as much a social history of

Shakespeare's time as a biography of his wife. Hathaway is used as a vehicle to show the life, customs, and rituals of the time. While scholars may rightly find fault in certain liberties that Greer takes in her eager defense of Hathaway, the majority of the assertions are clearly based on more solid evidence than are the majority of facts used to disparage her.

---

(28) What does Greer say about the image that scholars have drawn of Anne Hathaway?
  1 It is fairly accurate in most regards, except that Hathaway loved Shakespeare more than Shakespeare loved her.
  2 It is primarily based on the model of women that Shakespeare drew for many of his plays.
  3 It is too simplistic, for the image is derived only from known facts of their early marriage.
  4 It is overly negative and does not reflect the facts reported in texts from Shakespeare's period.

(29) Greer argues that scholars have created the common image of Hathaway because
  1 their assumptions are based on misleading documentary evidence.
  2 they are jealous of the intimacy and personal knowledge she had of the playwright.
  3 it makes a more entertaining story than a portrait of a common wife.
  4 Hathaway is a convenient scapegoat for some negative stories about Shakespeare.

(30) What does Greer suggest about the marriage of Shakespeare and Hathaway?
  1 There is no evidence indicating that Hathaway could possibly profit from forcing Shakespeare to marry her.
  2 Though there are indications she did seduce Shakespeare against his will, they actually loved each other at the time of their marriage.
  3 Hathaway was 26 years old at the time of their marriage and, worried about her age, she likely prodded Shakespeare to marry her.
  4 Shakespeare was not well educated and poor, so it was more likely he, rather than Hathaway, who pushed for marriage.

筆記試験

Day 1
Day 2
Day 3
Day 4
Day 5
Day 6
Day 7

(31) What does the author of the passage imply about Greer's interpretation of Hathaway?

1 It is clearly supported by Greer's in-depth research so scholars are beginning to accept it.

2 Despite Greer's bias, it is more credible than the more common, negative assertions about Hathaway.

3 In Greer's eager pursuit of Hathaway's defense, her interpretation is fundamentally flawed and not worthy of serious consideration.

4 It paints too demeaning a picture of Hathaway, though many of her facts are clearly accurate.

4 English Summary

● Instructions: Read the article below and summarize it in your own words as far as possible in English.

● Suggested length: 60-70 words

● Write your summary in the space provided on your answer sheet. <u>Any writing outside the space will not be graded.</u>

Around 85 million years ago, New Zealand became separated from an ancient supercontinent. For ages, there were no land animals that would eat birds, and it is believed that this caused a number of native bird species to become flightless. In the modern era, humans inhabited the country and introduced non-native species such as rats and stoats, wiping out nearly a third of native flightless bird species. In response to this, in the 2010s, the government began taking steps to remove animals that hunt birds.

The plan to get rid of these predators is showing success, as New Zealand's population of native birds is recovering in some areas. Over time, this will help reduce the decline of native birds and increase their numbers further. It also has the additional benefits of protecting native plants and trees, where the birds often nest.

Nevertheless, some critics think that the mass destruction of intelligent creatures like rats is cruel. Additionally, the plan is to exterminate the pests by 2050, which will require a long-term commitment for the organizations involved. Most critics agree that this will end up becoming extremely expensive, costing millions of dollars for staff and equipment.

Day 1
Day 2
Day 3
Day 4
Day 5
Day 6
Day 7

5 English Composition

- Write an essay on the given **TOPIC**.
- Use TWO of the **POINTS** below to support your answer.
- Structure: introduction, main body, and conclusion
- Suggested length: 120-150 words
- Write your essay in the space provided on your answer sheet. <u>Any writing outside the space will not be graded.</u>

TOPIC
Should companies in Japan take action to reduce plastic waste?

POINTS
- *Cost*
- *Environment*
- *Excess packaging*
- *Reuse*

リスニングテスト

試験時間 リスニング約30分

There are three parts to this listening test.

Part 1	**Dialogues:** 1 question each	Multiple-choice
Part 2	**Passages:** 2 questions each	Multiple-choice
Part 3	**Real-Life:** 1 question each	Multiple-choice

※Listen carefully to the instructions.

Part 1 ◀﮿) 001～013

No. 1
1 Extend a deadline for his thesis.
2 Accept his absence for a week.
3 Allow him to send his work by e-mail.
4 Let him take a computer home.

No. 2
1 Discuss the matter with their son.
2 Hire a private teacher for their son.
3 Consult with their son's brass band instructor.
4 Ask their son's teacher about his grades.

No. 3
1 He is nervous about his new job.
2 He is unhappy about a job change.
3 Living abroad will be exciting.
4 Renting a house will cost money.

No. 4
1 Megan's behavior is out of character.
2 Megan's manners need to improve.
3 Megan is behaving normally for her age.
4 Megan is unhappy with her parents' reaction.

No. 5
1 Shorten the proposal.
2 Attend the meeting.
3 Make some phone calls.
4 Arrive at work later than usual.

No. 6	**1** Meet her downtown for dinner.
	2 Pick her up at the suburban office.
	3 Bring the food she wants home.
	4 Cook her a meal at their house.

No. 7	**1** He cannot take vacations during the holiday season.
	2 He does not take enough vacations.
	3 His vacations coincide with tourist seasons.
	4 His company provides a lot of vacation time.

No. 8	**1** She works for Japan Network Communications.
	2 She produces Internet communication systems.
	3 She has recently joined a new company.
	4 She is in the international sales office.

No. 9	**1** The man had some trouble at the hospital.
	2 The man's shoulder bone does not hurt anymore.
	3 The man is no longer in rehabilitation.
	4 The man will recover in another half year.

No. 10	**1** The New York office is doing better than his office.
	2 He hopes to work in the New York office next year.
	3 Sales in his office are actually dropping.
	4 He is not enjoying the conference.

No. 11	**1** The couple was not home at the time.
	2 The delivery has been delayed.
	3 It was delivered to the wrong address.
	4 The delivery person thought the couple was out.

No. 12	**1** It is the latest model.
	2 It was not so expensive.
	3 He is not very happy with it.
	4 The woman paid for it.

Part 2   ◀»)) 014～020

(A) *No. 13*   **1** It was built using the oldest way of construction.
　　　　　　　2 It transports both people and vehicles on a gondola.
　　　　　　　3 It connects two World Heritage sites.
　　　　　　　4 It is the most utilized bridge in the world.

　　　　No. 14   **1** To enable ferries to cross the broad Nervion River.
　　　　　　　2 To create a scenic spot for pleasure boats.
　　　　　　　3 To allow ferries to pass the bridge while in use.
　　　　　　　4 To save on the cost of transportation.

(B) *No. 15*   **1** He asked study participants to select a picture.
　　　　　　　2 He conducted a survey about photography.
　　　　　　　3 He asked volunteers how they make a decision.
　　　　　　　4 He picked out volunteers who answered correctly.

　　　　No. 16   **1** Investigate their perception of feelings.
　　　　　　　2 Pay attention to actions more than thoughts.
　　　　　　　3 Think ahead and make conclusive plans.
　　　　　　　4 Focus on conducting rational self-analysis.

(C) *No. 17*   **1** It started accepting animals and birds in need.
　　　　　　　2 It started keeping pets temporarily.
　　　　　　　3 It started breeding wildlife and farm animals.
　　　　　　　4 It started protecting endangered species of plants.

　　　　No. 18   **1** It tells visitors where to find good stories.
　　　　　　　2 It educates people about signs of wildlife.
　　　　　　　3 It provides opportunities to help other zoos.
　　　　　　　4 It seeks new homes for sheltered cats and dogs.

Day 1
Day 2
Day 3
Day 4
Day 5
Day 6
Day 7

No. 19 1 He put on a pair of black gloves.
2 He wore an accessory to support racial equality.
3 He refused to stand on the winners' podium.
4 He wore a badge to represent his nationality.

No. 20 1 The Australian parliament declared a Peter Norman Day.
2 Two monuments were built in Australia.
3 An apology was given by the Australian parliament.
4 His action was recognized in Australia immediately.

(E) *No. 21* 1 Their production continued to increase.
2 They began to appear in ordinary households.
3 They were bought and sold at reduced prices.
4 They began to lose popularity to radio and television.

No. 22 1 Print newspapers were the most preferred news source.
2 Many people stopped watching television.
3 The number of newspaper readers increased.
4 News via social media is more popular than newspapers.

(F) *No. 23* 1 Whether or not they had concepts of good and bad.
2 At what age they were capable of playing with dolls.
3 Whether or not they would copy the dolls' actions.
4 At what age they could learn social skills.

No. 24 1 The way the experiment was set up.
2 The use of such young infants.
3 The actual results of the study.
4 The researchers' conclusions.

(G) | **No. 25** | **Situation:** You have had a runny nose for more than a week. You visit your doctor and receive the following advice.

Question: What should you do first?

1 Switch to a different medication.
2 Have your nose checked.
3 Come back for allergy tests.
4 Stop taking allergy medication.

(H) | **No. 26** | **Situation:** You are a college student. You need help finding research materials for a paper you are writing. You want to work from your computer at home as well. You talk to one of your professors, who gives you the following advice.

Question: Where should you go first?

1 To the writing resource center.
2 To the university computer center.
3 To another professor's office.
4 To the university library.

(I) | **No. 27** | **Situation:** You are shopping at the supermarket and are looking for cheese. You hear the following directions from a store clerk.

Question: Where can you find the cheeses?

1 In aisle 1.
2 In aisle 12.
3 In the dairy section.
4 Next to the delicatessen.

(J) *No. 28* ***Situation:*** You have submitted a résumé to a job recruitment agency. You receive the following voice mail regarding your application.

Question: What should you do to complete your application?

1 Send an e-mail to Tarryton Employment.

2 Submit another online application.

3 Fill in an online survey.

4 Provide a paper copy of your résumé.

(K) *No. 29* ***Situation:*** You live in Miami, Florida and hear a long-term weather forecast on the radio. You want to prepare for the hurricane season.

Question: What should you do?

1 Listen to future reports.

2 Be prepared to evacuate.

3 Have some boards on hand.

4 Purchase extra-strength windows.

筆記試験

試験時間 筆記**90**分

1　*To complete each item, choose the best word or phrase from among the four choices. Then, on your answer sheet, find the number of the question and mark your answer.*

---

(1)　It took three weeks of hard bargaining for the union and the company to (　　　) a new agreement, but to the relief of all, they finally succeeded.

1 admonish　　**2** forge　　　**3** haunt　　　**4** inhibit

(2)　Despite the scandal, the politician eventually won the people's respect. He had the courage to (　　　) his mistakes.

1 retrieve　　**2** acknowledge　**3** browse　　**4** embellish

(3)　The economist argued that more banks would have to (　　　) to avoid bankruptcy. There were simply too many banks in a highly competitive market.

1 circulate　　**2** merge　　**3** blend　　**4** mingle

(4)　The lawyer presented solid evidence to prove that the (　　　) against his client were false, so the case was dismissed.

1 initiatives　　**2** expectations　**3** allegations　**4** contemplations

(5)　When the guest was asked to make a speech at the party, he had to (　　　) because he had not prepared anything.

1 ascend　　**2** improvise　　**3** assume　　**4** inoculate

(6)　Robots are replacing humans in such (　　　) jobs as automobile assembly. Therefore, factory workers need retraining to obtain higher skill levels so that they can take on more challenging work.

1 gratifying　　**2** reassuring　　**3** tender　　**4** tedious

(7)　*A:* I usually write my reports by hand before I type them up.
　　B: That sounds very (　　　). You would waste less time if you just typed them in the first place.

1 inefficient　　**2** unassuming　　**3** inevitable　　**4** unoriginal

(8)   The President has some (   ) critics in Congress who aim to block his every move, if not force him out of office.
1 fierce   **2** sympathetic   **3** fraudulent   **4** striking

(9)   The gangsters kidnapped the son of a wealthy businessman and demanded a (   ) of one million dollars.
1 revenue   **2** debt   **3** bond   **4** ransom

(10)   Robert often gets into arguments with his colleagues because he insists on his way and seldom changes his opinion. He needs to be less (   ) if he wants to get along with them.
1 productive   **2** startling   **3** portable   **4** stubborn

(11)   The latest edition of the magazine offers revealing new (   ) into the political campaign.
1 insights   **2** advocates   **3** telescopes   **4** revisions

(12)   The executive was dismayed to learn that his proposal for a new branch office had been (   ). It was considered too expensive in the currently sluggish market.
1 floored   **2** walled   **3** booked   **4** shelved

(13)   Everyone admits that (   ) changes are needed to democratize the country, which has long been dominated by a dictator.
1 drastic   **2** fragile   **3** illiterate   **4** lethal

(14)   Thanks to the in-depth study, there is now sufficient data to (   ) prove that eating fresh tomatoes lowers the risk of cancer.
1 intimately   **2** disdainfully   **3** perversely   **4** convincingly

(15)   The environmental conference ended last week, concluding with a resolution to (   ) gases that damage the ozone layer.
1 adhere to   **2** drag along   **3** phase out   **4** work out

(16)   *A:* Tom's decided to (   ) class president for the third time.
B: Oh, dear. I'm afraid he'll be defeated again.
1 think up   **2** feel for   **3** make up   **4** run for

(17) It came as quite a shock to learn that our company would have to (　　) half of its employees in the next three months.

1 break into　　**2** fall through　　**3** lay off　　**4** kick up

(18) Nowadays most banks around the world are required to (　　) international banking regulations and agreements.

1 allude to　　**2** conform to　　**3** testify for　　**4** substitute for

Day 1

Day 2

Day 3

Day 4

Day 5

Day 6

Day 7

Read each passage and choose the best word or phrase from among the four choices for each blank. Then, on your answer sheet, find the number of the question and mark your answer.

Surfing

Surfing is often seen as a recently-invented extreme sport, pitting courageous humans against nature. Its origins, however, are far different and stretch back much further than many imagine. Rather than being (**19**), surfing emerged in antiquity as a spiritual pursuit dominated by the aristocracy and upper classes. It is thought that the Polynesian people have been surfing for over 2,000 years in one form or another, and the ancient practice has been especially woven into the fabric of Hawaiian culture.

The first surfboards were often very long, made from wood, and could weigh up to 35kg. That is a far cry from today's lightweight carbon fiber shortboards, and it is not the only thing to have changed drastically. Modern surfers have rigorous training regimens and travel the world to compete in international competitions. For those who reach the top, the development of professional surfing has brought with it all the perks of other modern professional sports. While (**20**), today's top-level surfers can often be treated as such.

Those at the pinnacle of the sport can become world-famous and earn millions of dollars in prize money and sponsorship deals. Some, like 11-time world champion Kelly Slater, branch out into fields as varied as entrepreneurship, acting, writing, and modeling. For professionals at this level, recent developments have helped raise their profile and the profile of the sport. (**21**), the inclusion of surfing as an Olympic sport is seen by many as the ultimate validation of their dedication and lifestyle.

---

(19)   **1** a restrictive hobby of the rich and famous
         2 a modern adrenaline-fueled pastime open to everyone
         3 an ancient practice from Polynesia
         4 a noble endeavor by religious leaders

(20)   **1** some professional surfers used to be amateurs
         2 most surfers were low achievers
         3 the original surfers were actual royalty
         4 all surfers became wealthy people

(21)   **1** For instance   **2** Even so
         3 On the contrary   **4** In exchange

Two Island Nations

Japan and the British Isles are separated by a vast distance, each with their own unique culture. Superficially, the countries appear to be completely different, but scratch under the surface and some very interesting patterns manifest themselves.

Both are of a similar size, located not far off the coasts of much larger land masses. (22) has helped to protect them from many of the wars fought throughout the years, which ravaged their more-exposed neighbors, wherein entire cities were razed to the ground and several empires were shattered.

In particular, the inhabitants of these two small island nations share many common traits. They can trace their histories far back into the mists of time. They developed hierarchical societies based around the family and strong codes of honor. Both nations excel at trade and have forged strong commercial links with other countries all over the world. People who cling to their traditions are often very (23) change; however, they are certainly capable of dealing with it when absolutely necessary.

One problem both now find themselves facing is how to deal with the future which is certain to be less illustrious than their past. Their continued acceptance of this reality and the resolve to embrace (24) will be of the utmost importance in the future. The two nations must find the willpower to steer a steady course through these uncharted waters and their ability to rise to this challenge will determine their fates.

---

(22)　**1** Their relatively higher latitudes
　　　2 Their proximity to nearby islands
　　　3 This dependence on their neighbors
　　　4 This geographical isolation

(23)　**1** bent on　　　　　　**2** motivated by
　　　3 exempt from　　　　**4** resistant to

(24)　**1** a new world order　　**2** their valued traditions
　　　3 a hierarchical society　**4** isolationist policies

Read each passage and choose the best answer from among the four choices for each question. Then, on your answer sheet, find the number of the question and mark your answer.

Biodiversity Loss

Biodiversity refers to the variety and variability of life on Earth. It involves all species, from the largest to the microscopic, and the many ecosystems they form. Its importance cannot be overestimated as the air we breathe, the food we eat, and the water we drink all rely on it in one way or another. However, problems such as urban sprawl, climate change, and deforestation are threatening biodiversity, and the consequences could be disastrous. The loss of biodiversity could impact everything from food production and medicine, to the loss of ecosystems and the survival of species.

Unlike climate change, however, it is difficult to feel biodiversity loss in our everyday lives. Extreme weather, wildfires, droughts, floods, and rising temperatures are all signs of climate change that populations around the world are experiencing first-hand. The extinction of a species may not be so noticeable, but the chain reaction it causes could be devastating. Changes in biodiversity could, for example, see a microbe or insect that helps kill harmful bacteria disappear. This could in turn lead to disease, food shortages, and malnutrition. As resources become scarcer, the chain of events could lead to global shortages, price increases, political turmoil, and even war.

As a result, biodiversity loss has been referred to as a "silent killer," although increased awareness could help lead to solutions. Crucially, scientific and business interests are converging in the field to help ensure the problem is not either dominated by financial interests or simply ignored. As our lives depend on biodiversity in ways we often fail to understand, many hope that efforts to protect it will be backed by international political efforts. We are already losing troubling amounts of biodiversity, but there is room for optimism. A number of agreements have been proposed and signed which seek to underline the importance of protecting biodiversity as vital to the survival of life on Earth.

At an international level, at least, efforts to protect biodiversity have thankfully tended to be apolitical. This is important as the more the problem is politicized, the less likely it is that agreements will be ratified and repeated. That is often not the case at domestic levels, where the issues are used to score political points. Whether politically motivated or not, a concerted effort will hopefully not doom us to the prospect of perhaps being the first species to not only comprehend, but also witness our own extinction.

(25) What does the passage tell us about the importance of biodiversity?

1 The importance of biodiversity has perhaps been overestimated when discussing natural disasters.

2 All forms of life are interdependent and any damage we create could imperil our own survival.

3 Biodiversity can be enhanced through human interventions such as urbanization and intensive food production.

4 Biodiversity is considered important enough to develop new medicines to protect it.

(26) Why is biodiversity loss sometimes referred to as a "silent killer"?

1 Malnutrition is seen as a bigger threat to society, therefore the effects of biodiversity loss tend to be underplayed.

2 The effects of biodiversity loss, while serious, tend to go unnoticed by most people as they are not immediately obvious.

3 People do not see or hear insects and microbes dying, therefore they do not care about the consequences.

4 People have more important things to worry about, like fires and droughts, meaning there is a shortage of information.

(27) What problems could potentially weaken efforts to deal with biodiversity loss?

1 The science behind biodiversity loss is difficult to understand, so governments cannot attract funding for research.

2 Conflict between financial and political interests suggests that meaningful progress is unlikely.

3 The rush to politicize circumstances we do not understand highlights the level of ignorance surrounding the problem.

4 A collective international effort could be hindered by disagreements at the domestic level.

Day 1
Day 2
Day 3
Day 4
Day 5
Day 6
Day 7

The Inside Truth about Teamwork

The importance of building good teamwork for a more efficient workforce dates back to the Hawthorne studies of the 1920s and 1930s, when Harvard Business School Professor Elton Mayo conducted a series of studies to determine the relationship between the working environment and productivity. Mayo changed a number of variables in the work environment, like lighting, for instance. What he discovered was at first contradictory. No matter how he changed the lighting, whether it became darker or brighter, the workers studied showed increased productivity. The same went for other environmental variables. Mayo finally realized something quite profound: environmental variables in the workplace are far less important than teamwork. The teams in Mayo's research seemed to strengthen under the researcher's attention and imposed changes.

The Hawthorne studies spotlighted the significance of interpersonal relationships in the work environment. Since then, corporations have spent billions of dollars on team-building exercises such as team retreats and various other team exercises. However, MIT Professor Deborah Ancona and INSEAD Assistant Professor Henrik Bresman argue in their book, *X-Teams: How to Build Teams That Lead, Innovate and Succeed*, that the time and money spent on corporate teambuilding might actually be better spent elsewhere, for their decades-long research indicated that a team's external relationships are just as important as internal bonds. The authors state that more focus should be paid to external relations such as proving a team's effectiveness and value to upper management, making closer bonds with customers and others whom a team depends on, and searching for outside ideas and approaches that could effectively be adopted or implemented by the team.

Ancona discovered that the more traditional concepts of effective teamwork rested on such characteristics as team spirit and clearly delineated work roles, but that in the real business world, these characteristics had little to do with such success markers as production and sales revenue. "The internal model is burned into our brain, but research and the actual experience of many managers demonstrate that a team can function very well internally and still not deliver the desired results. In the real world, good teams, according to our own definition, often fail," says Ancona.

The authors stress that the work world has changed dramatically since Hawthorne's time. The knowledge-driven global economy of today relies more on loose hierarchies rather than tightly controlled centralized authority. Companies are more complex and, with information and strategies often changing, they must be more flexible. The distributed yet interconnected nature of global task forces and clients requires increased networking with outside people and groups. The authors do not argue that the internal team-building model is completely outdated, for they freely admit that relationships between team members are important, but they believe the inner bonds are best understood in the context of how teams effectively reach outward. The internal bonds of teamwork are the overrated half of the equation, and are not by themselves a useful indicator without looking at how that team builds bridges with those outside the team in efforts to become more productive and successful.

---

(28) In the Hawthorne studies, Elton Mayo first set out to show how
   1 teamwork is vital for an organization's effectiveness.
   2 teamwork has little to do with environmental variables in the workplace.
   3 environmental factors in the workplace affect productivity.
   4 environmental variables in the workplace affect the building of teamwork.

(29) The quote by Ancona can basically be summed up by stating that
   1 the internal model of teamwork has survived the test of time, though it should be measured by external factors as well as internal.
   2 external success will likely not be achievable unless the team strives to build strong internal bonds first.
   3 teamwork is a relative term, and that companies actually require different types of teamwork to be successful.
   4 effective internal teamwork may well not be so effective in terms of achieving success in the real world.

(30) What do Ancona and Bresman say about the current business environment?
   1 It is more complex and fluid than in Hawthorne's time, requiring businesses to be more flexible.
   2 Teams must accept that the businesses environment has become increasingly hierarchical in the global community.
   3 It relies more on information and strategies than in Hawthorne's time, making team-building irrelevant.
   4 The knowledge-based global economy has not significantly changed the demands on companies' teams.

Day 1
Day 2
Day 3
Day 4
Day 5
Day 6
Day 7

(31) What do Ancona and Bresman believe about internal team building?
  1 It is no longer a relevant or useful concept in today's real business world.
  2 It is just as important today as Hawthorne first indicated, though the concept needs adjustment.
  3 It is overvalued compared to building better ties with outside groups.
  4 It has actually proven to be counterproductive in the current global economy.

4 English Summary

- Instructions: Read the article below and summarize it in your own words as far as possible in English.
- Suggested length: 60-70 words
- Write your summary in the space provided on your answer sheet. <u>Any writing outside the space will not be graded.</u>

People who follow a vegan lifestyle do not consume any foods that come from animals, such as meat, fish, eggs, dairy products and honey. They also avoid products from animals, including leather and fur. Despite such restrictions, the number of people becoming vegan is rising for a number of reasons.

Supporters of veganism claim that it is healthier than consuming animal products as it is based on vegetables, whole grains, fruit, and plant-based oils. Additionally, since veganism does not involve any cruelty, and no animals are harmed or killed, many choose this lifestyle.

Nonetheless, some people who engage in a vegan lifestyle fail to eat a balanced diet, which can result in a lack of nutrition. The human body requires nutrients such as protein and various kinds of minerals like iron or zinc, which are commonly derived from animal products in traditional human diets. Some vegans, however, may not eat enough of their alternative foods that contain these nutrients. In addition, some vegan foods can be harder to find, and could be more expensive, so maintaining a restrictive vegan diet can be difficult.

Day 1
Day 2
Day 3
Day 4
Day 5
Day 6
Day 7

5 English Composition

- Write an essay on the given **TOPIC**.
- Use TWO of the **POINTS** below to support your answer.
- Structure: introduction, main body, and conclusion
- Suggested length: 120-150 words
- Write your essay in the space provided on your answer sheet. <u>Any writing outside the space will not be graded.</u>

TOPIC

Agree or disagree: Companies should promote workers on performance rather than seniority

POINTS

- *Motivation to work*
- *Loyalty*
- *Experience*
- *Fairness*

リスニングテスト

試験時間 リスニング約30分

There are three parts to this listening test.

Part 1	Dialogues: 1 question each	Multiple-choice
Part 2	Passages: 2 questions each	Multiple-choice
Part 3	Real-Life: 1 question each	Multiple-choice

※Listen carefully to the instructions.

Part 1　◀))027〜039

No. 1
1 He tends to repeat the same mistakes.
2 His boss will not listen to him.
3 He is frustrated with his superior.
4 His boss has been very helpful.

No. 2
1 She got a higher score than he did.
2 She was planning to cheat on a test.
3 She would not let him copy her answers.
4 She did not tell him the test has changed.

No. 3
1 He quickly gets upset at small things.
2 He has a gentle personality.
3 He was the cause of the problem.
4 He should talk to his ex-girlfriend.

No. 4
1 Begin to eat dinner.
2 Put dinner in the oven.
3 Prepare some snacks.
4 Go shopping for vegetables.

No. 5
1 Find someone with good people skills.
2 Improve his skills as a salesperson.
3 Apply for a position in her department.
4 Consider working for another company.

No. 6	**1** It might be too late for him to start skiing.
	2 Her husband might be too strict with him.
	3 She has seen other children get injured skiing.
	4 She has heard him say he does not like skiing.

No. 7	**1** The man said her dress is too expensive.
	2 The man does not like her new dress.
	3 The dress does not fit her properly.
	4 The dress is too formal for the party.

No. 8	**1** It is too expensive at this time of year.
	2 It is hard to find at nearby supermarkets.
	3 He might get sick from eating it.
	4 He prefers a different kind of lettuce.

No. 9	**1** Lend him some money.
	2 Give him back the money she borrowed.
	3 Lend him some textbooks.
	4 Give him a ride to the Student Union.

No. 10	**1** He was in bad physical condition.
	2 He did not get along with his co-workers.
	3 He was not suited to being an accountant.
	4 He had to take over his father's business.

No. 11	**1** She is not interested in marketing.
	2 Her boss is difficult to work for.
	3 Her new position is challenging.
	4 She is looking for a new job.

No. 12	**1** Talk their daughter out of going to art school.
	2 Voice her concerns to their daughter.
	3 Wait and see if their daughter maintains her art interest.
	4 Persuade their daughter to change her career.

Part 2 🔊 040〜046

(A) *No. 13* **1** They move by moving joints in legs.
2 They move by using bones and muscles in legs.
3 All eight legs are moved in the same way.
4 Half of the legs perform a different action from the other half.

No. 14 **1** Perform missions in dangerous places.
2 Help develop 3-D printing technology.
3 Assist people in using measuring devices.
4 Use sensors to detect other robots.

(B) *No. 15* **1** There were only a few communities.
2 Its writing system is too complicated.
3 It completely died out thousands of years ago.
4 Evidence that shows cultural information is limited.

No. 16 **1** They help explain the stone pyramids around the area.
2 There was a system for working together.
3 The Norte Chico civilization began in Peru.
4 The lifestyle during that period in time was very simple.

(C) *No. 17* **1** To make cups from a variety of materials.
2 To dispose of unnecessary cups.
3 To reduce the amount of waste.
4 To subscribe to a coffee service.

No. 18 **1** Collect the tags in each cup and lid.
2 Present them to make a donation to the club.
3 Wash and reuse them for themselves.
4 Bring them to the stores participating in the service.

Day 1
Day 2
Day 3
Day 4
Day 5
Day 6
Day 7

(D) *No. 19* **1** Wander from one island to the next.
2 Care for its babies on Amsterdam Island.
3 Use its large wing span to create nests.
4 Migrate to Canada every other year.

No. 20 **1** They only lay a single egg at a time.
2 There is not enough nesting space for all the birds.
3 Food has been scarce for the past decade.
4 They are having trouble finding a place to live.

(E) *No. 21* **1** An online catalog of annual publications.
2 Recommendations from a major bookstore.
3 Information posted in a local library.
4 A list of books published during the year.

No. 22 **1** Paper was easy to get to make books.
2 The government passed a law promoting books.
3 Books were imported in large quantities.
4 There was a shortage of delivery services.

(F) *No. 23* **1** Most factories, offices, and shops are open then.
2 They are often on Saturdays or Sundays.
3 All banks and post offices are closed then.
4 Britain has more of them than other European countries.

No. 24 **1** They have one more bank holiday than England.
2 They have fewer bank holidays overall.
3 They share few bank holidays with England.
4 They hope to add some new bank holidays.

(G)   *No. 25*   ***Situation:*** You want to go hiking with your four-year-old son in Sycamore Woodland Park. You want to have lunch along the way. A guide gives you the following advice on park routes.

Question: Which route should you take?

1 Woodhaven Road.

2 Windhill Summit Trail.

3 Seaview Trail.

4 Lighthouse Walk.

(H)   *No. 26*   ***Situation:*** You are due to return home to New York in three days. You call Skyways Airlines to check your return reservation and hear the following message.

Question: What should you do?

1 Press 1.

2 Press 2.

3 Press 3.

4 Press 4.

(I)   *No. 27*   ***Situation:*** You are stopping by a printing company before you go to work. You expect to arrive at your office at about 10:30 a.m. You receive a voice mail from a co-worker.

Question: What should you do?

1 Print a pamphlet for yourself.

2 Read an e-mail from the printing office.

3 Get some office supplies on the way.

4 Postpone a department meeting.

Day 1
Day 2
Day 3
Day 4
Day 5
Day 6
Day 7

45

(J)   *No. 28*   ***Situation:*** You are at a camping goods store and are looking at a shoulder bag for a trip this weekend. You see a bag with a nice design on display, but you want to buy one with dark colors. A clerk tells you the following.

Question: What should you do?

1 Choose a bag that is available now.
2 Try another store nearby.
3 Come back to the store next week.
4 Order a bag on the store's website.

(K)   *No. 29*   ***Situation:*** You are shopping at the department store and discover that your four-year-old daughter has wandered away. You hear the following announcement about a lost child.

Question: Where should you go to get her?

1 The information booth on the first floor.
2 The service desk on the second floor.
3 The lost and found counter on the third floor.
4 The confectionery section on the third floor.

筆記試験＆リスニングテスト

試験時間 筆記 **90分** リスニング約**30分**

1 *To complete each item, choose the best word or phrase from among the four choices. Then, on your answer sheet, find the number of the question and mark your answer.*

---

(1) As a result of recent restructuring, more than 2,000 workers in the automobile company were made ( ).

1 synthetic **2** optional **3** redundant **4** potent

(2) The cancer patient was found to have a heart problem. This ( ) prevented the doctors from operating as soon as they had wanted to.

1 abbreviation **2** complication
3 application **4** contrivance

(3) The university's opening ceremony is to be held in the Campus Stadium, which has a seating ( ) of 25,000.

1 adversity **2** commission **3** capacity **4** redemption

(4) Mike studied so hard during high school that he was able to ( ) admission to a top university.

1 secure **2** surpass **3** concede **4** reflect

(5) After the boys finished raking the garden, they put the ( ) of leaves into a large plastic bag for disposal.

1 clamp **2** heap **3** blaze **4** grave

(6) When Mrs. Edwards found out that her husband had been cheating on her for over a year, she demanded a ( ) and talked to a lawyer.

1 retreat **2** divorce **3** recess **4** diversion

(7) After working hard all day long without taking a single break, the construction engineer felt completely ( ).

1 deplored **2** crouched **3** immersed **4** drained

Day 1
Day 2
Day 3
Day 4
Day 5
Day 6
Day 7

(8)   *A:* Do you still write for several different newspapers?

        B: No, I write (   ) for *The News Today* now. It's become a full-time job.

        1 exclusively   **2** disdainfully   **3** superficially   **4** attentively

(9)   The major errors in this report will have to be (   ) before the meeting with the president on Monday.

        1 reclaimed   **2** exempted   **3** rectified   **4** exceeded

(10)   Adults who commit crimes against children should be severely punished as children are (   ). They require the protection of adults.

        1 variable   **2** fascinating   **3** vulnerable   **4** filthy

(11)   Customers shouldn't (   ) at a restaurant after they have paid their bill.

        1 swindle   **2** pluck   **3** linger   **4** flirt

(12)   Julie stayed at a (   ) hotel in the countryside. The rooms were small, but they were nicely decorated and very comfortable.

        1 vague   **2** dire   **3** quaint   **4** crucial

(13)   *A:* Carl just bumped into me and spilled his juice all over me. Look at my shirt.

        B: I bet it was (   ). He's a bully.

        1 watchful   **2** deliberate   **3** functional   **4** serene

(14)   The two political parties decided to join in order to form a (   ) government. Otherwise, they would have had no chance of leading the country.

        1 collision   **2** coalition   **3** compression   **4** consolation

(15)   Sources said that, after a very bad year, the company faced bankruptcy and was likely to (   ) its loans.

        1 round off   **2** skim over   **3** default on   **4** scratch out

(16)   The reporter tried to (   ) everything the witnesses were saying, but it was impossible. They were not only speaking quickly, but they often spoke at the same time.

        1 make over   **2** jot down   **3** put up   **4** write off

(17) In response to local residents' frequent complaints, police promised to ( ) on illegal parking on streets and in private driveways.

1 knock down   **2** strike out   **3** break out   **4** crack down

(18) After lengthy negotiations between representatives from the two companies, their major problems were ( ) so that their partnership on the project could continue.

1 carried through   **2** hung up

3 ironed out   **4** washed up

Day 1
Day 2
Day 3
Day 4
Day 5
Day 6
Day 7

Read each passage and choose the best word or phrase from among the four choices for each blank. Then, on your answer sheet, find the number of the question and mark your answer.

Cashmere — A Delight to the Senses

Cashmere is sheer magic. With its uniquely soft and velvety touch, it has become a supreme symbol of luxury and opulence. The hard-wearing quality, colors, and design of cashmere clothing produced in Scotland have given it undisputed leadership in the world's knitwear markets. Some designers will only work with cashmere made in Scotland.

Expensive? Of course. The reason for its high cost (*19*) the difficulty of obtaining the raw material. The word cashmere is an Anglicization of Kashmir, the province of India where the goats that supply the wool used to be. Today the necessary undercoat of the fleece is provided by goats from China and Russia. Great expense is involved, not only because the animals roam high up in the mountains of nations distant from Scotland, but also because so much time and skill is required in the manufacturing process. The matching and seaming carried out during assembly is a skilled process (*20*) quality checks. The frequent checks assure that the highest standards are met at each and every stage. Training for the assembly process takes about one to one and a half years.

The development and availability of cashmere can be traced to the conglomerate known as Dawson International. In 1901, Joseph Dawson invented a machine which could separate the hair of the goat, a process that had previously been done entirely by hand, in preparation for yarn-spinning. (*21*), the company became one of the largest cashmere processors in the world. It was not until the 1950s, however, that cashmere became the status symbol it is today.

---

(19) **1** has little to do with   **2** complies with
      3 lies partly in   **4** is overshadowed by

(20) **1** compared with   **2** free from
      3 necessary for   **4** subject to

(21) **1** In addition   **2** As a result
      3 Ironically   **4** Before that

Emotional Intelligence

In 1996, Daniel Goleman published a book called *Emotional Intelligence*. The book puts forth the view that conventional measures of intelligence such as IQ tests are totally inaccurate when used to predict an individual's success or failure in life. Goleman believes that a person's emotional make-up is (22) indicator of how well that person will do in the real world.

Goleman's ideas (23) to most of us. We have all met people who seem to be intellectually superior but have difficulty dealing with fellow human beings. Difficulty in dealing with people is equivalent to difficulty in dealing with society. And common sense tells us that an inability to deal with society is a large stumbling block to achieving personal or professional success.

The controversy over conventional IQ tests has been raging since they were first invented. Do they have any validity at all? If so, what exactly do they measure and what does it mean? Goleman hoped to set the record straight but, unfortunately, his book gives us no methods of measuring emotional intelligence.

(24), the fact that he addresses the question is enough to get us thinking. People who are likable tend to like other people. People who are withdrawn and defensive find few friends and allies at home or at work. It stands to reason that people who deal well with other people are going to find more satisfaction and success than those who don't.

Balance is essential for our well-being and, in a way, this is the essence of what Goleman is saying. IQ can be a useful tool, but without a balanced, more humanistic perspective, it is simply not enough.

筆記試験＆リスニングテスト

Day 1
Day 2
Day 3
Day 4
Day 5
Day 6
Day 7

| (22) | **1** a somewhat outdated | **2** a much more troublesome |
| | **3** a far more reliable | **4** a relatively unrelated |

| (23) | **1** are not surprising | **2** seem rather contradictory |
| | **3** appear revolutionary | **4** may not ring true |

| (24) | **1** Furthermore | **2** However |
| | **3** For example | **4** As a result |

Read each passage and choose the best answer from among the four choices for each question. Then, on your answer sheet, find the number of the question and mark your answer.

The "Me Too" Movement

The "Me Too" movement began to attract widespread attention in 2017, but the use of the phrase and the reasons behind it began just over a decade before. Before the hashtag #MeToo went viral on social media, a civil rights activist from New York had been using the phrase as part of her activities to highlight abuse suffered by women and to help victims. Following a number of high-profile accusations of sexual abuse in Hollywood, an actress encouraged others to share their experiences using the hashtag, causing it to go viral.

The results were immediate and far-reaching, with many women sharing stories of exploitation and abuse at the hands of powerful men. As noted by the woman who started the movement, women from minority backgrounds remain particularly vulnerable, a fact that some critics have claimed has been overlooked. The woman behind the original movement had been working to improve gender equality, especially for young women of color, for many years before the movement she created gained widespread attention. Since 2017, however, a great deal of media attention has focused on abuse claims from within Hollywood, and those who control the entertainment industry.

The focus on Hollywood is understandable as it involves many famous people, whose lives tend to attract a great deal of attention. This attention has helped to raise the profile of the original movement, in turn helping to fund efforts to support victims. More than ever, the plight of people suffering abuse has been brought into the public eye and that is having many positive consequences for those who felt that their voices were not being heard before. Sadly, it has also unearthed a litany of abuses involving both women and men who have suffered injustices.

The movement has also expanded far beyond New York and Hollywood, with translations of "Me Too" being used on social media around the world. The conversation surrounding the movement now encompasses a number of issues addressing inequality and injustice, although its core problem remains sexual abuse and harassment. Although many abusers have been brought to justice thanks to the movement, many believe it is still in its infancy. That idea is bolstered by the fact that it has led to similar movements highlighting other forms of abuse. Others, however, are wary that spurious claims aimed at destroying reputations, which spread quickly over social media, could undermine the good work being done.

(25) How did the "Me Too" movement start and subsequently develop?

1 It originally started purely on social media and became a provider of welfare services.

2 Women from ethnic minorities shared their stories on social media and it grew from there.

3 An activist worked with abused women and then it attracted attention on social media.

4 Abused women from New York took action against their abusers, and it spread virally.

(26) In what ways has the amount of attention on social media affected the movement?

1 Despite the enormous amount of attention, the movement has been unable to benefit in any tangible way.

2 Although the attention has helped to support victims of abuse, some feel the focus is too narrow.

3 Social media attention means that fewer victims are willing to come forward and tell their stories.

4 The social media attention has meant that men from minority backgrounds are getting fewer jobs in Hollywood.

(27) What might the future hold for the "Me Too" movement and other similar movements?

1 Now that these movements have gained traction, there is considerable scope for them to combat social ills.

2 The movements look set to remain localized due to the poor reputation of the people behind them.

3 Although some people are wary of false accusations, the movements are spreading and are already producing results.

4 While the movements have attracted a lot of attention, the fact that they undermine genuine attempts at justice means they will soon run out of steam.

Day 1
Day 2
Day 3
Day 4
Day 5
Day 6
Day 7

Eating Less for a Longer Life

A number of research studies have revealed that rodents and primates have benefited from a highly restricted diet, meaning a diet with 20 to 30 percent fewer calories than normally consumed. Underfed lab animals lived longer and healthier lives. Now, a growing number of people are taking the findings of the research at face value, and are restricting their own calorie intake by 20 to 30 percent. Calorie restriction, commonly called CR, is not as popular as many other diet plans, but it has generated a number of books, including *The Longevity Diet* and *Beyond the 120 Year Diet*.

While most diets are all about losing weight, CR is primarily about living longer, healthier lives. Since followers of CR diets eat less, they are often highly concerned with food quality, assuring they receive sufficient nutrients. Saturated fats, sugars, and dairy products are usually reduced or cut out of the diet. The diet does generally lead to weight loss and a lower metabolic rate, which may in turn lead to a longer life span.

However, there are no long-term studies that have proven that CR actually lengthens one's lifespan, but there are numerous studies that indicate it may well actually do that. One study published in the *American Journal of Physiology-Endocrinology and Metabolism* in 2007 showed that a CR diet consuming 20 percent less calories, combined with an exercise regimen, resulted in burning 20 percent more calories, lowered bad cholesterol, and increased the amount of good cholesterol. Even CR without exercise resulted in a significant lowering in the risk of heart disease.

But CR can also lead to some serious risks. Many CR dieters quickly lose weight, and for those who already have little body fat, the loss can be dangerous. The CR diet can attract the wrong kind of people, including those with such eating disorders as anorexia. And many on CR diets complain of feeling hungry at all times, so much so that they become obsessed with food. One study showed that those who have followed a CR diet for one year have less muscle mass and a lesser ability to exercise compared to those who have lost weight by exercise alone. Another study showed that those who lost weight from CR as opposed to those who lost weight through exercise developed weaker bones in the hip and spine. Other effects of a CR diet include increased colds and infertility. Washington University School of Medicine researchers found that major calorie reductions lead to a host of ailments, including malnutrition, anemia, muscle loss, weakness, and even depression. Fortunately, recent research shows no evidence that CR negatively affects memory or attention issues.

While proponents of CR feel certain they are on track to greater health and longer life, it's important to seek medical advice about how fast and how far to go. Cutting more than 500 calories per day off your diet may not only be unhealthy in the short term, it could have negative long-term consequences impacting longevity.

---

(28) Dieters who have decided to follow the CR approach
1 were convinced by long-term studies of humans that CR is the most effective.
2 were initially attracted by the findings of CR research on animals.
3 are rapidly gaining in number, making the plan one of the most popular.
4 have found that other diet plans do not work as well for them.

(29) The passage implies that CR diets may not be healthy for those people who
1 hope to lower current conditions of high cholesterol or heart disease.
2 have never had any success with any other kind of diet.
3 already have serious psychological issues concerned with food and dieting.
4 are clearly obese or who have high amounts of body fat.

(30) Which of the following would be an unlikely result from a CR diet?
1 Mood swings, including feelings of despair.
2 A fixation on food and food consumption.
3 Weaker bones and loss of muscle mass.
4 Mental slowness and a loss in concentration.

(31) What does the author imply about CR diets?
1 CR diets are basically only successful when people adhere to the 20 to 30 percent calorie restriction.
2 CR diets have been shown to be effective for most people, and may become a very popular way to reduce weight.
3 Research indicates that CR diets could be healthy, but there are also dangers to consider.
4 Research shows that the risks of CR diets far outweigh any benefits, so the diets are best avoided by most people.

Day 1
Day 2
Day 3
Day 4
Day 5
Day 6
Day 7

English Summary

- Instructions: Read the article below and summarize it in your own words as far as possible in English.
- Suggested length: 60-70 words
- Write your summary in the space provided on your answer sheet. <u>Any writing outside the space will not be graded.</u>

In the past, the only way to follow the latest fashion trends was to buy brand-name clothes, which were mainly available in expensive stores. However, in the late twentieth century, companies began quickly producing similar designs in large quantities and selling them at low prices. This business model became known as fast fashion.

Supporters of fast fashion claim that it has made it possible for everyone, not only the wealthy, to buy and wear the most current and stylish clothes. Fast fashion brands can now look just as good as designer brands. The growth of fast fashion has also provided employment for people all over the world, including those who work to design, produce, and sell the clothing.

Despite this, some people say that fast fashion encourages people to waste money on clothing and dispose of it quickly. Consequently, the waste produced by the production of the clothes is seen as bad for the environment. On top of that, there are concerns that people employed to make the clothes often work long hours for low pay in dangerous conditions, such as being exposed to harmful chemicals.

5   English Composition

- Write an essay on the given **TOPIC**.
- Use TWO of the **POINTS** below to support your answer.
- Structure: introduction, main body, and conclusion
- Suggested length: 120-150 words
- Write your essay in the space provided on your answer sheet. <u>Any writing outside the space will not be graded.</u>

TOPIC

Do you think children should have homework during summer vacation?

POINTS

- *Children's happiness*
- *Teacher's workload*
- *Preparation*
- *Academic competitiveness*

Day 1
Day 2
Day 3
Day 4
Day 5
Day 6
Day 7

Listening Test

Part 1	Dialogues: 1 question each	Multiple-choice
Part 2	Passages: 2 questions each	Multiple-choice
Part 3	Real-Life: 1 question each	Multiple-choice

※Listen carefully to the instructions.

Part 1　◀)) 053~065

No. 1
1 The man bought the woman a new car.
2 The man has just sold his own car.
3 The man's company loaned him a car.
4 The man's company has only one car.

No. 2
1 She does not enjoy traveling.
2 She does not like cold climates.
3 She is a fan of art and culture.
4 She wants to stay at her current office.

No. 3
1 She has been involved in various sports.
2 She used to weigh more.
3 Her skis are uncomfortable.
4 Her friend enjoys running in marathons.

No. 4
1 The game was exciting.
2 It rained during the game.
3 Their team played well.
4 The game was canceled.

No. 5
1 Exercise is more effective than diet products.
2 Jogging outside is possible year-round.
3 Going on a diet is expensive.
4 Workouts should not be done for a long time.

No. 6	**1** The woman did not watch the game.
	2 The referee was unfair to United.
	3 Several United players were injured.
	4 He could not watch the whole game.

No. 7	**1** She has gained weight rapidly recently.
	2 She eats a lot of high cholesterol foods.
	3 She does not exercise very often.
	4 She has not had an annual checkup.

No. 8	**1** The man contacted the wrong person.
	2 The man will drop by Ms. Daniels' office later today.
	3 Ms. Daniels does not have a work phone.
	4 Ms. Daniels will be in the office this afternoon.

No. 9	**1** He is rather hopeless at French.
	2 His pronunciation is actually quite good.
	3 She can help him with his accent.
	4 Her French is actually worse than his.

No. 10	**1** Pay for two shirts.
	2 Ask for a discount.
	3 Look for a different store.
	4 Shop for more items.

No. 11	**1** Reschedule the meeting.
	2 Take the woman home.
	3 Come up with some new ideas.
	4 Meet the client for the woman.

No. 12	**1** Talk to someone about a celebrity.
	2 Take a picture of a building.
	3 Wait outside of an entryway.
	4 Complain to someone in the crowd.

Day 1
Day 2
Day 3
Day 4
Day 5
Day 6
Day 7

(A)	*No. 13*	**1** She found a role model.
		2 She beat her own path.
		3 She followed other female players.
		4 She was inspired by great athletes.

No. 14
1 She established a foundation related to education.
2 She fought for gender equality in the workplace.
3 She started to support people from a poor background.
4 She actively promoted sports for girls.

(B)   *No. 15*
1 It is a contemporary singing style.
2 It is traditionally sung by most Nordic people.
3 It is a musical form that is sung with no words.
4 It is a musical instrument invented in Russia.

No. 16
1 It became part of popular culture.
2 It was not allowed in many places.
3 Only older Sami people could do it.
4 It spread to non-Sami people.

(C)   *No. 17*
1 With a focus on practical skills.
2 By teachers with technical knowledge.
3 By using many learning materials.
4 In big classrooms with many teachers.

No. 18
1 Students are guided through a fixed program.
2 Teachers attend to each student the same way.
3 Students are finding school education more demanding.
4 Teachers help students with their individualized learning.

(D) *No. 19* **1** It was common for long flights.

2 People only carried cold food when traveling.

3 The crew could only handle cold meals for food safety.

4 Airplanes did not have enough energy for heat.

No. 20 **1** More kinds of foods appeared on the menu.

2 It took more time to heat up the food.

3 The quality of the food went down.

4 Passengers started needing silver cutlery to eat.

(E) *No. 21* **1** It provides wild animals with food.

2 It is a big market in most developed countries.

3 It offers experiences of living in the wilderness.

4 It makes money as a business.

No. 22 **1** Wildlife may not be treated well when shown to tourists.

2 Natural environment can be lost to lodging development.

3 Animals may become violent towards people.

4 Tourism guarantees sustainable wildlife conservation.

(F) *No. 23* **1** During a time of war centuries ago.

2 During the early days of photography.

3 During the signing of a peace treaty.

4 During archery contests hundreds of years ago.

No. 24 **1** To make a sign of good luck before a battle.

2 To motivate their fellow soldiers.

3 To show they could shoot arrows.

4 To make peace with the French.

(G)   *No. 25*   ***Situation:*** You are a college student and talking to an academic advisor. You have good grades, but are interested in switching majors.

                        Question: What should you do first?

                        1 Take a few extra basic-level classes.
                        2 Talk to the Humanities head.
                        3 Pay a fee for a copy of a transcript.
                        4 Bring some completed paperwork to the advisor.

(H)   *No. 26*   ***Situation:*** You are driving on Highway 280 and will arrive in San Francisco in about 20 minutes. You listen to the following information on the radio.

                        Question: What are you advised to do?

                        1 Take the off ramp to Highway 101.
                        2 Take the off ramp to Highway 1.
                        3 Turn off Highway 280 at Market Street.
                        4 Proceed carefully on Highway 280.

(I)   *No. 27*   ***Situation:*** You have a problem with your credit card. A company representative leaves you the following voice mail.

                        Question: What should you do next?

                        1 Call a toll-free number.
                        2 Send an application for a new card.
                        3 Reset the card's password.
                        4 Visit the credit card company office.

(J) *No. 28* ***Situation:*** You have just moved to the United States, and want to buy an old house. A friend gives you the following advice.

Question: What should you do first?

1 Talk to a specialist at a bank.

2 Check the house's foundation for cracks.

3 Repair any leaky pipes.

4 Hire a roof inspector.

(K) *No. 29* ***Situation:*** You purchased some First Rate ground beef with a best by date of March 3, but have not yet consumed it. You hear the following warning on TV.

Question: What are you advised to do?

1 See a physician immediately.

2 Return the beef for a refund.

3 Cook the beef thoroughly.

4 Throw the beef away.

Day 1
Day 2
Day 3
Day 4
Day 5
Day 6
Day 7

筆記試験＆リスニングテスト

試験時間 筆記90分 リスニング約30分

1 *To complete each item, choose the best word or phrase from among the four choices. Then, on your answer sheet, find the number of the question and mark your answer.*

---

(1) Tom received a letter from the electricity company informing him that his payment was two weeks (　　　) and that he must pay it immediately.
   1 unbalanced　　**2** underdone　　**3** overdue　　**4** premature

(2) According to the traffic report, more than thirty cars (　　　) on the freeway due to the dense fog.
   1 collided　　**2** diverged　　**3** disputed　　**4** violated

(3) The woman tried to (　　　) the fire in the kitchen, but it was no use. She finally had to run from the house and call the fire department.
   1 ambush　　**2** extinguish　　**3** encounter　　**4** stimulate

(4) The soccer team was overjoyed because, after its poor start at the beginning of the season, it now had five (　　　) wins.
   1 dubious　　**2** crippling　　**3** secluded　　**4** consecutive

(5) *A:* My finger is (　　　), doctor.
   B: Yes, it looks painful. We'll need to take an x-ray to see if it's broken.
   1 flimsy　　**2** stale　　**3** invalid　　**4** swollen

(6) Park rangers observed that the park's (　　　) changed significantly after reintroducing wolves. The population of deer decreased, while certain species of plants and trees returned.
   1 format　　**2** proposal　　**3** habitat　　**4** theory

(7) If you would like to add a second story to your house, you'll have to (　　　) the walls of the first story so they can support the additional weight.
   1 prearrange　　**2** reinterpret　　**3** reinforce　　**4** predetermine

(8) Due to political unrest, the nation fell into years of (   ) and economic collapse. As a result, many citizens emigrated to nearby countries to find better opportunities.

1 disorder **2** evasion **3** intention **4** clamor

(9) By almost any (   ), Roger Morton's literary career was a huge success. He wrote over 15 best sellers and was given numerous literary awards.

1 censure **2** ratio **3** felony **4** measure

(10) Your paper did have some interesting points, John, but it was rather disorganized. You should rewrite it to make it more (   ).

1 awkward **2** coherent
3 contradictory **4** rebellious

(11) Police said the suspected drug dealers had been arrested at dawn as part of a police (   ) of the inner city.

1 sweep **2** brush **3** pat **4** rub

(12) A group of consumers hired a lawyer to help them (   ) the manufacturers of the faulty product.

1 deed **2** cue **3** sue **4** hail

(13) The researchers' latest findings are significant and are expected to be a (   ) in the treatment of cancer.

1 bundle **2** breakthrough **3** condolence **4** dropout

(14) Engineers check the assembly line (   ) throughout the day to make sure that it is functioning properly.

1 periodically **2** annually **3** impulsively **4** erratically

(15) *A:* I'm exhausted. I've been working for over a year without a decent vacation.
B: You need to (   ) some time for yourself, Kyle. It's not good for your health to work so hard.

1 give off **2** hand out **3** set aside **4** set off

(16) If your name or address on the form is incorrect, please (   ) with a red pen and print the correct version below.

1 check it out **2** cross it out **3** hold it up **4** make it up

Day 1
Day 2
Day 3
Day 4
Day 5
Day 6
Day 7

(17) "I cannot (   ) such a small pension with prices continually going up," complained the retired military officer.

1 see through   **2** give in   **3** try out   **4** live on

(18) The runner was well ahead during most of the race, but as he approached the finish line, the other runners (   ) him. He barely won the race.

1 benefited from   **2** gained on

3 stirred up   **4** grew over

筆記試験＆リスニングテスト

Day
1

Day
2

Day
3

Day
4

Day
5

Day
6

Day
7

（筆記試験の問題は次のページに続きます。）

Read each passage and choose the best word or phrase from among the four choices for each blank. Then, on your answer sheet, find the number of the question and mark your answer.

Food for Thought

In his book *Stuffed and Starved*, researcher Raj Patel of the University of KwaZulu-Natal in South Africa provides an overview of (**19**). He delves into the complex web of reasons why one billion people, mostly in the developed world, are almost drowning in calories while 800 million people in the world go to bed each night hungry. It's a Gordian knot of a problem, a knot that cannot be untied until we gain a broader understanding of how this gross inequity came about.

However, it is exactly this understanding that Patel believes is key to motivate the over-indulged to change their ways. He cajoles readers to fight for debt relief of countries exploited by corporate food giants exporting products to the West and to support worker's rights for fair pay. (**20**), he makes the case for greater reliance on locally grown foods with an emphasis on organically grown and environmentally sustainable crops.

Patel questions our current food-trade system, which relies on massive corporations motivated more by greed than support of nature or nurture. He shows how and why farmers in the U.S. and Korea suffer from debt and despair, and analyzes the disastrous epidemic of farmer suicides in India. He further examines how the efforts of such organizations as the World Bank and the WTO to level the playing field for the world's farmers by lowering trade tariffs and opening agricultural markets have actually (**21**). Large corporations and government bureaucracies have benefited from the changes at the expense of the masses of small farmers.

(19) **1** modern healthy diets   **2** hunger in the developed world
     3 the world's food imbalance   **4** the benefits of agricultural trade

(20) **1** On the other hand   **2** Based on this
     3 As a result   **4** In addition

(21) **1** helped those farmers   **2** impaired world trade tremendously
     3 had the opposite effect   **4** equalized opportunities

A Human's Humor

Today, the word humor is mostly associated with jokes and laughter, but it wasn't always so. Humor had much more to do with body fluids and the nature of people in medieval physiology. Man was thought to have four humors, or body fluid types: blood, phlegm, choler, and melancholy. A person's physical and mental qualities and disposition were held to be determined by the (22) of the four humors that flowed into and throughout the body.

Ben Jonson, an Elizabethan dramatist, wrote a play, *Every Man in His Humor*. The phrase, "in his humor" expresses which humor he has most and what kind of man he is. If a man was fat and merry, he was thought to have more blood than the other three humors. (23), if a person was thin and gloomy, he was considered to contain a lot of the melancholy humor. And it follows that a person of sound mind and body was believed to have the four humors in the right proportions.

Then what was the function of laughter with regard to the humors? Foolish people were considered the source of laughter. People who were laughed at were deemed to have exhibited bizarre behaviors under the influence of too much of one of the humors. The persons laughing were seen to be able to rightly judge such excessive and abnormal actions because their humors were thought to have been well balanced. Today, humor is (24) body fluids. Instead, it more often implies a sense of humor. But the function of laughing, which helps us maintain a balanced mind, has never changed. Many people around the world believe that a sense of humor is essential to a healthy and enjoyable life, almost as essential to us as our body fluids.

---

(22)　**1** almost total absence　　**2** clearly defined colors
　　　 3 relative proportions　　　**4** overall endurance

(23)　**1** In return　　　　　　　　**2** In contrast
　　　 3 As a result　　　　　　　 **4** Just as importantly

(24)　**1** rarely associated with　　**2** seen as directly affecting
　　　 3 primarily a medical term for　**4** increasingly related to

Read each passage and choose the best answer from among the four choices for each question. Then, on your answer sheet, find the number of the question and mark your answer.

Made for Music

For the overwhelming majority of people, music has an important role to play in their lives. As well as entertaining and fostering a real sense of togetherness, music has been shown to evoke many emotions. Hearing particular songs from our past can conjure up sharp images and sentiments of days gone by. A favorite tune can turn despair into happiness in an instant. Music is an important part of our existence and is with us throughout our daily lives.

Researchers have concluded that our love of music begins while we are still in the womb. The rhythmic beat of our mothers' heart is the first sound we hear. For many of us, from when we enter the world to when we leave it, we are exposed to music in an ever-increasing number of guises and locations. How have recent social changes, coupled with technological advancements, exerted a strong influence over the music that we listen to in the twenty-first century?

Greater cultural integration throughout the world in the last century has meant music that had previously been confined to one corner of the globe can now be enjoyed by a much wider audience. Moreover, as these groups are pulled closer together, musicians are increasingly able to draw on a large number of artistic influences. Culturally distinct styles can now be blended into exciting new fusions, offering the public further genres from which to choose. A notable example being the marriage between Afro-American popular music and that of European origin, which in the 1950s saw the birth of rock'n'roll in the U.S.A. Furthermore, ever-expanding towns and cities have brought together creative talents in even greater numbers. History tells us that New Orleans was the birthplace of jazz, while soul music originated from Detroit.

The mediums through which music can enter our homes became widely available in the twentieth century, touching all but those living in remote, isolated communities. This began with the radio. People no longer had to leave their homes to be musically entertained. The turning of a dial was all that was now required. Television took this a stage further by adding a visual dimension, enabling viewers to see a variety of popular artists regularly from the comfort of their armchairs. The advent of portable devices in the 1970s and 1980s gave us the freedom to listen to music as we traveled from one place to another.

(25) According to research, when do humans first gain an appreciation for music?

1 When we are growing inside our mothers.

2 When we are born and exposed to the various sounds around us.

3 When we are taught to associate certain sounds as music by our parents.

4 After first being exposed to songs throughout our daily life.

(26) What factor does the author suggest accelerated the integration of musical styles into new fusions?

1 Greater integration of culturally diverse groups, exposing musical artists to new sounds.

2 The fusion of Afro-American music and European music, which gave birth to jazz.

3 The invention of the radio, which brought music to rural communities.

4 The desire of people in the 1950s to hear new styles of music from all over the world.

(27) According to the passage, how has technology in the twentieth century changed our experience of music?

1 It has given people greater access to music.

2 It has changed our appreciation for music.

3 It has enabled modern music to reach even isolated communities.

4 It has enabled common people to create their own music.

筆記試験&リスニングテスト

Day 1

Day 2

Day 3

Day 4

Day 5

Day 6

Day 7

Cleaner Diagnoses

Technetium-99m (Tc-99m) is a radioisotope, a form of the chemical element called technetium that gives off energy as it breaks down. It is widely used in medical imaging for the diagnosis of cancers, including hard-to-detect cancers. Patients receive an injection of Tc-99m, which gives off gamma rays. These gamma rays are detected by a special gamma camera that can then produce an image—higher concentrations of the gamma rays indicate the location of a tumor. Over 40 million procedures utilize Tc-99m per year, making it the most common radioisotope used in diagnoses worldwide. This is because it is a relatively safe radioisotope. Tc-99m has a short half-life of about 6 hours, meaning that it only takes this long for the radioactivity to decrease to half its original value. Therefore, not only are patients' bodies free from the radioactivity quickly but people around them are exposed to only a small amount of secondhand radiation, and there is no radioactive waste that would harm the environment. The production of Tc-99m, however, is another story.

Molybdenum-99 (Mo-99) is the base ingredient required to produce Tc-99m and must be created in a nuclear reactor using highly enriched uranium-235 (U-235). The radioactive byproducts of this process have extremely long half-lives, making disposal an environmental hazard and very costly. Now, only 4 nuclear reactors in the world produce Mo-99, some of which are unreliable and shut down suddenly for months at a time, causing a shortage of the radioisotope. Luckily, NorthStar Medical Radioisotopes (NorthStar), a company based in Beloit, Wisconsin, in the U.S., recognized the challenges this presented, and in 2006, began work to secure a domestic, reliable, and environmentally friendly supply of medical radioisotopes.

NorthStar has developed a way to create Mo-99 from the naturally occurring mineral molybdenite, found in the earth's crust. This eliminates U-235 from the process as well as the radioactive byproducts. Furthermore, while Tc-99m's half-life renders transportation to hospitals extremely expensive or even impossible in some cases, Mo-99 has a half-life of 66 hours, a timeframe much more convenient for transportation across the country or even the world. NorthStar has invented a machine called the RadioGenix System that hospitals can purchase to easily transform Mo-99 into Tc-99m onsite. In this way, hospitals around the globe can have a ready supply of Tc-99m for all of their diagnostic needs.

NorthStar's new technology is making it possible to begin tackling the production of other radioisotopes as well. For instance, actinium-225 (Ac-225) and bismuth-213 (Bi-213) have been found to bind to and kill cancer cells in a patient's body, then allowing the body to excrete them as waste. Unfortunately, the supply of these radioisotopes is severely limited, meeting the demand for only a small fraction of patients annually. NorthStar is currently developing a process to produce large amounts of these radioisotopes for clinical research and treatment. With these developments, it seems that NorthStar's efforts are changing the history of medical imaging and treatment in a way that satisfies the needs of the patient while successfully keeping the environment clean.

---

(28) Why is technetium-99m (Tc-99m) considered a safe radioisotope?

1 Smaller amounts of it are necessary for successful medical imaging than other typically used radioisotopes.

2 The gamma rays that it emits travel directly to a patient's tumor but leave no trace after the tumor is surgically removed.

3 It is injected into the upper layer of a patient's skin rather than deep tissues where it can cause harm.

4 Its radioactivity disappears rapidly, causing little or no harm to the patient, others, and the Earth.

(29) What problem arises when one of the nuclear reactors shuts down?

1 Fewer patients around the world are able to receive the diagnostic imaging they need for proper treatment in a timely manner.

2 Radioisotopes that are less stable than uranium-235 (U-235) must be used, which produces Mo-99 of lesser quality.

3 Special equipment for making Mo-99 is transported to a different nuclear reactor to get production started again.

4 Radioactive byproducts leak out of the nuclear reactor and thus require excessive time and effort to clean up the surrounding environment.

(30) What is special about the Mo-99 produced by NorthStar?

1 It has properties similar to Tc-99m, making it possible for hospitals to use the two radioisotopes interchangeably.

2 It has an extremely long half-life that allows facilities to purchase large amounts every once in a while and store it long term.

3 Its production does not require the use of either U-235 or a nuclear reactor, making it environmentally friendly.

4 It is not radioactive and therefore does not require special receptacles or equipment for safe transport.

Day 1
Day 2
Day 3
Day 4
Day 5
Day 6
Day 7

(31) According to the article, in the future, it is likely that NorthStar will

1 expand into the mining industry in order to locate new areas with naturally occurring radioisotopes and extract them for use in the medical field.

2 develop ways to provide the global medical industry with a sufficient amount of important radioisotopes to meet demands.

3 begin to research other deadly diseases in the hopes that they can adapt their products and help to bring about cures.

4 help patients who live far away to reach research facilities where they can participate in medical trials with radioisotopes.

4 English Summary

- Instructions: Read the article below and summarize it in your own words as far as possible in English.
- Suggested length: 60-70 words
- Write your summary in the space provided on your answer sheet. <u>Any writing outside the space will not be graded.</u>

In 1983, China opened its first university for the elderly, based on similar schools in Europe. Thousands of such universities have opened since then, offering traditional academic courses alongside skills-based courses. They are open to students over the age of 60 and, as China has the world's fastest aging population, they have proven to be extremely popular.

The benefits for students, through various classes, include learning new skills and memory improvement, both of which can help to slow the decline of the brain. The universities also give students a chance to meet people and be part of a community, thereby lowering the risk of loneliness.

On the other hand, not everybody who wants to attend the universities can do so. With such a high number of applicants who wish to be admitted, there is now the need for admission lotteries and entrance competitions. In addition, the funding of the universities is primarily provided by the government, so the demand for more universities would require further amounts of money, putting pressure on the welfare system.

Day 1
Day 2
Day 3
Day 4
Day 5
Day 6
Day 7

English Composition

- Write an essay on the given **TOPIC**.
- Use TWO of the **POINTS** below to support your answer.
- Structure: introduction, main body, and conclusion
- Suggested length: 120-150 words
- Write your essay in the space provided on your answer sheet. <u>Any writing outside the space will not be graded.</u>

TOPIC

Agree or disagree: The Japanese government needs to encourage young people to live in rural areas

POINTS
- *Lifestyle*
- *Education*
- *The economy*
- *Elderly care*

Listening Test

There are three parts to this listening test.

Part 1	Dialogues: 1 question each	Multiple-choice
Part 2	Passages: 2 questions each	Multiple-choice
Part 3	Real-Life: 1 question each	Multiple-choice

※Listen carefully to the instructions.

Part 1　◀))079～091

No. 1
1 She would rather spend time indoors.
2 She will allow the man to go to work.
3 She has never been camping before.
4 She likes to take naps on the beach.

No. 2
1 She does not have an entrance ticket.
2 She was not aware of a policy.
3 She neglected to recycle her utensils.
4 A server was unhelpful.

No. 3
1 He takes risks on motorcycles.
2 He was in a serious accident.
3 He is planning to buy a new motorcycle.
4 He paid too much for his motorcycle.

No. 4
1 The instructor gives unremarkable lectures.
2 The textbook is difficult to understand.
3 The instructor has a good reputation.
4 The subject material is extensive.

No. 5
1 Give the driver the exact fare.
2 Go get some change.
3 Give the driver five dollars.
4 Take another form of transportation.

Day 1
Day 2
Day 3
Day 4
Day 5
Day 6
Day 7

No. 6	1 Attend a meeting.
	2 Retrieve a brochure from the woman.
	3 Obtain a memory stick from the woman.
	4 Provide the woman with an updated file.

No. 7	1 Locate a credit card.
	2 Submit an application.
	3 Obtain a higher score.
	4 Contact his credit company.

No. 8	1 Meeting with a client.
	2 Preparing an advertising plan.
	3 Having a job interview.
	4 Reporting to his company manager.

No. 9	1 He is grieving over the loss of his wife.
	2 He has never liked social gatherings.
	3 He likes to argue with people.
	4 He was reminded by Steve why he got married.

No. 10	1 Her boyfriend ended their relationship.
	2 She just heard that her friend broke a leg.
	3 She no longer wants to go out with Jeremy.
	4 She has been feeling ill recently.

No. 11	1 Retrieve his bags from the hotel.
	2 Return the hotel's call.
	3 Send his smartphone through the mail.
	4 Visit the hotel in person.

No. 12	1 Having a nice flight.
	2 Returning to Los Angeles.
	3 Taking a three-month vacation.
	4 Seeing the man again in July.

(A)   *No. 13*   **1** A giant monster that lives in the forest.
                     2 A mythical spirit with a red animal.
                     3 A child-like creature with unusual feet.
                     4 A hunter with great physical strength.

         No. 14   **1** It leaves footprints to guide people who get lost home.
                     2 It protects forests against damage from humans.
                     3 It uses special abilities to confuse forest inhabitants.
                     4 It informs people of information on hunting grounds.

(B)   *No. 15*   **1** It has rock art scattered across a wide area.
                     2 All of the images on the rocks were painted in red.
                     3 The paintings were made during various eras.
                     4 Most paintings were found underground.

         No. 16   **1** Historical documents from different ages.
                     2 Artifacts from different layers.
                     3 Jewelry pieces in the deepest layer.
                     4 The full remains of a human settlement.

(C)   *No. 17*   **1** Having an animal that became extinct there.
                     2 Being the only protected area for the Arabian oryx.
                     3 Having an ecosystem with a diverse plant life.
                     4 Being a protected zone for hunted animals.

         No. 18   **1** Hunters started coming close to it.
                     2 The number of Arabian oryx increased.
                     3 Oil drilling income in Oman was reduced greatly.
                     4 It was soon taken off from the World Heritage list.

Day **1**
Day **2**
Day **3**
Day **4**
Day **5**
Day **6**
Day **7**

(D)	*No. 19*	**1** She adapted navigation systems into cars.
		2 She invented an early model of the smartphone.
		3 She was mostly unknown until recent times.
		4 She is known to be an African-American activist.

	No. 20	**1** She earned a scholarship to learn about computers.
		2 She collected satellite data to study the Earth.
		3 She improved the existing computer system.
		4 She discovered a new theory in mathematics.

(E)	*No. 21*	**1** Being able to work in various locations.
		2 Only accepting temporary contracts.
		3 Moving with their co-workers to various offices.
		4 Working in a permanent physical residence.

	No. 22	**1** Jobs that require creativity and teamwork.
		2 Jobs that have many restrictions in offices.
		3 Jobs that depend on communication skills.
		4 Jobs that can be done solely on a computer.

(F)	*No. 23*	**1** The destructive nature of humans.
		2 Dust in the sky, which blocked the sun.
		3 Asteroids and comets, which almost collided with the Earth.
		4 Earthquakes and volcanic eruptions.

	No. 24	**1** They are not in reality threatened by extinction.
		2 They are carefully observing objects in space.
		3 They are making the best use of technology.
		4 They lack the motivation to protect themselves.

(G)	*No. 25*	***Situation:*** You are a college student talking with a housing consultant about nearby accommodations. You want to live alone, within walking distance of the university, but don't have a lot of money.

Question: Which living arrangement should you choose?
1 The house on Bixby Road.
2 The apartment on Bixby Road.
3 The house on Exeter Way.
4 The apartment on Molton Avenue.

(H)	*No. 26*	***Situation:*** You are planning to buy a new car. You would like an insurance plan that covers damage to your car for under $150 per month. You talk with an auto insurance agent.

Question: Which plan should you choose?
1 Basic Liability.
2 Comprehensive Collision.
3 Family Coverage.
4 Economy Plus.

(I)	*No. 27*	***Situation:*** You will soon arrive at London's King's Cross Train Station and then want to go to Heathrow Airport. You hear the following announcement on the train.

Question: What are you advised to take to get to the airport?
1 The train from platform 26.
2 The Tube.
3 A taxi from the taxi stand.
4 The express from platform 17.

Day **1**
Day **2**
Day **3**
Day **4**
Day **5**
Day **6**
Day **7**

(J)   *No. 28*   ***Situation:*** You purchased a new table at a furniture store, but when you unbox it you notice a large scratch on the top. You call the store's customer service center.

Question: What number should you press?

1 One.

2 Two.

3 Three.

4 Four.

(K)   *No. 29*   ***Situation:*** You plan to hike on the trail from Stanley Park to Ridgeway Golf Course. You hear this announcement at Stanley Park.

Question: What should you do?

1 Wear rubber boots or hiking boots.

2 Wait until noon to start your hike.

3 Be careful when stepping over fallen branches.

4 Take the alternative route for part of the trail.

筆記試験＆リスニングテスト

試験時間 筆記**90**分 | リスニング約**30**分

1 *To complete each item, choose the best word or phrase from among the four choices. Then, on your answer sheet, find the number of the question and mark your answer.*

---

(1) The insurance company rewards drivers who have no speeding tickets and no automobile ( ) for a three-year period by lowering the cost of their insurance.

1 intrusions **2** collisions **3** temptations **4** illusions

(2) Needless to say, technological innovation is ( ) to our continuing leadership in the semiconductor field.

1 intensive **2** extensive **3** overall **4** integral

(3) If ( ) persist, please consult your physician immediately.

1 contrivances **2** menaces **3** symptoms **4** outcomes

(4) *A:* Hi, Mary!
B: What a ( ) ! I didn't expect to see you here in New York.

1 benevolence **2** coincidence **3** prosperity **4** motivation

(5) *A:* I heard you were offered the position of general manager but you turned it down. Was it a difficult decision?
B: Well, it was ( ), but to be honest, I prefer working more directly on product development.

1 expressive **2** tempting **3** obnoxious **4** numbing

(6) Don't worry about making spelling errors. The software on this computer will ( ) most of them from your drafts automatically.

1 adhere **2** eliminate **3** foster **4** relieve

(7) Defense lawyers proved at last that the prisoner, who had been ( ) of murder 20 years earlier, was innocent.

1 ascribed **2** distilled **3** convicted **4** corrupted

Day **1**
Day **2**
Day **3**
Day **4**
Day **5**
Day **6**
Day **7**

(8) They say the young man is sure to win the tennis tournament at Wimbledon this year, but I'm (   ). He's too inexperienced.

1 affirmative   **2** decisive   **3** faithful   **4** skeptical

(9) Mark woke up this morning with a cold, so he didn't go to school. He now has a sore throat and his nose is (   ).

1 congested   **2** dreary   **3** ominous   **4** enviable

(10) I don't trust that politician. He often (   ) himself and makes impossible promises to please everybody.

1 acclaims   **2** contradicts   **3** embraces   **4** interrogates

(11) A (   ) of the interview can be obtained by phoning or e-mailing KNTV before June 3.

1 transcript   **2** transaction   **3** confession   **4** circumstance

(12) The inhabitants near the river demand that the proposed dam's impact on the environment be carefully (   ) before construction starts.

1 assessed   **2** invoiced   **3** smeared   **4** ventured

(13) Having stories read to them (   ) a love of reading in young minds. Therefore, it is highly recommended that all parents read stories to their children.

1 converts   **2** crumbles   **3** nurtures   **4** presides

(14) It took Paul several months to (   ) to living in Germany. So many things were different from his home country of Australia.

1 display   **2** adapt   **3** adjourn   **4** subsist

(15) Josh has (   ) a small fortune. His grandmother passed away and left him a sizable inheritance.

1 come into   **2** held out   **3** dragged out   **4** turned out

(16) Due to the prolonged recession, many companies in Japan have had no alternative but to (   ) on salaries.

1 catch hold   **2** cut back   **3** end up   **4** get away

(17) The government recently (　　　　) with many outdated laws that had been passed in the 1800s.

1 did away   **2** threw up   **3** made up   **4** fell back

(18) *A:* It's time for you to (　　　　), John. It's already past eleven.
B: OK, Mom. Good night.

1 turn in   **2** hold up   **3** leave out   **4** hand over

Day 1
Day 2
Day 3
Day 4
Day 5
Day 6
Day 7

Read each passage and choose the best word or phrase from among the four choices for each blank. Then, on your answer sheet, find the number of the question and mark your answer.

Bonfire Night

Every November 5, Britons brave the chill evening air to stand in a park or field to watch firework displays and gather around large fires known as bonfires. This is in celebration of the capture of Guy Fawkes. He was part of a four-man plot to blow up the Houses of Parliament, the seat of government. History tells us that he was apprehended by guards in the cellars of Parliament on November 5, 1605, with a considerable amount of gunpowder. Under duress, he revealed that this was part of a wider plot to kill the reigning monarch, James I.

A year from his capture, Parliament decreed that from then onwards, the day should be marked with an annual (*19*). The fireworks aspect of the festivities represents the fate that Parliament had barely escaped. However, the burning of bonfires stretches further back in time, to an era when people perceived them as the most effective way of warding off evil spirits. The fires formed an integral part of ancient New Year festivals. Over time, these (*20*) have evolved into the present celebration known as Guy Fawkes Day.

No bonfire night is complete without the burning of the guy. This is a large effigy, which initially represented Guy Fawkes. However, over the last hundred years, all manner of unpopular public figures have (*21*).

Safety has a large influence on the planning of any Bonfire Night. Increasingly, people have chosen not to have their own private celebrations but to attend large organized ones.

(19) **1** display of public thanksgiving   **2** time of quiet reflection
       3 period of private mourning   **4** show of individual anger

(20) **1** early records   **2** combined traditions
       3 crime enactments   **4** sacrificial rites

(21) **1** evaded the same fate   **2** had their turn as the guy
       3 attended the celebrations   **4** burned their own Guy effigies

Population — Past and Present

The world's population now stands at over 7 billion people. Most of us have become accustomed to the crowds and the crush in our daily lives as we go about our business. But it has not always been this way. (22), such a huge population is a recent phenomenon in demographics, the study of population.

For most of human history, the number of people alive on Earth at any one time was only several hundred million, a total easily surpassed by some countries today. It is only in the last two centuries that the population reached the 1 billion mark.

This information often gives rise to the question "how many people have lived on Earth since the beginning of humankind?" The exact answer is, of course, (23). After all, records have only been kept for the last one percent of human history. Intrigued by the question, demographers at the United Nations have attempted to reach an approximate answer using the best available data and current theories of population growth. Various assumptions and estimates of specific figures had to be made, such as the life span of previous generations, the number of children born to each woman, and even when exactly Homo sapiens are thought to have first appeared.

After taking into account the above assumptions and many others, the total number is estimated by the most reputable scientists to be approximately 105 billion. This in turn leads to another very interesting figure, namely that six percent of all the people ever born are alive today. Considering the length of time humans have been on Earth, which is thought to be about fifty thousand years, this is a (24). But then when you are caught in rush-hour crowds day after day, you cannot avoid the fact of just how crowded our planet has become in modern times.

---

(22) **1** However   **2** Indeed   **3** Moreover   **4** Nevertheless

(23) **1** of little use to anyone   **2** easy to guess with modern tools
      3 predictable with effort   **4** difficult to accurately estimate

(24) **1** rather weak indicator   **2** surprisingly large figure
      3 highly precise estimate   **4** very suspect number

筆記試験＆リスニングテスト

Day 1
Day 2
Day 3
Day 4
Day 5
Day 6
Day 7

Read each passage and choose the best answer from among the four choices for each question. Then, on your answer sheet, find the number of the question and mark your answer.

How a Microwave Works

Microwaves are a form of electromagnetic energy moving through space. They are useful in cooking because they are absorbed by foods but reflected by metal and because they pass through glass, paper, plastic, and similar materials.

Produced by a magnetron electron tube, microwaves bounce around inside the metal oven until they are absorbed by food. They cause food molecules such as water, a very efficient microwave absorber, to vibrate at high speeds and thus produce heat to cook the food. This is why foods high in water content, such as fresh vegetables, can be cooked more quickly in a microwave than other foods. Microwaved food retains more vitamins and minerals than food cooked in other ways because microwaving takes less time and does not require additional water. Most people agree, however, that traditionally cooked food tastes better.

Though microwaves produce heat directly in the food, they really do not cook food from the inside out, according to Joanne Barron, who heads the television, acoustic, and microwave products branch at the Food and Drug Administration's Center for Devices and Radiological Health. "With thick foods like roasts," she says, "microwaves generally cook only about an inch of the outer layers. The heat is then slowly conducted inward, cooking along the way."

An area of food where there is increased moisture will heat more quickly than other areas. So when heating up a jelly roll, for instance, it is a good idea to let the food stand after cooking for a minute or two until the heat disperses throughout. To promote uniform cooking, recipes for the microwave usually include directions such as "turn the food midway through cooking" and "let stand after cooking."

Though microwave ovens are found in roughly 90 percent of American homes today, not everyone is a fan. Several research studies show that the rapid spinning of the microwave-heated molecules actually tears molecules from their neighbors, creating damaging effects in food. In one short-term study, volunteers ate various combinations of the same food cooked in different ways. The food cooked in microwaves caused disturbing changes in the blood of the volunteers. Hemoglobin levels decreased and overall white cell levels and cholesterol levels increased. In 1991, Dr. Hans Ulrich Hertel, a Lausanne University professor, published a research paper that showed that microwave cooking causes changes in the makeup and nutrients of food, which may pose a risk to health, including having cancerous effects on the blood.

However, other studies have concluded that microwave cooking is safe, so the decision about microwave usage is left up to consumers.

---

(25) Microwaves heat food by

  1 causing water molecules to oscillate at high speeds.
  2 being absorbed by food containers made of glass, paper, or plastic.
  3 passing through food molecules at rapid speeds.
  4 instantly turning water molecules into steam.

(26) Based on the passage, we can infer that

  1 microwaved food often tastes better than food cooked by other means.
  2 microwaves are absorbed deep within food first, so they cook food from the inside out.
  3 microwaved food can retain more nutrients than food cooked conventionally.
  4 microwaved food should not be allowed to stand after they have been cooked.

(27) The author of the passage implies that

  1 findings of various studies on microwaved food contradict each other.
  2 the majority of research on microwaved food show that they are unsafe to eat.
  3 some studies have shown conclusively that microwaved food causes cancer.
  4 consumers are advised not to use microwaves until the evidence is clearer.

Day 1
Day 2
Day 3
Day 4
Day 5
Day 6
Day 7

Environmental Racism

Environmental concerns such as climate change are among the most pressing issues we face today. While these problems ultimately affect us all, some groups and regions are being disproportionately affected. In many cases, the results are not only devastating, but deliberate. It is this imbalance, and the systematic abuse behind it, that has given rise to the problem of environmental racism. The term "environmental racism" was first coined in the 1980s, but examples of environmental injustices affecting racial groups stretch back to many centuries ago.

While environmental racism often takes the form of exposing certain communities to pollution and other hazardous materials, there are other factors to be considered. For example, actions including placing communities in areas vulnerable to natural disasters, or far from accessible potable water can be regarded as being environmentally racist. Others include discriminatory waste management processes and unfair exploitation of natural resources leading to environmental damage. In times of war, locating military bases and storage facilities near certain communities has also been described as acts of environmental racism.

Unsurprisingly, victims of environmental racism tend to be ethnic minorities and low-income communities. Historical examples of the practice were often linked to colonization and industrialization, although it is ongoing and, in many cases, becoming even worse. Rich western governments, for example, are often unwilling to dispose of the hazardous waste their industries produce within their own countries, therefore they ship it to developing countries willing to accept the risks. However, the reality is not as simple as a country being "willing," as connected trade deals and offers of social support act as a form of coercion. While the governments may profit, the areas in which the waste is located and disposed of often suffer terrible consequences. Such consequences include high infant mortality rates, huge rises in instances of cancer, cardiovascular disease, and physical abnormalities.

However, environmental racism and the ill effects it brings are not confined to developing nations. Even countries like the United States still suffer from it, as a number of recent cases have shown. The devastation wrought by Hurricane Katrina in 2005, and the reaction of the government, disproportionately affected ethnic minorities as a result of racial segregation policies. Another more recent example has seen the predominantly African American population of Flint, Michigan drinking and bathing in water that contains enough lead to meet the Environmental Protection Agency's definition of "toxic waste." There are many other examples in developed nations where ethnic minorities are exposed to levels of air and water pollution which far exceed the levels the ruling majorities are exposed to.

Unfortunately, as it tends to be the rich and powerful controlling the processes that lead to environmental racism, it is often hard to bring them to justice. However, that has not stopped environmental justice groups and civil rights movements from pursuing successful actions. In turn, affected communities and marginalized groups have successfully campaigned to improve conditions in the areas in which they live. With increased exposure through social media and the involvement of international organizations like the United Nations, instances of environmental racism may hopefully one day be a thing of the past.

---

(28) What is true about environmental racism?
 1 As with most environmental problems, environmental racism affects every region on Earth.
 2 The problem of environmental racism has spread all over the world since it started in the 1980s.
 3 Abuses by certain judicial systems are often mistakenly characterized as environmental racism.
 4 Environmental racism results from the systematic oppression of certain racial groups.

(29) What factors can help detect instances of environmental racism?
 1 The fact that any policies dealing with natural resources or natural disasters are not considered.
 2 Poor management by environmental protection agencies and governmental departments.
 3 Any circumstances leading to certain groups being at special risk from their environment.
 4 The placement of military bases near national parks and other protected areas.

(30) What are the ruling elite doing to exacerbate the problems connected with environmental racism?
 1 They are proving to be willing to learn from historical mistakes and make reparations.
 2 They often ignore the issues at home or use coercive tactics to force other nations to take risks.
 3 They are helping foreign companies make major financial deals while not addressing domestic issues.
 4 They are trying to use any profits made to help treat diseases like cancer and cardiovascular disease.

Day 1
Day 2
Day 3
Day 4
Day 5
Day 6
Day 7

(31) According to the passage, how may the issue of environmental racism be solved?

1 By finding support from major organizations or the Internet.

2 By letting the wealthy control civil rights movements.

3 By spreading the movements of the rich and powerful on social media.

4 By asking environmental justice groups to build new communities.

4 English Summary

- Instructions: Read the article below and summarize it in your own words as far as possible in English.
- Suggested length: 60-70 words
- Write your summary in the space provided on your answer sheet. <u>Any writing outside the space will not be graded.</u>

For many years, scientists have been concerned about the environmental impact of fossil fuels like oil, coal, and gas. As such, there has been a need for alternative sources of energy that are renewable, economical, and less harmful to the planet. One such alternative is biofuels, which are fuels created mainly from plant sources.

Biofuels are considered to be a cleaner source of energy than fossil fuels. One main reason is that they have much lower carbon dioxide emissions. Also, biofuels do not require special equipment to produce and can be reliably stored for later use. In this way, the effectiveness of biofuels is unaffected by weather conditions, unlike wind or solar power systems.

Although biofuels may be renewable, critics argue that growing the plants used for producing them requires harmful chemicals that kill insects and a large amount of water, and this is not good for the environment. In addition, this type of farming requires a great deal of land and can be expensive, which may affect the economic advantages of biofuels.

Day 1
Day 2
Day 3
Day 4
Day 5
Day 6
Day 7

5 English Composition

- Write an essay on the given **TOPIC**.
- Use TWO of the **POINTS** below to support your answer.
- Structure: introduction, main body, and conclusion
- Suggested length: 120-150 words
- Write your essay in the space provided on your answer sheet. <u>Any writing outside the space will not be graded.</u>

TOPIC
Should Japan introduce a system of giving tips for good service?

POINTS
- *Motivation*
- *Stress for customers*
- *Lower wages*
- *Encouragement of better service*

Listening Test

There are three parts to this listening test.

Part 1	Dialogues: 1 question each	Multiple-choice
Part 2	Passages: 2 questions each	Multiple-choice
Part 3	Real-Life: 1 question each	Multiple-choice

※Listen carefully to the instructions.

Part 1 ◀))105~117

Day 1
Day 2
Day 3
Day 4
Day 5
Day 6
Day 7

No. 1
1 Consult with a car salesperson.
2 Consider purchasing a used car.
3 Inspect a variety of brand new cars.
4 Find someone to repair their car.

No. 2
1 Board his flight.
2 Go to his departing gate.
3 Find out which gate to go to.
4 Go through the security check.

No. 3
1 It will damage their living space.
2 It might hurt their daughter.
3 The man will not offer his support.
4 The man has never had a pet before.

No. 4
1 Give a sales report at a meeting.
2 Complete a slideshow for him.
3 Postpone a presentation.
4 Take a rest in the office.

No. 5
1 It features a variety of boutiques and delis.
2 It is convenient for grocery shopping.
3 There is an inexpensive supermarket nearby.
4 Most businesses cost too much.

No. 6	**1**	She often gets lost.
	2	She is going to Steve's place.
	3	She does not have a map.
	4	She is a student.
No. 7	**1**	Have a yard for garden space.
	2	Find out what houses are currently available.
	3	Move to a house that has lower rent.
	4	Build a new house with room for their children.
No. 8	**1**	It is a good opportunity.
	2	He should stay in Tokyo.
	3	Los Angeles is an outstanding city.
	4	It comes at a bad time.
No. 9	**1**	Refund the price of the cleaning.
	2	Provide an additional service.
	3	Return the man's suit early.
	4	Finish the work by Sunday.
No. 10	**1**	Booking a hotel room.
	2	Canceling his flight.
	3	Reserving a flight.
	4	Contacting a guest.
No. 11	**1**	It will likely be demanding.
	2	He could not get the job he wanted.
	3	He will have no co-workers.
	4	It was not chosen by his team.
No. 12	**1**	The man is being overly pessimistic.
	2	The man did better than she did.
	3	She found the exams challenging.
	4	She will help the man to do better next time.

(A) *No. 13* **1** They need more time to eat.
2 They process calories better than meat-eaters.
3 They follow the example of the giraffe.
4 They spend more energy asleep than awake.

No. 14 **1** Giraffes do not need any sleep.
2 Giraffes can only sleep standing up.
3 Giraffes only sleep for about half an hour a day.
4 Giraffes can get up quickly to escape attacks.

(B) *No. 15* **1** It has become too dangerous for children.
2 It has not changed much over the years.
3 It is vital for future professional racers.
4 It is available in too few countries.

No. 16 **1** Professional racers becoming national heroes.
2 Winners of kart races making a lot of money.
3 Karts becoming more reasonably priced.
4 Kart racing becoming a professional sport.

(C) *No. 17* **1** People thought the items at street markets had fleas.
2 Certain sellers started selling fleas at a market.
3 Sellers began to offer their goods at a city named "Flea."
4 They originated from markets where people collected blood from fleas.

No. 18 **1** It features antiques from France.
2 It is smaller than the original market.
3 It consists of multiple small markets.
4 It mainly targets wealthy people.

Day 1
Day 2
Day 3
Day 4
Day 5
Day 6
Day 7

(D)	*No. 19*	**1** By listening to other similar songs.
		2 By not listening to it for a while.
		3 By telling others that they like it.
		4 By listening to it several times.
	No. 20	**1** Companies often change their logos to maximize the effects of advertising.
		2 Well-known themes are incorporated into products.
		3 Most companies sell products recommended by famous people.
		4 Stores play various kinds of music to make customers comfortable.
(E)	*No. 21*	**1** It is a mythical creature that lives in a valley.
		2 It is a person wearing a mask and animal fur.
		3 It is a group of robbers stealing from the rich.
		4 It is a young man that only scares children.
	No. 22	**1** Only married couples can participate.
		2 They celebrate the birth of Switzerland.
		3 Participants have fun in the traditional costume.
		4 Costumes no longer look scary.
(F)	*No. 23*	**1** A little stress is actually healthy.
		2 Stress is naturally damaging.
		3 Strong people can handle more stress.
		4 It is not a natural part of the human body.
	No. 24	**1** They often fail to recognize signs of stress.
		2 They frequently complain about it to others.
		3 They can actually become addicted to it.
		4 They may become more efficient at handling it.

(G)　**No. 25**　*Situation:* You are on vacation, walking around a busy tourist area. You want to take a break for a couple of hours in a spot with Internet access which is not too noisy. You stop by an information center and ask for advice.

Question: Which place should you choose?

1 Mark's Café on Portner Road.
2 O'Toole's Coffee in the business district.
3 Margaret's Café on Eleanor Avenue.
4 The library on Eleanor Avenue.

(H)　**No. 26**　*Situation:* You are attending a college orientation. You hear the following instructions.

Question: To have your picture taken, where should you go?

1 To the Administration Building.
2 To Hancock Student Union.
3 To Steinbeck Library.
4 To the Registration Office.

(I)　**No. 27**　*Situation:* You have sent a vacuum cleaner to be repaired. If it cannot be fixed within two weeks, you would prefer to dispose of it. You receive a voice mail from the manufacturer.

Question: What should you do?

1 Send the warranty certificate.
2 Pick up the product at the factory.
3 Call the manufacturer within three days.
4 Wait for the repairs to finish.

(J) **No. 28** ***Situation:*** You notice a service fee of $50 on your monthly bank account statement. You do not know what it is for. You call your bank's customer service hotline.

Question: What number should you press?

1 One.
2 Two.
3 Three.
4 Four.

(K) **No. 29** ***Situation:*** You are at your dentist's clinic to have a check-up. After your check-up, you are listening to the dentist's explanation.

Question: What should you do before your next appointment?

1 Brush your teeth harder.
2 Purchase some dental floss.
3 Get a softer toothbrush.
4 Have your teeth x-rayed.

筆記試験＆リスニングテスト

Day
1

Day
2

Day
3

Day
4

Day
5

Day
6

Day
7

準1級の面接（スピーキングテスト）は どんなテスト？

面接（スピーキングテスト）では，
問題カードのイラストについて説明をしたり，
質問に対して自分自身の意見を述べたりします。
まず面接の流れをつかみ，予想問題を確認しましょう。

スピーキングテスト
対策はこちら ▶ ▶ ▶

1 入室

係員の指示に従い，面接室に入ります。あいさつをしてから，面接委員に面接カードを手渡し，指示に従って，着席しましょう。

2 氏名・受験級の確認と日常会話

面接委員があなたの氏名と受験する級の確認をします。その後，簡単な会話をしてから試験開始です。

3 ナレーションの考慮時間（1分間）

問題カードを手渡されます。指示文を黙読し，4コマのイラストについてナレーションの準備をします。時間は1分間です。
※問題カードには複数の種類があり，面接委員によっていずれか1枚が手渡されます。

4 ナレーション（2分間）

ナレーションをするよう指示されるので，問題カードで指定された言い出し部分から始めます。時間は2分間です。超過しないよう時間配分に注意しましょう。

┌─ **ナレーションのポイント** ──────────────
│ ☐ 問題カードで指定された文から始める
│ ☐ イラスト内にある時間や場所を示す表現，せりふ，登場人物の表情などを活用する
│ ☐ 各コマ2〜3文程度で描写する（ナレーション時間は全体で2分）
└──────────────────────────────

5 4つの質問

面接委員の4つの質問に答えます。イラストやトピックに関連した質問です。1つ目の質問に答える際には問題カードを見ても構いませんが，2つ目以降は問題カードを裏返して答えます。また，自然な聞き返しであれば減点の対象になりません。積極的に自分の意見を話しましょう。

質問への返答のポイント

- ☐ No.1は多くの場合，イラストのうちの4コマ目に登場した人物の立場に立ち，受験者自身がその人物だったらどう思うかといった質問に答える
- ☐ No.2/3はカードのトピックに関連した内容について自分の意見を求められる
- ☐ No.4はカードのトピックにやや関連した，社会性のある内容についての質問に答える

6 カード返却と退室

試験が終了したら，問題カードを面接委員に返却し，あいさつをして退室しましょう。

ナレーション 🔊131

問題カード

You have **one minute** to prepare.

This is a story about a man who watched a TV program about plastic pollution.
You have **two minutes** to narrate the story.

Your story should begin with the following sentence:
One day, a man was at home with his wife.

Questions

No. 1   Please look at the fourth picture. If you were the man, what would you be thinking?

No. 2   Do you think many young people these days are concerned about environmental issues?

No. 3   Should the government introduce a carbon tax?

No. 4   Some say that Japan's media needs to change the way it reports the news. Should the Japanese media report on a wider range of issues that affect people's lives?

解答解説

ナレーション　🔊 133

解答例

One day, a man was at home with his wife. They were watching a program about plastic waste on TV. They both felt very shocked to see that the amount of plastic waste that is thrown away every year is increasing. Later that evening, the man suggested they do something to reduce plastic waste. The woman said she would start using an eco-bag. The man said he was going to start using a reusable coffee tumbler. Two days later, the man was in a café ordering coffee. Smiling, the man asked the server to put his coffee into his reusable tumbler. A few seconds later, the man was shocked to see the server measure his coffee out in a disposable cup, pour the coffee into his reusable tumbler, and then throw the cup into the trash.

解答例の訳

ある日，1人の男性が妻と一緒に家にいました。彼らはテレビでプラスチック廃棄物に関する番組を見ていました。彼らは2人とも，毎年捨てられるプラスチック廃棄物の量を見て非常にショックを受けました。その晩の後ほど，男性はプラスチック廃棄物を減らすために何かをしようと提案しました。女性はエコバッグを使い始めると言いました。男性は，再利用可能なコーヒータンブラーを使い始めるつもりだと言いました。2日後，男性はカフェにいて，コーヒーを注文していました。ほほえみながら男性は，自分の再利用可能なタンブラーにコーヒーを入れるよう，店員に頼みました。数秒後，男性は，その店員が使い捨てのカップに入れてコーヒーを計量し，そのコーヒーを彼の再利用可能なタンブラーに注ぎ，それからそのカップをごみ箱に捨てるのを見てショックを受けました。

> **解説** 解答に含めるべき点は，①夫婦が自宅でテレビの画面に映ったプラスチック廃棄量の増加を示すグラフを見ている，②その晩の後ほど，男性がプラスチック廃棄物を減らそうと提案し，妻はエコバッグを，夫は再利用可能なコーヒータンブラーの使用を考えている，③2日後，夫はカフェでコーヒーを注文しており，タンブラーにコーヒーを入れてもらおうとしている，④店員が使い捨てのカップで計量してから夫のタンブラーにコーヒーを入れ，そのカップをごみ箱に捨てるのを見て驚いている，の4つ。1コマ目は，They were looking at a graph showing that the amount of plastic waste was increasing. のような表現も可能。2コマ目の男性のせりふは They were talking about ways to reduce plastic waste. のように表すこともできる。

4つの質問　🔊 134

No. 1

解答例

I'd be thinking that the server doesn't understand why I'm using a reusable tumbler. If she understood, she would measure out my coffee in a regular cup.

> **解説** 「4番目の絵を見てください。もしあなたが男性なら，どのようなことを考えているでしょうか」という質問。解答例の第2文は，仮定法を使って「店員がもし理解していたら通常の（使い捨てではない）カップで計量

するだろう」という意味。よりストレートに, It makes no sense to bring a reusable tumbler. 「再利用可能なタンブラーを持参しても意味がない」なども可能だろう。

No. 2

解答例

Yes, these days more and more young people are becoming aware of environmental issues such as climate change. Some are making real efforts to reduce their impact on the environment by changing their diets and buying more eco-friendly products. Others are starting to campaign for change.

解説 「最近の多くの若者は環境問題に関心があると思いますか」という質問。解答例はYesの立場で, 気候変動などの環境問題に気付いている若者が増えていることに言及した後, 具体的にどんな努力をしているかを説明している。Noの立場では, 若者は「忙しくて考える時間がない」「環境よりも利便性に関心がある」などの意見が可能。

No. 3

解答例

Yes, the government should do so. A carbon tax would encourage individuals and businesses to reduce consumption and increase energy efficiency. Carbon taxes also make alternative energies more cost-competitive.

解説 「政府は炭素税を導入すべきですか」という質問。解答例はYesの立場で, 炭素税は「個人と企業が消費を減らし, エネルギー効率を高める」「代替エネルギーをよりコスト競争力のあるものにする」という2つの理由を述べている。個人の視点で「化石燃料を多く使った製品は買わなくなるだろう」などのより具体的な意見も可能だろう。

No. 4

解答例

Yes. I think the media has a responsibility to report on all kinds of issues that affect our lives. In Japan there are fewer TV documentaries about environmental, political and social issues than in many other countries.

解説 「日本のメディアはニュース報道の仕方を変える必要があると言う人がいます。日本のメディアは人々の生活に影響を与えるより広い範囲の問題を報道すべきですか」という質問。1文目の話題導入文で現況や事実が紹介され, 2文目でそれに関するYes/No質問がなされる。ほかの質問と同様, この2文目の質問に適切な内容を答えよう。解答例はYesの立場で,「メディアは生活に影響を与えるあらゆる種類の問題を報告する責任がある」と主張した後, 他国と比べて少ないテレビキュメンタリーの例を挙げている。「少ない(からもっと広範囲の問題を報道すべき)」という主張の仕方である。

MEMO

MEMO

MEMO

MEMO

4 English Summary

Write your English Summary in the space below. (Suggested length: 60-70 words)

5
10
15
20

Day 1 解答用紙（準1級）

筆記解答欄

問題番号	1	2	3	4
(1)	①	②	③	④
(2)	①	②	③	④
(3)	①	②	③	④
(4)	①	②	③	④
(5)	①	②	③	④
(6)	①	②	③	④
(7)	①	②	③	④
(8)	①	②	③	④
(9)	①	②	③	④
(10)	①	②	③	④
(11)	①	②	③	④
(12)	①	②	③	④
(13)	①	②	③	④
(14)	①	②	③	④
(15)	①	②	③	④
(16)	①	②	③	④
(17)	①	②	③	④
(18)	①	②	③	④

1

問題番号	1	2	3	4
(19)	①	②	③	④
(20)	①	②	③	④
(21)	①	②	③	④
(22)	①	②	③	④
(23)	①	②	③	④
(24)	①	②	③	④
(25)	①	②	③	④
(26)	①	②	③	④
(27)	①	②	③	④
(28)	①	②	③	④
(29)	①	②	③	④
(30)	①	②	③	④
(31)	①	②	③	④

2 (19)–(24)
3 (25)–(31)

リスニング解答欄

	問題番号	1	2	3	4
Part 1	No.1	①	②	③	④
	No.2	①	②	③	④
	No.3	①	②	③	④
	No.4	①	②	③	④
	No.5	①	②	③	④
	No.6	①	②	③	④
	No.7	①	②	③	④
	No.8	①	②	③	④
	No.9	①	②	③	④
	No.10	①	②	③	④
	No.11	①	②	③	④
	No.12	①	②	③	④
A	No.13	①	②	③	④
	No.14	①	②	③	④
B	No.15	①	②	③	④
	No.16	①	②	③	④
C	No.17	①	②	③	④
	No.18	①	②	③	④
D	No.19	①	②	③	④
	No.20	①	②	③	④
E	No.21	①	②	③	④
	No.22	①	②	③	④
F	No.23	①	②	③	④
	No.24	①	②	③	④
G	No.25	①	②	③	④
H	No.26	①	②	③	④
I	No.27	①	②	③	④
J	No.28	①	②	③	④
K	No.29	①	②	③	④

Part 2 (A–F), Part 3 (G–K)

注意事項

（HBの）黒鉛筆またはシャープペンシル以外の筆記
具を使用してマーク・記入した場合、解答が無効と
なるので、注意してください。

※ 5 の解答欄は裏面にあります。

記入上の注意（記述形式）

・太枠に囲まれた部分のみが採点の対象です。

・指示事項を守り、文字は、はっきりと分かりやすく、濃く、書いてください。

・数字の１と小文字のl（エル）、数字の２とＺ（ゼット）など似ている文字は、判別できるよう書いてください。

・消しゴムで消す場合は、消しくず、消し残しがないようしっかりと消してください。

・解答が英語以外の言語を用いている、質問と関係がない、テストの趣旨に反すると判断された場合、０点と採点される可能性があります。

5 English Composition

Write your English Composition in the space below. (Suggested length: 120-150 words)

5

10

15

20

25

4 English Summary

Write your English Summary in the space below. (Suggested length: 60-70 words)

5
10
15
20

Day 2 解答用紙（準1級）

筆記解答欄

問題番号	1	2	3	4
(1)	①	②	③	④
(2)	①	②	③	④
(3)	①	②	③	④
(4)	①	②	③	④
(5)	①	②	③	④
(6)	①	②	③	④
(7)	①	②	③	④
(8)	①	②	③	④
(9)	①	②	③	④
(10)	①	②	③	④
(11)	①	②	③	④
(12)	①	②	③	④
(13)	①	②	③	④
(14)	①	②	③	④
(15)	①	②	③	④
(16)	①	②	③	④
(17)	①	②	③	④
(18)	①	②	③	④

1

問題番号	1	2	3	4
(19)	①	②	③	④
(20)	①	②	③	④
(21)	①	②	③	④
(22)	①	②	③	④
(23)	①	②	③	④
(24)	①	②	③	④
(25)	①	②	③	④
(26)	①	②	③	④
(27)	①	②	③	④
(28)	①	②	③	④
(29)	①	②	③	④
(30)	①	②	③	④
(31)	①	②	③	④

2

3

リスニング解答欄

	問題番号	1	2	3	4
Part 1	No.1	①	②	③	④
	No.2	①	②	③	④
	No.3	①	②	③	④
	No.4	①	②	③	④
	No.5	①	②	③	④
	No.6	①	②	③	④
	No.7	①	②	③	④
	No.8	①	②	③	④
	No.9	①	②	③	④
	No.10	①	②	③	④
	No.11	①	②	③	④
	No.12	①	②	③	④
Part 2	A No.13	①	②	③	④
	No.14	①	②	③	④
	B No.15	①	②	③	④
	No.16	①	②	③	④
	C No.17	①	②	③	④
	No.18	①	②	③	④
	D No.19	①	②	③	④
	No.20	①	②	③	④
	E No.21	①	②	③	④
	No.22	①	②	③	④
	F No.23	①	②	③	④
	No.24	①	②	③	④
Part 3	G No.25	①	②	③	④
	H No.26	①	②	③	④
	I No.27	①	②	③	④
	J No.28	①	②	③	④
	K No.29	①	②	③	④

注意事項

（HBの）黒鉛筆またはシャープペンシル以外の筆記具を使用してマーク・記入した場合、解答が無効となるので、注意してください。

4 English Summary

Write your English Summary in the space below. (Suggested length: 60-70 words)

_____ 5

_____ 10

_____ 15

_____ 20

Day 3 解答用紙（準1級）

筆記解答欄

問題番号	1	2	3	4
(1)	①	②	③	④
(2)	①	②	③	④
(3)	①	②	③	④
(4)	①	②	③	④
(5)	①	②	③	④
(6)	①	②	③	④
(7)	①	②	③	④
(8)	①	②	③	④
(9)	①	②	③	④
(10)	①	②	③	④
(11)	①	②	③	④
(12)	①	②	③	④
(13)	①	②	③	④
(14)	①	②	③	④
(15)	①	②	③	④
(16)	①	②	③	④
(17)	①	②	③	④
(18)	①	②	③	④

1

問題番号	1	2	3	4
(19)	①	②	③	④
(20)	①	②	③	④
(21)	①	②	③	④
(22)	①	②	③	④
(23)	①	②	③	④
(24)	①	②	③	④
(25)	①	②	③	④
(26)	①	②	③	④
(27)	①	②	③	④
(28)	①	②	③	④
(29)	①	②	③	④
(30)	①	②	③	④
(31)	①	②	③	④

2 ((19)–(24))
3 ((25)–(31))

リスニング解答欄

	問題番号	1	2	3	4
Part 1	No.1	①	②	③	④
	No.2	①	②	③	④
	No.3	①	②	③	④
	No.4	①	②	③	④
	No.5	①	②	③	④
	No.6	①	②	③	④
	No.7	①	②	③	④
	No.8	①	②	③	④
	No.9	①	②	③	④
	No.10	①	②	③	④
	No.11	①	②	③	④
	No.12	①	②	③	④
Part 2 A	No.13	①	②	③	④
	No.14	①	②	③	④
B	No.15	①	②	③	④
	No.16	①	②	③	④
C	No.17	①	②	③	④
	No.18	①	②	③	④
D	No.19	①	②	③	④
	No.20	①	②	③	④
E	No.21	①	②	③	④
	No.22	①	②	③	④
F	No.23	①	②	③	④
	No.24	①	②	③	④
Part 3 G	No.25	①	②	③	④
H	No.26	①	②	③	④
I	No.27	①	②	③	④
J	No.28	①	②	③	④
K	No.29	①	②	③	④

注意事項

（HBの）黒鉛筆またはシャープペンシル以外の筆記
具を使用してマーク・記入した場合、解答が無効と
なるので、注意してください。

※ 5 の解答欄は裏面にあります。

切り取り線

5　English Composition

Write your English Composition in the space below. (Suggested length: 120-150 words)

5

10

15

20

25

4 English Summary

Write your English Summary in the space below. (Suggested length: 60-70 words)

(writing lines marked at 5, 10, 15, 20)

Day 4 解答用紙（準1級）

リスニング解答欄

	問題番号	1	2	3	4
Part 1	No.1	①	②	③	④
	No.2	①	②	③	④
	No.3	①	②	③	④
	No.4	①	②	③	④
	No.5	①	②	③	④
	No.6	①	②	③	④
	No.7	①	②	③	④
	No.8	①	②	③	④
	No.9	①	②	③	④
	No.10	①	②	③	④
	No.11	①	②	③	④
	No.12	①	②	③	④
Part 2 A	No.13	①	②	③	④
	No.14	①	②	③	④
B	No.15	①	②	③	④
	No.16	①	②	③	④
C	No.17	①	②	③	④
	No.18	①	②	③	④
D	No.19	①	②	③	④
	No.20	①	②	③	④
E	No.21	①	②	③	④
	No.22	①	②	③	④
F	No.23	①	②	③	④
	No.24	①	②	③	④
Part 3 G	No.25	①	②	③	④
H	No.26	①	②	③	④
I	No.27	①	②	③	④
J	No.28	①	②	③	④
K	No.29	①	②	③	④

筆記解答欄

	問題番号	1	2	3	4
1	(1)	①	②	③	④
	(2)	①	②	③	④
	(3)	①	②	③	④
	(4)	①	②	③	④
	(5)	①	②	③	④
	(6)	①	②	③	④
	(7)	①	②	③	④
	(8)	①	②	③	④
	(9)	①	②	③	④
	(10)	①	②	③	④
	(11)	①	②	③	④
	(12)	①	②	③	④
	(13)	①	②	③	④
	(14)	①	②	③	④
	(15)	①	②	③	④
	(16)	①	②	③	④
	(17)	①	②	③	④
	(18)	①	②	③	④

	問題番号	1	2	3	4
2	(19)	①	②	③	④
	(20)	①	②	③	④
	(21)	①	②	③	④
	(22)	①	②	③	④
	(23)	①	②	③	④
	(24)	①	②	③	④
3	(25)	①	②	③	④
	(26)	①	②	③	④
	(27)	①	②	③	④
	(28)	①	②	③	④
	(29)	①	②	③	④
	(30)	①	②	③	④
	(31)	①	②	③	④

注意事項

（HBの）黒鉛筆またはシャープペンシル以外の筆記具を使用してマーク・記入した場合、解答が無効となるので、注意してください。

4 English Summary

Write your English Summary in the space below. (Suggested length: 60-70 words)

(解答欄：罫線あり、5・10・15・20行の目盛り付き)

Day 5 解答用紙（準1級）

筆記解答欄

問題番号	1	2	3	4
(1)	①	②	③	④
(2)	①	②	③	④
(3)	①	②	③	④
(4)	①	②	③	④
(5)	①	②	③	④
(6)	①	②	③	④
(7)	①	②	③	④
(8)	①	②	③	④
(9)	①	②	③	④
(10)	①	②	③	④
(11)	①	②	③	④
(12)	①	②	③	④
(13)	①	②	③	④
(14)	①	②	③	④
(15)	①	②	③	④
(16)	①	②	③	④
(17)	①	②	③	④
(18)	①	②	③	④

（上記 (1)〜(18) は **1**）

問題番号	1	2	3	4
(19)	①	②	③	④
(20)	①	②	③	④
(21)	①	②	③	④
(22)	①	②	③	④
(23)	①	②	③	④
(24)	①	②	③	④
(25)	①	②	③	④
(26)	①	②	③	④
(27)	①	②	③	④
(28)	①	②	③	④
(29)	①	②	③	④
(30)	①	②	③	④
(31)	①	②	③	④

（(19)〜(24) は **2**、(25)〜(31) は **3**）

リスニング解答欄

	問題番号	1	2	3	4
Part 1	No.1	①	②	③	④
	No.2	①	②	③	④
	No.3	①	②	③	④
	No.4	①	②	③	④
	No.5	①	②	③	④
	No.6	①	②	③	④
	No.7	①	②	③	④
	No.8	①	②	③	④
	No.9	①	②	③	④
	No.10	①	②	③	④
	No.11	①	②	③	④
	No.12	①	②	③	④
A	No.13	①	②	③	④
	No.14	①	②	③	④
B	No.15	①	②	③	④
	No.16	①	②	③	④
C	No.17	①	②	③	④
	No.18	①	②	③	④
D	No.19	①	②	③	④
	No.20	①	②	③	④
E	No.21	①	②	③	④
	No.22	①	②	③	④
F	No.23	①	②	③	④
	No.24	①	②	③	④
G	No.25	①	②	③	④
H	No.26	①	②	③	④
I	No.27	①	②	③	④
J	No.28	①	②	③	④
K	No.29	①	②	③	④

（No.13〜No.24 は Part 2、No.25〜No.29 は Part 3）

注意事項
（HBの）黒鉛筆またはシャープペンシル以外の筆記具を使用してマーク・記入した場合、解答が無効となるので、注意してください。

※ **5** の解答欄は裏面にあります。

記入上の注意（記述形式）

・太枠に囲まれた部分のみが採点の対象です。

・指示事項を守り、文字は、はっきりと分かりやすく、濃く、書いてください。

・数字の1と小文字のl（エル）、数字の2とZ（ゼット）など似ている文字は、判別できるよう書いてください。

・消しゴムで消す場合は、消しくず、消し残しがないようしっかりと消してください。

・解答が英語以外の言語を用いている、質問と関係がない、テストの趣旨に反すると判断された場合、0点と採点される可能性があります。

5 English Composition

Write your English Composition in the space below. (Suggested length: 120-150 words)

5

10

15

20

25

切り取り線

4 English Summary

Write your English Summary in the space below. (Suggested length: 60-70 words)

(lined answer space with line markers at 5, 10, 15, 20)

Day 6 解答用紙（準1級）

筆記解答欄

問題番号	1	2	3	4
(1)	①	②	③	④
(2)	①	②	③	④
(3)	①	②	③	④
(4)	①	②	③	④
(5)	①	②	③	④
(6)	①	②	③	④
(7)	①	②	③	④
(8)	①	②	③	④
(9)	①	②	③	④
(10)	①	②	③	④
(11)	①	②	③	④
(12)	①	②	③	④
(13)	①	②	③	④
(14)	①	②	③	④
(15)	①	②	③	④
(16)	①	②	③	④
(17)	①	②	③	④
(18)	①	②	③	④

（1）

問題番号	1	2	3	4
(19)	①	②	③	④
(20)	①	②	③	④
(21)	①	②	③	④
(22)	①	②	③	④
(23)	①	②	③	④
(24)	①	②	③	④

（2）

問題番号	1	2	3	4
(25)	①	②	③	④
(26)	①	②	③	④
(27)	①	②	③	④
(28)	①	②	③	④
(29)	①	②	③	④
(30)	①	②	③	④
(31)	①	②	③	④

（3）

リスニング解答欄

	問題番号	1	2	3	4
Part 1	No.1	①	②	③	④
	No.2	①	②	③	④
	No.3	①	②	③	④
	No.4	①	②	③	④
	No.5	①	②	③	④
	No.6	①	②	③	④
	No.7	①	②	③	④
	No.8	①	②	③	④
	No.9	①	②	③	④
	No.10	①	②	③	④
	No.11	①	②	③	④
	No.12	①	②	③	④
Part 2　A	No.13	①	②	③	④
	No.14	①	②	③	④
B	No.15	①	②	③	④
	No.16	①	②	③	④
C	No.17	①	②	③	④
	No.18	①	②	③	④
D	No.19	①	②	③	④
	No.20	①	②	③	④
E	No.21	①	②	③	④
	No.22	①	②	③	④
F	No.23	①	②	③	④
	No.24	①	②	③	④
Part 3　G	No.25	①	②	③	④
H	No.26	①	②	③	④
I	No.27	①	②	③	④
J	No.28	①	②	③	④
K	No.29	①	②	③	④

注意事項
（HBの）黒鉛筆またはシャープペンシル以外の筆記具を使用してマーク・記入した場合、解答が無効となるので、注意してください。

※ 4 の解答欄は裏面にあります。

記入上の注意（記述形式）

・太枠に囲まれた部分のみが採点の対象です。

・指示事項を守り、文字は、はっきりと分かりやすく、濃く、書いてください。

・数字の1と小文字のl（エル）、数字の2とZ（ゼット）など似ている文字は、判別できるよう書いてください。

・消しゴムで消す場合は、消しくず、消し残しがないようしっかりと消してください。

・解答が英語以外の言語を用いている、質問と関係がない、テストの趣旨に反すると判断された場合、0点と採点される可能性があります。

5 English Composition

Write your English Composition in the space below. (Suggested length: 120-150 words)

5

10

15

20

25

4 English Summary

Write your English Summary in the space below. (Suggested length: 60-70 words)

（解答欄：5 / 10 / 15 / 20 行）

Day 7 解答用紙（準1級）

筆記解答欄

問題番号	1	2	3	4
(1)	①	②	③	④
(2)	①	②	③	④
(3)	①	②	③	④
(4)	①	②	③	④
(5)	①	②	③	④
(6)	①	②	③	④
(7)	①	②	③	④
(8)	①	②	③	④
(9)	①	②	③	④
(10)	①	②	③	④
(11)	①	②	③	④
(12)	①	②	③	④
(13)	①	②	③	④
(14)	①	②	③	④
(15)	①	②	③	④
(16)	①	②	③	④
(17)	①	②	③	④
(18)	①	②	③	④

問題番号	1	2	3	4
(19)	①	②	③	④
(20)	①	②	③	④
(21)	①	②	③	④
(22)	①	②	③	④
(23)	①	②	③	④
(24)	①	②	③	④
(25)	①	②	③	④
(26)	①	②	③	④
(27)	①	②	③	④
(28)	①	②	③	④
(29)	①	②	③	④
(30)	①	②	③	④
(31)	①	②	③	④

1 … (1)～(18)　　2 … (19)～(24)　　3 … (25)～(31)

リスニング解答欄

	問題番号	1	2	3	4
Part 1	No.1	①	②	③	④
	No.2	①	②	③	④
	No.3	①	②	③	④
	No.4	①	②	③	④
	No.5	①	②	③	④
	No.6	①	②	③	④
	No.7	①	②	③	④
	No.8	①	②	③	④
	No.9	①	②	③	④
	No.10	①	②	③	④
	No.11	①	②	③	④
	No.12	①	②	③	④
Part 2 A	No.13	①	②	③	④
	No.14	①	②	③	④
B	No.15	①	②	③	④
	No.16	①	②	③	④
C	No.17	①	②	③	④
	No.18	①	②	③	④
D	No.19	①	②	③	④
	No.20	①	②	③	④
E	No.21	①	②	③	④
	No.22	①	②	③	④
F	No.23	①	②	③	④
	No.24	①	②	③	④
Part 3 G	No.25	①	②	③	④
H	No.26	①	②	③	④
I	No.27	①	②	③	④
J	No.28	①	②	③	④
K	No.29	①	②	③	④

注意事項

（HBの）黒鉛筆またはシャープペンシル以外の筆記具を使用してマーク・記入した場合、解答が無効となるので、注意してください。

※ 5 の解答欄は裏面にあります。

記入上の注意（記述形式）

・太枠に囲まれた部分のみが採点の対象です。

・指示事項を守り、文字は、はっきりと分かりやすく、濃く、書いてください。

・数字の1と小文字のl（エル）、数字の2とZ（ゼット）など似ている文字は、判別できるよう書いてください。

・消しゴムで消す場合は、消しくず、消し残しがないようしっかりと消してください。

・解答が英語以外の言語を用いている、質問と関係がない、テストの趣旨に反すると判断された場合、0点と採点される可能性があります。

5 English Composition

Write your English Composition in the space below. (Suggested length: 120-150 words)

5

10

15

20

25

7日間完成

文部科学省後援

英検®準1級
予想問題ドリル
[6訂版]

解答と解説

Contents 解答と解説

英検®は、公益財団法人 日本英語検定協会の登録商標です。

旺文社

筆記試験
解答と解説

1

問題	1	2	3	4	5	6	7	8	9	10	11	12	13	14	15	16	17	18
解答	4	1	3	3	3	1	3	1	1	4	2	2	4	2	4	4	2	2

2

問題	19	20	21	22	23	24
解答	1	4	3	4	3	2

3

問題	25	26	27	28	29	30	31
解答	1	1	3	4	2	1	2

4 解説内にある解答例を参照してください。

5 解説内にある解答例を参照してください。

Day
1

1

(1) 解答 **4**
A「ヒューストン・ヘルスクリニック＆ジムへようこそ。目標は何ですか」
B「夏までに30ポンド減らしたいです」
解説 Bの「30ポンド減らしたい」は，運動をして体重を減らすことを意味しており，これはジムに来た目標（objective）である。observation「観察」，reflection「反射」，reaction「反応」

(2) 解答 **1**
「その女性議員は保全において優れた記録を残している。彼女はしばしば環境保護に対する規制を提案，支持している」
解説 第2文のenvironmental protectionと結び付くのはconservation「（自然・文化財などの）保護，保存」である。corruption「汚職・腐敗」，exploration「探査」，extension「拡張」

(3) 解答 **3**
「その歴史学の教授は初代アメリカ大統領ジョージ・ワシントンについて講義をした」
解説 lecture「講義」が目的語なので，動詞はdeliver「（講義・講演など）を行う」。besiege「包囲する」，congregate「召集する」，indent「（段落の最初の語）を字下げにする」

(4) 解答 **3**
「カレンはボートに乗り込んだとき，自分が一生の冒険に乗り出していたとは思いも寄らなかった」
解説 直後のon the adventureがポイント。embark onで「（冒険など）に乗り出す」という意味。filter「ろ過する」，portray「肖像を描く」，intervene「介入する」

(5) 解答 **3**
「若者の間で腰の問題の発生率が増加している理由の1つは，彼らが通学時に背負う重いバックパックであると医者たちは考えている」
解説 重い荷物が原因で増加するのは，腰の問題のincidence「発生率」である。intolerance「不寛容」，inheritance「相続」，insertion「挿入」

1

(6) 解答 **1**

「彼女は夫に無条件の愛を与えた。彼女は彼が大変なときも, 彼を信じ, 支えた」

解説 夫が大変なときも与える妻の愛を説明するものを探すと, **1**の「無条件な」(unconditional) 愛とわかる。unauthorized「権限のない」, exaggerated「誇張された」, expedient「都合の良い」

(7) 解答 **3**

「数週間に及ぶ激しい論争の末, 国会は最終的には政府の年度予算案を承認した」

解説 endorse は「(提案・計画など) を是認する」という意味。approximate「近づける」, embezzle「横領する」, admonish「警告する」

(8) 解答 **1**

「警察は暴動を鎮圧し, デモ参加者が街路を暴れ回るのをやめさせるために催涙ガスを発射した」

解説 tear gas「催涙ガス」を発射するのは, 暴動をquell「鎮圧する」ためだと考えられる。rouse「目を覚まさせる」, stir「かき回す」, incite「扇動する」

(9) 解答 **1**

「膝の問題は軽く考えてはいけません。きちんとした治療を受けないと, 慢性的になりますよ」

解説 治療しないと, chronic「慢性的な」になると推測できる。reckless「向こう見ずな」, neutral「中立の」, expectant「期待している」

(10) 解答 **4**

「クラブの会則によれば, ダイニングホールではネクタイと上着の着用が義務付けられている。選択の余地は本当にない」

解説 第2文の「選択の余地がない」を言い換えたcompulsory「義務的な」が適切。collective「集団の」, nomadic「遊牧の」, protective「保護の」

(11) 解答 **2**

A「新しい仕事に就くことをなぜそんなに急いでいるの?」

B「外国人だから, 就労ビザの期限が切れるまでに, 常勤の仕事に就きたいんだ」

解説 主語のvisa「ビザ」に合う動詞はexpire「期限が切れる」。assert「主張する」, insert「差し込む」, inspire「鼓舞する」

(12) 解答 **2**

A「両親は私が大学で経済学を学ぶよう強要しました。私は本当に音楽家になりたかったのです」

B「だからあなたはそんなに勉強に無関心なんですね」

解説 音楽家になりたかったのに親が大学進学を強要した結果, 勉強に無関心 (indifferent) なのである。vigorous「元気いっぱいの」, enduring「我慢強い」, meager「やせ衰えた」

(13) 解答 **4**

「窃盗の容疑者の自宅を調べるために, 警察は裁判所から家宅捜索の令状を得なければならなかった」

解説 家宅捜索に必要なものは裁判所からのwarrant「令状」である。citation「引用」, grant「補助金」, deed「権利書, 行為」

(14) 解答 **2**

「東京の電車は時々通勤客でぎっしり満員なので, プラットホームで待っている人が電車に乗り込めないことがある」

解説 通勤客で満員の状態なので, densely「ぎっしりと」がふさわしい。sparsely「まばらに」, clumsily「不器用に」, devoutly「敬虔に」

(15) 解答 **4**

「早々にいくつか敗戦した後, チームは立ち直り, その大会で優勝した」

解説 「いくつかの敗戦」と「優勝した」の間に起こったこととして, bounced back「(打撃から) 回復した」が適切。pass down「〜を (次世代に) 伝える」, drop in「立ち寄る」, mix up「〜を混同する」

(16) 解答 **4**

「私は授業で手を挙げ続けたが, 先生は決して私を当てなかった。私は授業の後で先生と話し, 先生はより内気な生徒たちに話す機会をもっと与えたいと説明した」

解説 butがあるので「手を挙げ続けたが当ててくれなかった」という流れ。〈call on+人〉「(授業で) (人) に当てる」。〈tell off+人〉「(人) に文句を言う」, speak out「遠慮なく言う」, 〈talk+人+through〉「(人) に理解できるように説明する」

(17) 解答 **2**

「メーガンは頭痛がひどく, 鎮痛剤を飲んだ。しかし, 数時間後に薬の効果が消えたので, 彼女はもう1錠飲

まなければならなかった」

解説 soに着目。薬をもう1錠飲んだのは，薬の効果が「消えた」からである。wear off「（痛み・効果が）徐々に消える」。drop out「脱落する」，take off「離陸する」，fall out「（外へ）落ちる」

2

全訳

変わりゆく世界

　近年，企業にとって最大の課題の1つは，例えば科学技術や法律，流行などの変化についていくことである。これに成功するには，企業には非伝統的な手法を採用することを恐れない，柔軟に物事を考える人が必要である。しかしながら，これらの役割に合う人を見つけるのは難しい。そのため，ぴったりの人材を新しく雇用しようとする代わりに，企業は即興を使って現従業員の技能を磨いている。

　即興は，アドリブとしても知られているが，役者によって自発的に，すなわち台本なしで生み出される舞台演技の一種である。一般的に信じられていることとは反対に，アドリブは，その瞬間に行動し，反応する能力を培うための計画性と練習を必要とする。アドリブで最も重要なルールは，すべての発言に対して「はい，そして」で返答することである。「はい」と言うことは，話し手の考えに対するオープンスと受け入れを示し，コミュニケーションのための好意的な場を作り出す。「そして」を追加して発言を続けることで，相手の発言を足掛かりにさらに発展させる。これはチームワークと共同作業の基礎である。ビジネスにおけるこの「はい，そして」ルールは協調を促進し，ブレインストーミングと問題解決のために従業員たちがアイデアを出し合うことを助長する。

　アドリブ手法は，現世代の大学生から未来のリーダーを育成するのに特に有益だと見込まれる。この世代は，前の世代よりも感情面でオープンであるだけでなく，実践からよく学び，優れた協力者でもあり，社会的な交流を楽しむが，これらはアドリブで必要なものを反映する特徴である。カリキュラムにアドリブの課程を組み入れるアメリカのビジネススクールが増えるにつれ，このアイデアがより主流となることが見込まれる。

---

(18) **解答** **2**

「ハイキングで小道を歩く際は，特に崖の下を歩くような場所では，落石に注意してください」

解説 落石が続くので，look out for「～に注意する」。make out「～を理解する」，catch up「追いつく」，see off「～を見送る」

---

(19) **解答** **1**

解説 Thereforeがあるので，その前の内容と因果関係になる。前の「柔軟に物事を考える人を見つけるのは難しい」から，instead ofを入れて，そういった人材を新しく雇用しようとする「代わりに」とすると文意が通る。

(20) **解答** **4**

解説 Thisは前の内容を指す。すべての発言に対して"yes, and"と言うアドリブ手法がコミュニケーションにおいてどんな効果があるかを考えると，**4**が適切。空所後の「協調を促進し，従業員がアイデアを出し合うことを助長する」にもうまくつながる。

(21) **解答** **3**

解説 段落冒頭の「アドリブ手法は現世代に有益」という内容から，「感情面でオープン，実践からよく学ぶ，優れた協力者，社会的な交流を楽しむ」といった現世代の特徴は，**3**「アドリブで必要なものを反映する」特徴である。

全訳

セネガルのピンク色の湖

　セネガルのレトバ湖は，そのピンク色の水により世界中で有名である。この色は，高濃度のベータカロテンを持つドナリエラ・サリナと呼ばれる藻に由来する。レトバ湖でドナリエラ・サリナが繁茂する理由は，その水の高い塩分含有量のためである。1970年代に起こった深刻な干ばつにより，漁場としての湖が，塩の収穫のための湖に変わった。

　これらの環境上の変化に対応して，近くに会社が次々に設立されて，湖から塩を取って販売した。湖底にある塩を男たちが棒で割り，潜って集めた。これが重労働であることに加え，塩分量の多い水の腐食性が皮膚障害を引き起こした。これを避けるため，塩採掘

者は湖に入る前に体にシアバターを塗った。ボートを塩でいっぱいにして，男たちは浜に戻り，そこで女たちが塩を降ろして湖沿いに積み上げ，山を作った。塩は，ヨウ素という元素と混ぜ合わされ，袋詰めにされ，ほとんどが魚を保存するために漁師に売られた。

　残念ながら，問題がすぐに生じた。不誠実な会社が給料を支払わず，労働者の権利を常に侵害した。レトバ湖周辺の建設により，水の流出が妨げられた。場所の回復を待つことなく，塩が湖全体から採取されていた。その結果，1994年には地域社会が自ら責任を負った。レトバ湖沿岸の５つの村が代表者を選出し，管理委員会を設立した。この委員会のおかげで，今では労働者と環境の両方に擁護者がいる。まだ対処しなければならない課題はあるものの，行動を起こすという地域社会の決断は，正しい方向への力強い一歩であった。

(22)　解答　**4**

解説　空所にはレトバ湖でドナリエラ・サリナが繁茂する理由が入る。空所後の「干ばつによって塩の収穫のための湖に変わった」という内容から，**4**「その水の高い塩分含有量」が適切。

(23)　解答　**3**

解説　空所には後の To avoid this の this に当たる内容が入る。塩採掘者が湖に入る前に体にシアバターを塗った理由を考えると，塩分量の多い水の腐食性が**3**「皮膚障害を引き起こした」からである。

(24)　解答　**2**

解説　空所後の「地域社会が自ら責任を負った」は，空所前の「不誠実な会社が労働者の権利を侵害した」「水の流出が妨げられた」などの問題が生じた結果である。よって，**2**「その結果」が適切。

3

全訳
健康と強引な売り込み

　インターネット上における商品広告の違いは，アメリカとイギリスの健康文化が同じものではないことを浮き彫りにする。インターネットにアクセスすれば，ユーザーは非常に広範囲にわたる健康の専門家がその治療を宣伝し，想像し得る限りのありとあらゆる症候群，病気，異常について声高に語っていることに気が付く。あらゆるアメリカの雑誌，特にライフスタイルを扱ったものを手にすれば，そこには医者や医療，処方箋がなければ買えない薬についての広告がたっぷりある。これらの薬の広告は，イギリスでは医学雑誌でしか見られない種類のものである。テレビをつければ，さらに多くの製薬会社の宣伝や，著名な医師が最新の著書について語っているトークショーにさらされることになる。イギリス人の観点からすると，アメリカ人はあまりにも多くの健康情報を砲撃のように浴びせかけられているので，彼らの健康管理に関する判断は過度に複雑になっているように思える。

　アメリカの良心的な医者の中には，こういう形での広告は倫理に反するものであり，欲しいような気にさせられたがきっと必要ないであろう薬について表面的に情報を与えられただけの患者に対し，自分の処方の選択を擁護しなければならない立場に医者を追い込ん

でいると考える人も多い。これは中途半端な情報を持った患者とプロの医者の対立という問題となる。一方，可能な限りの情報を与えられるのは患者にとって良いことであり，もしインターネットや広告全般がこれを促進できるのなら，悪いことではないと信じる医者もいる。

　このようなアメリカの健康消費者，すなわち患者の姿は，イギリスのものとはまったく異なっている。イギリス人は列を作り，国民健康保険による診療を受けるために予約待ちをし，医者の時間を無駄にしているのではないかと心配をする。さらに非常に異なるのは，イギリスにいまだに残る，医者が一番わかっているという姿勢であり，これが医療分野における新たな発展に関して患者と医者の間で質問したり，話し合ったりすることをしばしばやめさせてしまう。

　イギリスでは，全国医学協議会（GMC）が最近ガイドラインを改定して，医者に広告することを許可したが，保守的な医者はこのような自己宣伝は適切でないという強い見解を一般に持っている。しかし，広告はとても必要とされている情報を人々に提供する手段の１つである。したがって，商業主義と結び付けられるのを恐れるのは，気取りの表れの１つと見なす者もいる。インターネットを利用して医学的なウェブサイトにアクセスすることが増え，テレビドラマによって

医学用語が家庭に持ち込まれ，医療サービスで受けられるものに対する意識が高まるにつれ，イギリスでも徐々に変化は起きているのである。

(25) 解答 **1**

「この文章によると，次のどれが正しいか」

1 アメリカでの方が患者に対する広告に焦点が置かれる。

2 メディアの医療情報はイギリスでより容易に入手可能である。

3 アメリカの医師の大多数は，薬物と医師の宣伝が患者に利益をもたらすことで意見が一致している。

4 アメリカ人はイギリス人よりもメディアの情報にはるかに強い疑いを抱いている。

解説 第1段落に，アメリカでは雑誌の広告やテレビの宣伝を通して消費者はたっぷりの情報が得られるという内容があり，また，第3段落第1文に This portrait of the American health consumer or patient「このようなアメリカの健康消費者，すなわち患者の姿」とあることから，アメリカでは患者は消費者と考えられていることがわかる。したがって**1**が正解。

(26) 解答 **1**

「多くのイギリス人はアメリカ人をどのように見ているか」

1 アメリカ人は医療に関する情報に圧倒されているため，選択が不必要に難しくなっている，と思っている。

2 アメリカ人は運良く非常に多くの医療情報が自由に入手でき，またイギリスの患者よりも幸せだ，と思っている。

3 アメリカ人がインターネットから得た情報は，彼らが代わりに医者に頼るべきであるときに彼らに誤った専門知識の感覚を与えている，と思っている。

4 アメリカ人を健康管理に対してあまりに無頓着だと見ており，アメリカ人は広告にもっと懐疑的であるべきだ，と思っている。

解説 イギリス人がアメリカ人をどう見ているかについては，第1段落最終文で From the British point of view, it would seem ... become overly complex. とあり，この部分と**1**が一致する。

(27) 解答 **3**

「イギリスの医療ではどのような変化が起きているか」

1 医師が患者にもっと多くの質問をしてもっと情報を得るよう促している。

2 大多数の医師がメディアで宣伝をし始めている。

3 医学と健康管理に関する情報を知らされる人が増えている。

4 保守的な医者が医療広告を阻止する新しい法律を要請した。

解説 医療情報に関するイギリスでの変化については，最終段落最終文の Change is also gradually happening in Britain ... の部分にインターネットやテレビ経由で情報が増えたことが説明されている。

全訳

アン・ハサウェーの新しい見方

　ウィリアム・シェークスピアに携わるジャーナリストと学者の批評家はシェークスピアの妻，アン・ハサウェーにこれまで好意的ではなかった。彼らは彼女を，26歳のときに18歳のウィリアムを誘惑し，妊娠によって自分と結婚することを強制した器量の良くない女性に仕立て上げている。シェークスピアは，ストラットフォード・アポン・エーボンでの不幸な家庭生活から，より刺激的で自由なロンドンの生活へ逃れ，脚本家として成功を収めたと言われていた。彼らは，シェークスピアが彼の遺書にはアンを含めなかったことを，結婚生活の仲たがいの証拠として引用している。

　しかしながら，伝記作家でフェミニストのジャーメイン・グリアはこの描写に異議を唱える。エリザベス朝時代からの証拠書類を引用して，グリアは，ハサウェーは実際はシェークスピアに愛されていたと『シェークスピアの妻』の中で主張した。事実彼女は，シェークスピアの劇中の，長い別離にもかかわらず愛にいちずな真面目な女性たちのモデルだったのかもしれない。ではシェークスピアの学者たちによるハサウェーの否定的な印象はなぜなのだろう？「妻の方が，彼ら（学者たち）が近づき得るよりも偶像（シェークスピア）に近く，彼らが理解し得るよりもよく彼を理解していたという可能性は面白くなかったのでしょう」とグリアは言う。若いウィリアムは実際に年上のアンと恋に落ちたが，彼女にとってその結婚は理想の結婚からはほど遠かった，と彼女（グリア）は考える。彼女は裕福な地主であり，金もほとんどなく初等教育しか受けていないティーンエージャーを誘惑することで得るメリットなどなかっただろう。彼女はよく描写されるように，26歳で相手を見つけることにそんなに必死ではなかったようだ。エリザベス朝時代の女性の結婚の平均年齢は成熟した27歳だったのだから。さらに，彼女がもし本当に彼の意思に逆らってティーンエージャーを誘惑したとしたら，彼女は村の法律官吏

と確実にもめていたであろう。そのような出来事の記録や言及はない。

シェークスピアとハサウェーは結婚生活のほとんどを別々に暮らしていたが，彼女が彼を非難したことはなく，彼もまた彼女を非難しなかった。ハサウェーはつらい時期を通してシェークスピアの3人の子供を誠実に育て，金貸しだけでなく麦芽の生産者としても独力で成功を収めた。ハサウェーはシェークスピアが戻って老後の生活を送ることになる大きくて優雅な家，「新居」を購入し，準備した人である。

グリアはハサウェーには欠点がないと示すようなことをして，強く出過ぎることはしないように注意している。彼女は，ハサウェーが夫との長年にわたる別離でおそらく孤独であり，村人たちやほかのロンドンを訪れた人たちがシェークスピアにはほかに女のみならず男がいると報告していたので，彼が彼女に対していつも誠実なのではないことを心配していたと認めている。さらに，シェークスピアの，欲望に満ちた年上の女性についての官能的な詩「ビーナスとアドニス」の発表の後，ハサウェーは世間の物笑いの種になったと予想される。

グリアの本はシェークスピアの時代の社会史であり彼の妻の伝記でもある，非常に研究された作品である。ハサウェーはその時代の生活，習慣，しきたりを示す手段として用いられている。グリアがハサウェーを熱心に擁護するあまりに行ったいくつかの強引な解釈について，学者は当然批判するだろうが，彼女の主張の大部分は明らかに，彼女をけなすのに用いられた事実より確かな証拠に基づいている。

(28)　解答　4

「グリアは，学者がアン・ハサウェーについて描いたイメージについて何と言っているか」

1 シェークスピアがハサウェーを愛していたよりもハサウェーはシェークスピアを愛していたことを除けば，ほとんどの点でかなり正確である。

2 主に，シェークスピアが自分の劇の多くのために描いた女性たちのモデルに基づいている。

3 イメージは2人の早婚の既知の事実にのみ基づいているために単純過ぎる。

4 過度に否定的で，シェークスピア時代の文献に書かれた事実を反映していない。

解説　学者の否定的なアン・ハサウェー像については第1段落に，グリアが唱えている異議の内容が第2段落に述べられている。グリアはエリザベス朝時代からの証拠書類を引用することで意義を唱えていることか

ら，**4** が正解。

(29)　解答　2

「グリアは，学者たちがハサウェーの共通のイメージを作り上げたと異議を唱える。その理由は」

1 彼らは誤解を招く証拠書類に基づいて仮定したから。

2 彼らは彼女がその作家について持っていた知識と親密さに嫉妬しているから。

3 そのイメージが普通の妻の肖像よりももっと面白い話を作るから。

4 ハサウェーはシェークスピアについての否定的な話に便利な身代わりだから。

解説　学者に共通したハサウェー像の成立原因については，第2段落中ほどのグリアの発言 "The possibility that a wife may be closer to their idol ... could not be entertained." にヒントがある。the playwright はシェークスピアのことで，**2** が正解。

(30)　解答　1

「グリアはシェークスピアとハサウェーの結婚について何を示唆しているか」

1 シェークスピアに結婚を強要することでハサウェーが得るだろうメリットを示す証拠はない。

2 彼女がシェークスピアを彼の意思に反して誘惑した兆候はあるが，2人は実際には結婚当時は互いに愛し合っていた。

3 ハサウェーは結婚当時26歳であり，自分の年齢を心配してシェークスピアに自分と結婚するように勧めた可能性がある。

4 シェークスピアは十分に教育を受けず，また貧しかったため，結婚を推し進めたのはハサウェーよりむしろ彼だった可能性が高い。

解説　結婚については，グリアは第2段落後半で She was a wealthy landowner who would benefit little from seducing a teenager ... と言っている。a teenager はシェークスピアのことで，**1** が正解。benefit を選択肢では profit に言い換えている。

(31)　解答　2

「この文章の筆者は，グリアのハサウェーの解釈について何をほのめかしているか」

1 グリアの綿密な研究によって明確に裏付けられているので，学者はそれを受け入れ始めている。

2 グリアの持つ先入観にもかかわらず，ハサウェーに関するより一般的で否定的な見解よりも信頼できる。

3 グリアはハサウェーを熱心に擁護しており，彼女の

解釈は根本的に欠陥があって真剣に検討する価値がない。

4 彼女の事実の多くは明らかに正確であるが，それはハサウェーの像をあまりにも卑劣に描いている。

解説 最終段落最終文のthe majority of the assertions are clearly based on more solid evidence than are the majority of facts used to disparage her から，**2**が正解。more solid evidenceを選択肢では more credibleと表している。

問題文の訳

　約8,500万年前，ニュージーランドは古代の超大陸から分離した。長い間，鳥類を食べる陸上動物がいなかったため，このことが多くの在来種の鳥が飛べなくなった原因だと考えられている。近代になって，人間がこの国に住み着きネズミやイタチなどの外来種を持ち込んだことで，在来種の飛べない鳥の3分の1近くが絶滅してしまった。これを受けて，2010年代に政府は鳥類を狩る動物を排除する対策を取り始めた。

　ニュージーランド在来鳥類の個体数が一部の地域では回復しつつあることから，これらの捕食動物を排除する計画は成功を収めつつある。長期的には，これは在来鳥類の減少を抑え，その数をさらに増やすことにつながるだろう。また，鳥がよく巣を作る在来の植物や樹木を保護するという，さらなる利点もある。

　とはいえ，ネズミのような知的な生き物の大量殺戮は残酷だと考える批評家もいる。さらに，この計画では2050年までに有害生物を駆除することになっており，関係組織の長期間にわたる関与が必要となる。ほとんどの批評家は，これは最終的には莫大な費用がかかり，スタッフや設備に何百万ドルもかかるだろうという点で意見が一致している。

解答例

　In the past, in New Zealand, many flightless birds became extinct because of humans, along with their introduction of foreign species. To handle this, the government began to eliminate animals that target birds. This plan is making progress, and it is also beneficial for native plants and trees. However, some point out the cruelty of killing so many intelligent animals and the significant expenses involved in this project. (68語)

解答例の訳

　かつてニュージーランドでは，人間や人間による外来種の導入により，多くの飛べない鳥が絶滅した。これに対応するために，政府は鳥類を狙う動物を排除し始めた。この計画は前進しており，在来の植物や樹木にも利点がある。しかし，これほど多くの知的な動物を殺すことの残酷さや，この計画に伴う多大な費用を指摘する人もいる。

解説　まず，英文を読んで，各段落の要点を押さえる。各要点を1（〜2）文でまとめ，展開を示す接続表現を用いながら，全体を3〜4文で書けば60〜70語に収まるだろう。解答例は，第1〜2文「トピック導入文（ニュージーランドの飛べない鳥の絶滅，政府の計画）」（第1段落），第3文「利点」（第2段落），第4文「欠点」（第3段落）の4文構成。第3段落のNeverthelessは計画の賛→否の展開を示す印で，解答例ではHoweverでつなげている。

　要点をまとめるポイントは，①重要な情報を見極め，細かい情報や具体例は省く，②具体的な情報を抽象化する，の2点。例えばnearly a third ofのような具体的な数字はあまり重要ではないため，解答に含む場合はmanyのように抽象化して表す。第1段落のsuch as rats and stoatsのような具体的な例や第2段落のwhere the birds often nestのような追加情報は重要ではないことが多い。主語と動詞を含む「文」を「名詞句」で表すことも端的に言い換えるコツである。第3段落では3文にわたり計画の負の側面として批評家の意見が複数書かれているが，これをpoint out A and B「AやBを指摘する」と名詞句で表すと少ない語数で複数の情報が盛り込める。

　評価観点の語彙では，英文の内容をできるだけ自分の言葉で表す力が求められる。別の表現に言い換えて，多種多様な語彙が使えることをアピールしよう。この問題では以下のようなパターンに分けることができる。ぜひ参考にしよう。

・同義表現の言い換え：wiping out→became extinct, non-native→foreign, In response to this→To handle this, get rid of→eliminate, showing success→making progress, mass destruction→killing so many
・派生語の言い換え：introduced（動詞）→introduction（名詞），cruel（形容詞）→cruelty（名詞），extremely expensive（副詞＋形容詞）→significant expenses（形容詞＋名詞）

5

TOPIC：日本の企業はプラスチック廃棄物を減らすための対応策を取るべきか。
POINTS：コスト・環境・過剰包装・再利用

<table>
<tr><td>

解答例

I believe companies in Japan should take action to reduce plastic waste. I have two reasons to support this: excess packaging and reuse.

First, many products in Japan are sold with excessive plastic packaging. Most of this is single-use plastic and is simply thrown away. Companies should not only reduce the amount of plastic packaging they use, but start to use more eco-friendly packaging materials.

Second, many companies have plenty of opportunities to find ways to encourage the reuse of plastic products. For example, many coffee shops still use plastic caps for takeout coffee cups. Instead, they should ask their customers to have their own reusable cups.

In conclusion, I feel companies in Japan should take steps to limit plastic waste because they still put too much packaging on many products and have ample opportunities to urge customers to use reusable products.（142語）

</td><td>

解答例の訳

　日本の企業はプラスチック廃棄物を減らすための対応策を取るべきだと思う。これを支持する2つの理由がある。過剰包装と再利用である。

　第1に，日本の多くの商品は過剰なプラスチック包装で販売されている。このほとんどは使い捨てのプラスチックであり，捨てられるだけである。企業は自分たちが使用するプラスチック包装の量を減らすだけでなく，より環境に優しい包装材料を使い始めるべきである。

　第2に，多くの企業はプラスチック製品の再利用を促す方法を見つける機会がたくさんある。例えば，多くのコーヒーショップでは，いまだにテイクアウト用のコーヒーカップにプラスチック製のふたを使用している。代わりに，客に再利用可能なカップを持つよう求めるべきである。

　結論として，日本の企業は，依然として多くの製品に過剰な包装を施しており，客に再利用可能な製品の使用を強く促す機会が十分にあることから，プラスチック廃棄物を制限するための措置を講じるべきだと思う。

</td></tr>
</table>

Day
1

解説　「日本の企業はプラスチック廃棄物を減らすための対応策を取るべきか」という質問に対し，解答例ではYesの立場を取っている。序論となる第1段落ではまず，I believe ... の形で立場を明らかにしている。その後I have two reasons to support this: A and B.「これを支持する2つの理由がある。AとBである。」という表現を使って，POINTSのExcess packagingとReuseを提示している。ほかにThey should do so for reasons such as A and B.「彼らはAやBなどの理由でそうすべきだ」のようなPOINTSを盛り込む定型表現をいくつか知っておくとよい。

　本論となる第2，3段落では，First, ... Second, ... などの構造で，取り上げた2つのPOINTSに沿って理由・根拠を詳しく述べる。解答例の第2段落はExcess packagingの観点で，not only A but Bの形を用いて，企業が「過剰なプラスチック包装を控える」こと，「環境に優しい包装材料を使う」ことの2点を挙げている。第3段落はReuseの観点で，「プラスチック製品の再利用を促す方法を見つける機会がたくさんある」と述べた後，For exampleを用いて具体的な対策の例を挙げている。結論となる最終段落では，自分の立場を再主張する。解答例では，再度2つのポイントを盛り込みながら，トピックのtake actionをtake stepsに言い換えて，「プラスチック廃棄物を制限するための措置を講じるべき」と締めくくっている。

　POINTSのCostとEnvironmentは，「環境に優しい素材にかかるコスト」「プラスチック廃棄物のリサイクルにかかるコスト」「プラスチック廃棄物が環境に与える影響」などの観点で意見を述べることができるだろう。

リスニングテスト
解答と解説

問題編 p.23〜28

Part 1	問題	*1*	*2*	*3*	*4*	*5*	*6*	*7*	*8*	*9*	*10*	*11*	*12*
	解答	1	1	3	3	1	3	1	3	4	1	4	2

Part 2	問題	*13*	*14*	*15*	*16*	*17*	*18*	*19*	*20*	*21*	*22*	*23*	*24*
	解答	2	3	1	2	1	4	2	3	4	4	1	4

Part 3	問題	*25*	*26*	*27*	*28*	*29*
	解答	1	2	4	1	3

Part 1 🔊 001〜013

No. 1　解答 **1**

☆：Your thesis drafts are due on Tuesday the 21st, so you all have exactly five days left. No exceptions. I'll accept e-mail attachments, as well as paper copies brought to my office in A-308. That's it for today.

★：Professor, can I ask a favor? Could I have two extra days? I'll be out of town this weekend since my aunt passed away. We're traveling to Cleveland and so I'll be away from my computer.

☆：Oh, I'm sorry to hear that. In that case, yes, Thursday is fine. Can you have it to me by 4 p.m.?

★：Absolutely. Thank you.

Question：What does the man ask his professor to do?

☆：皆さんの論文の原稿は21日の火曜日が期限なので，あと5日間ちょうどです。例外は認めません。A-308の私のオフィスに紙の原稿を持ってきてもいいですし，メールへの添付でも受け付けます。今日は以上です。

★：教授，お願いがあります。あと2日頂けないでしょうか。叔母が亡くなったので，今週末は不在にします。クリーブランドに行くので，パソコンから離れてしまいます。

☆：ああ，それは気の毒ですね。その場合はいいでしょう，木曜日で結構です。午後4時までにもらえますか。

★：もちろんです。ありがとうございます。

質問：男性は教授に何をするよう頼んでいるか。

1 論文の締め切りを延ばす。　　**2** 1週間の欠席を認める。
3 彼がメールで論文を送ることを許す。　　**4** 彼がパソコンを自宅に持ち帰ることを許す。

解説　男子学生の教授への頼み事は，can I ask a favor? の後に続く。Could I have two extra days? と言っているが，これは論文の原稿の期限についてなので，**1** が正解。

No. 2 解答 **1**

●：Mindy, is Alex doing all right in school these days? I noticed his report card on the table the other day. His grades have slipped a bit.

☆：I didn't see it yet. Have they?

●：A little. But he used to be a straight-A student. Did he say anything to you?

☆：Not recently, although now that I think about it, he did mention that brass band practice is hard, but he can't get out of it until the year is over.

●：If that's true, that's a problem. I'll talk to him and see what he says.

☆：So will I.

Question：What does the couple decide to do?

●：ミンディ，アレックスは最近学校でちゃんとやってる？　先日テーブルの上の成績表に気付いたんだけど。彼の成績は少し落ちたよ。

☆：まだ見ていないわ。落ちたの？

●：ちょっとね。でも以前はオールＡの生徒だったよ。君に何か言ってた？

☆：最近は言ってこないわね，でも今考えてみると，ブラスバンドの練習が厳しいのだけど，今年が終わるまでどうしようもないと言っていたわ。

●：それが本当なら問題だ。彼と話して何と言うか様子を見てみるよ。

☆：私もそうするわ。

質問：夫婦は何をすることにしたか。

1 問題について息子と話し合う。　　**2** 息子のために家庭教師を雇う。
3 息子のブラスバンドの先生に相談する。　　**4** 息子の先生に成績について尋ねる。

解説　夫婦が息子の成績が落ちたという問題（the matter）について話している。最後に夫がI'll talk to him and see what he says. と言うと妻はSo will I. と答えているので，**1**が正解。

No. 3 解答 **3**

☆：How did your meeting at work go today?

★：They told me I'll be transferring to the Singapore office.

☆：Wow, that's news. Are you upset?

★：No, quite the opposite. I've been putting in requests to go overseas for years now. Yumi and I don't have children yet, so this is our chance.

☆：Well, what does Yumi have to say about the matter? Didn't you two build a new house last year?

★：She's totally fine with it. We'll be back in three years, so we're thinking of renting out the house while we're gone.

Question：What does the man say about his situation?

☆：今日の仕事の会議はどうだった？

★：僕はシンガポールの事務所に転勤になると言われたよ。

☆：うわー，それは初耳だわ。動揺しているの？

★：いや，まったく逆だよ。もう何年もの間，海外への異動願いを出してきたからね。ユミと僕はまだ子供がいないから，これは僕たちのチャンスだ。

☆：それで，このことについてユミに何か言い分はないの？　あなたたち２人は昨年新しい家を建てなかった？

★：彼女は全然平気。３年後に戻ってくるから，僕たちがいない間は家を賃貸に出そうと考えているよ。

質問：男性は自分の状況について何と言っているか。

1 彼は新しい仕事について不安になっている。　　**2** 彼は転職に不満である。
3 海外に住むことはわくわくする。　　**4** 家を借りることはお金がかかる。

解説　冒頭部分から，男性が海外に転勤することがわかる。その気持ちを表したI've been putting in requests ..., so this is our chance. という発言から，**3**が正解。

No. 4　解答　3

● : These days Megan just stays in her room all day, honey. I'm worried. She doesn't talk to me much. I have no idea what she's up to.

☆ : She's a teenager, Joel. I was pretty much the same when I was her age. How about you? Did you have your own room when you were 14?

● : Well, yeah.

☆ : You spent time in it and didn't chit-chat with your parents, right?

● : OK, I get the picture. I'm just lonely, I guess. I miss the little girl I used to have.

☆ : Of course. I do too.

Question : What advice is the woman trying to give the man about their daughter?

● : ねえ，最近メーガンは一日中自分の部屋にいるね。心配だよ。僕とあまり話さないんだ。何を考えているのか見当が付かないよ。

☆ : 彼女はティーンエージャーよ，ジョエル。私も彼女くらいの年齢のときはあんな感じだったわ。あなたはどう？　14歳のときに自分の部屋はあった？

● : ああ，あったね。

☆ : 部屋の中で時間を過ごして，両親とはおしゃべりをしなかったでしょう？

● : そうか，わかったよ。僕は寂しいだけだと思う。以前の幼いあの子が懐かしいよ。

☆ : そうよね。私もよ。

質問 : 女性は娘について男性にどんな助言をしようとしているか。

1 メーガンの振る舞いは彼女らしくない。
2 メーガンの行儀は改善する必要がある。
3 メーガンの振る舞いは年齢を考えれば普通だ。
4 メーガンは両親の反応に不満を抱いている。

解説　部屋に閉じこもりがちな娘について，女性は，She's a teenager, ... の部分で，「娘はティーンエージャーで，自分もそうだった」→「年齢相応だ」と言っている。

No. 5　解答　1

★ : Helen, could you make this proposal a little shorter?

☆ : Sure, but I can't do it today. I've got to make some phone calls. When do you need it by?

★ : I need it for a meeting I'll attend tomorrow at nine. Could you come to the office earlier tomorrow morning?

☆ : What time?

★ : How about seven? Is it too early?

☆ : Yes, it's a little early. But I'll be sure to come before eight.

Question : What will the woman do tomorrow morning?

★ : ヘレン，この提案書をちょっと短くしてもらえないかな。

☆ : いいですけど，今日はできません。何本か電話をかけなければならないのです。いつまでに必要ですか。

★ : 明日9時に出席する会議に必要なんだ。明日の朝はいつもより早く事務所に来てもらえないかな。

☆ : 何時ですか。

★ : 7時はどうだろうか。早過ぎるかな。

☆ : ええ，それはちょっと早いですね。でも8時前には来るようにします。

質問 : 女性は明日の朝に何をするか。

1 提案書を短くする。
2 会議に出席する。
3 何本か電話をかける。
4 いつもより遅くに職場に着く。

解説　男性の could you make this proposal a little shorter? という依頼に対し，女性が Sure と答えている。その後の展開から，その仕事は明日の朝早めに出勤して行うので，明日の朝することとして **1** が正解。

No. 6　解答　3

☆：Hi honey, what's up?

●：Hey, Wendy. Listen, I just finished a meeting with a client whose office is near yours. What do you say you and I meet for dinner nearby? Chinese, maybe?

☆：Oh, George, I love the idea, but the timing couldn't be worse. I'm over at the suburban branch today. I'm just getting ready to leave for home.

●：Ah, no problem. Just thought I'd ask. Say, how about I get take-out? We can meet up at home.

☆：Awesome. Actually, I'd love Chinese tonight.

●：Consider it done.

Question：What does the man suggest that he do for the woman?

☆：あら，あなた。どうしたの？

●：やあ，ウェンディ。あのね，オフィスが君の職場の近くにあるクライアントとの会議が終わったところなんだ。この近くで落ち合って夕食を食べるっていうのはどう？　中華料理とか？

☆：まあ，ジョージ，ぜひそうしたいのだけど，タイミングが最悪だわ。今日は郊外の支店に来ているの。ちょうど家に帰る準備をしているところよ。

●：ああ，いいんだ。聞いてみようと思っただけ。じゃあ，僕が何か買って帰ろうか？　家で会ったらいいよね。

☆：いいわね。実のところ，今夜は中華がいいわ。

●：了解。

質問：男性は女性のために何をすることを提案しているか。

1 夕食を食べるのに繁華街で彼女に会う。　　**2** 郊外のオフィスに彼女を迎えに行く。
3 彼女が食べたい物を家に持ち帰る。　　**4** 自宅で彼女に食事を作ってやる。

解説　男性は最後の方で，how about I get take-out? We can meet up at home. と言って，テイクアウトの料理を家に持ち帰って女性と一緒に食べることを提案している。正解**3**の the food she wants は「中華料理」のこと。

No. 7　解答　1

☆：The vacation I just had was wonderful. It's always hard to go back to work after the holidays are over.

★：I guess that depends on what kind of work you have. I work in retail, and so the holidays are our busiest times of the year.

☆：I see what you mean. So, you can take vacations at any other time, right?

★：Yes. My family and I are planning to go and visit the Grand Canyon from Tuesday to Friday.

☆：That sounds good.

★：The best part is, since the holidays are over, there are fewer tourists, so the roads are wide open.

Question：What does the man imply about his vacations?

☆：今回の休暇は素晴らしかった。休日が終わって仕事に戻るのはいつもつらいわ。

★：それはどんな仕事をしているかによると思うな。僕は小売業で働いているから，休日は1年で最も忙しい時期だ。

☆：言いたいことはわかるわ。それで，ほかの時期にいつでも休暇が取れるわよね？

★：うん。家族で火曜日から金曜日までグランドキャニオンに行く予定なんだ。

☆：それはいいわね。

★：一番いい点は，休日が終わっているから，観光客が減って道が広々としていることだね。

質問：男性は自分の休暇について何をほのめかしているか。

1 彼は休暇シーズン中に休暇を取ることができない。
2 彼は十分な休暇を取らない。
3 彼の休暇は行楽シーズンと重なる。
4 彼の会社は多くの休暇日数を提供する。

解説　男性の発言内容から，男性は「小売業なので休日が忙しい」→「休日は休暇が取れない」と推測できる。最後の The best part is, ... も裏付けとなる。

No. 8　解答　3

●：Where were you before you joined our company last month?
☆：I was with Japan Network Communications. Do you know them?
●：No, I don't. What do they do?
☆：They produce Internet communication systems, mainly for teleconferencing.
●：And what exactly did you do?
☆：I was in the international sales office. My job was to make new contacts in other countries and create new business opportunities for the company.
Question：What do we learn about the woman?

●：先月この会社に入る前はどこにいらしたのですか。
☆：日本ネットワーク・コミュニケーションズにいました。ご存じですか。
●：いいえ。何をしている会社ですか。
☆：インターネットの通信システム，主にテレビ会議用のシステムを作っています。
●：それであなたは具体的に何をしていたのですか。
☆：私は国際販売の部署にいました。私の仕事はほかの国々で新たな関係を築き，会社のために新しいビジネスの機会を作ることでした。
質問：女性について何がわかるか。

1 彼女は日本ネットワーク・コミュニケーションズで働いている。
2 彼女はインターネットの通信システムを作っている。
3 彼女は最近，新しい会社に入社した。
4 彼女は国際販売の部署にいる。

解説　男性がWhere were you before you joined our company last month? と聞いていることから，女性は先月，2人の勤務する会社に入社したことがわかる。正解の**3**以外はすべて前職に関する内容。

No. 9　解答　4

☆：It's been almost half a year since that bicycle accident, but are you still going to physical therapy?
★：Yeah. They say my shoulder bone is healing nicely, but I was told that it takes about a year for it to get completely better.
☆：At least there were no major complications.
★：That's true, but to be honest, it's been half a year of poor sleep. You have to be really careful at night, to get just the right angle to fall asleep without pain.
Question：What do we learn from the conversation?

☆：例の自転車事故から半年近くたったけど，まだ理学療法を受けているの？
★：うん。肩の骨は順調に治っているようなんだけど，完全に良くなるには1年くらいかかると言われたよ。
☆：少なくとも大きな合併症はなかったのね。
★：そうなんだけど，正直に言うと，半年間よく眠れていないんだ。痛みを伴わずに眠るのにちょうどいい体勢を取るには，夜は本当に気を使わないといけないでしょ。
質問：会話から何がわかるか。

1 男性は病院で苦労した。
2 男性の肩の骨はもう痛みがない。
3 男性はもうリハビリ中ではない。
4 男性はあと半年で回復する。

解説　女性のIt's been almost half a year since ... と男性のit's been half a year of poor sleepから，事故から半年たっていることがわかるが，it takes about a year for it to ... から，完治まで1年かかる。これらの情報を統合して，**4**が正解。

No. 10　解答　1

☆：Hello. My name is Betty. I work in the New York office. I enjoyed your conference speech.

●：Pleased to meet you, Betty. As you probably know, I work here in the Tokyo office. I'm responsible for the Japan region.

☆：Yes, I heard. And how are things here?

●：Not bad, thanks. Sales are pretty good. I hear the New York office is doing very well this year.

☆：Yeah. Sales are up by 13 percent from last year. We're very pleased.

●：That's great! So your sales region will likely be number one again, then.

Question：What do we learn about the man?

☆：こんにちは。私はベティです。ニューヨークオフィスで働いています。会議でのあなたのスピーチ楽しかったわ。

●：お会いできてうれしいです，ベティさん。おそらくご存じでしょうが，私はこちら東京オフィスで働いています。日本地域の担当です。

☆：ええ，伺っています。こちらの調子はいかがですか。

●：おかげさまで悪くありません。売り上げは結構好調です。ニューヨークオフィスは今年はとても好調のようですね。

☆：ええ。売り上げが昨年より13％伸びました。私たちはとても喜んでいます。

●：それはすごい！すると，あなたの地域の売り上げがまた一番になりそうですね。

質問：男性について何がわかるか。

1 ニューヨークオフィスは彼のオフィスよりも好調である。
2 彼は来年，ニューヨークオフィスで働くことを望んでいる。
3 彼のオフィスの売り上げは実際低下している。
4 彼は会議を楽しんでいない。

解説 女性のニューヨークオフィスも男性の東京オフィスも好調だが，最後に男性がyour sales region will likely be number one againと言っており，ニューヨークオフィスの方がより好調であることがわかる。

No. 11　解答　4

★：Honey, did you get the mail?

☆：Yes. Why?

★：Was there a package? I ordered a new tool kit online. It was supposed to come today.

☆：No, but there was an undeliverable item notice. It says 3:30 p.m.

★：That's funny. That's just 20 minutes ago. I never heard the doorbell ring. They must have thought we weren't home.

☆：I'll give them a call. Maybe they can drive back here soon.

Question：Why was the package not delivered?

★：ねえ，郵便を受け取った？

☆：ええ。どうして？

★：荷物はなかった？　ネットで新しい工具セットを注文したんだ。今日届くはずだったんだけど。

☆：いいえ，でも不在届の通知があったわ。午後3時30分って書いてある。

★：それはおかしいな。ほんの20分前だよね。玄関のベルが鳴るのが聞こえなかった。僕たちが家にいないと思ったに違いない。

☆：電話するわ。すぐにここに戻ってこられるかもしれない。

質問：荷物はなぜ配達されなかったのか。

1 そのとき夫婦が家にいなかった。
2 配達が遅れた。
3 間違った住所に配達された。
4 配達員が夫婦は外出中だと思った。

解説 会話の前半から，届くはずの荷物が届いていないことがわかる。その理由は，後のThey must have thought we weren't home.から，**4**が正解。

No. 12 [解答] 2

●：Hi, Tina. Welcome to my humble home. Look at what I got today.

☆：Wow. What a fantastic computer! I bet that set you back a bit.

●：Actually, much less than you'd think. I got it on sale at Computer World. I'm going to have a new optical-fiber line installed here in my home office, though, and that will cost a lot.

☆：When will you have it installed?

●：Oh, next week sometime, if there are no problems.

Question：What do we learn about the man's new computer?

●：やあ，ティナ。つましいわが家にようこそ。今日買った物を見てよ。

☆：わあ。すごいコンピューターね！ ちょっとお金がかかったでしょ。

●：実は，君が思うよりずっと安かったよ。コンピューター・ワールドのセールで買ったんだ。もっともこの自宅オフィスに新しい光ファイバー回線を引くつもりで，そっちの方はだいぶかかるけどね。

☆：いつそれを引くの？

●：うーん，来週かな，何も問題なければね。

質問：男性の新しいコンピューターについて何がわかるか。

1 それは最新モデルである。　　　　　**2** それはさほど高価ではなかった。

3 彼はそれにあまり満足していない。　　**4** 女性がその支払いをした。

[解説]　女性の I bet that set you back a bit. の〈set＋人＋back〉は「（人）にお金がかかる」の意味。これに対する応答 much less than you'd think. I got it on sale ... から，男性の言いたいことをつかもう。

16

(A)

The Vizcaya Bridge

The Vizcaya Bridge in Spain is the world's oldest transporter bridge. It was built over the Nervion River in 1893. Unlike ordinary bridges that people and cars cross over, a transporter bridge has a gondola that moves back and forth, carrying people and vehicles across a body of water. The Vizcaya Bridge was the first to adopt this unique architecture and is still in use today. It was registered as a World Heritage site in 2006.

So how did such a design come to be used? Generally, a bridge needs long ramps on both sides to reach the height necessary to cross a river. However, the construction of an enormous structure with long ramps was too costly. Also, the Nervion River was a major traffic route for ferries. A suspension bridge would stop this traffic. The solution was to build an inexpensive bridge that lets ferries pass while people are transported across the river.

Questions

No.13 What is unique about the Vizcaya Bridge?

No.14 Why was the Vizcaya Bridge designed the way it is?

ビスカヤ橋

スペインのビスカヤ橋は世界最古の運搬橋である。これは1893年にネルビオン川に建設された。人と車が渡る通常の橋とは異なり，運搬橋には行き来するゴンドラがあり，人と車両を川の向こう岸へ運ぶ。ビスカヤ橋はこの独特な建築様式を採用した最初の橋で，現在も使用されている。2006年には世界遺産に登録された。

では，そのようなデザインはどのようにして使用されるに至ったのか。一般的に，橋は川を渡るのに必要な高さに達するために両側に長い傾斜路を必要とする。しかし，長い傾斜路を持つ巨大な建造物の建設は費用がかかり過ぎた。また，ネルビオン川はフェリーの主要な交通路だった。つり橋であればこの通行を止めてしまう。解決策は，人々が川を渡って運ばれる間にフェリーが通れるような安価な橋を建設することだった。

No. 13 解答 **2**

「ビスカヤ橋について独特な点は何か」

1 最古の建築方法で建設された。　　**2** ゴンドラで人と車両の両方を運ぶ。

3 2つの世界遺産を結んでいる。　　**4** 世界で最も利用されている橋である。

解説 Unlike ordinary bridges ... 以下に通常の橋とは異なる点，つまり運搬橋であるビスカヤ橋の特徴が述べられる。a transporter bridge has a gondola ... carrying people and vehicles across a body of water から，**2** が正解。

No. 14 解答 **3**

「なぜビスカヤ橋は今のようにデザインされたのか」

1 フェリーが広いネルビオン川を渡ることを可能にするため。

2 遊覧船のための景勝地を作り出すため。

3 利用中にフェリーが橋を通過できるようにするため。

4 交通費を節約するため。

解説 ビスカヤ橋ができた経緯については，最後の The solution was to ... にある。... lets ferries pass while people are transported across the river の言い換えである **3** が正解。節約したのは建設費なので **4** は不適。

(B)

The Illusion of Self

When you make a decision, you may be certain of the reason why you came to that conclusion. However, an experiment conducted by Timothy Wilson at the University of Virginia, as well as other similar tests, suggests that this reasoning may be unreliable. In Wilson's experiment, volunteers were shown two pictures of different people and asked to pick the one they thought was more attractive. Later, they were asked why they made their choice, but some were asked by being presented with the picture that they did not pick.

The outcome was that one out of four volunteers noticed that it was not the picture that they chose. However, the other respondents gave rational reasons for selecting the picture that they thought they had chosen, but had not. This result suggests that humans can simply make up believable stories in order to justify their decisions. Wilson argues that looking at what you do, rather than what you think and feel, may be a better way to learn about yourself.

Questions

No.15 What did Timothy Wilson do in his experiment?

No.16 According to Timothy Wilson, what should people do?

自己の幻想

　決断を下すとき，あなたはその結論に至った理由を確信しているかもしれない。しかし，バージニア大学のティモシー・ウィルソンによって行われた実験，およびほかの同様の検査は，この推論が信ぴょう性に欠けるかもしれないことを示唆している。ウィルソンの実験では，被験者は異なる人々の2枚の写真を見せられ，魅力的だと思う方を選ぶよう求められた。後ほど，被験者はなぜその選択をしたのかを尋ねられたが，何人かは自分が選ばなかった方の写真を提示されて尋ねられた。

　その結果，4人に1人の被験者が，自分が選んだ写真ではないことに気付いた。しかし，ほかの回答者は，自分が選んだと思っていたが実際選ばなかった写真について，それを選んだことに対する合理的な理由を述べたのだ。この結果は，人間が自分の決定を正当化するために単に信ぴょう性のある話を作り上げる可能性があることを示唆している。ウィルソンは，自分の考えと感情よりも，自分のしていることを見ることが，自分自身について知るより良い方法かもしれないと主張する。

No. 15　解答　1

「ティモシー・ウィルソンは実験で何をしたか」

1 彼は研究の参加者に1枚の写真を選ぶよう求めた。

2 彼は写真に関する調査を行った。

3 彼は被験者に決断を下す方法を尋ねた。

4 彼は正しく答えた被験者を選んだ。

解説　In Wilson's experiment, ... の部分に実験内容が詳しく述べられる。ウィルソンは被験者に2枚の人物写真を見せ，魅力的だと思う方を選ばせたことから，**1**が正解。

No. 16　解答　2

「ティモシー・ウィルソンによると，人々は何をすべきか」

1 感情に対する認識を調べる。　　　　**2** 考えよりも行動に注意を払う。

3 先を見越して決定的な計画を立てる。　**4** 合理的自己分析の実施に焦点を当てる。

解説　最後の Wilson argues that looking at what you do, rather than what you think and feel, may be a better way to learn about yourself. がポイント。**2**が正解で，what you do を選択肢では actions に，what you think and feel を thoughts に言い換えている。

(C)

Zoo for Rescued Animals

Popcorn Park Zoo in New Jersey is a special place for animals. Run by a non-profit organization, this unique zoo has been taking in injured, sick, or otherwise at-risk animals and birds since 1977. Visitors can see exotic animals that are not native to the U.S., such as tigers, monkeys, and turtles, as well as wildlife and farm animals. Astonishingly, some of these animals have been kept as pets by people and later abandoned or discovered mistreated.

While Popcorn Park Zoo operates like a normal zoo where visitors can see animals of different sorts, it also has programs that offer people opportunities to learn about these animals' situations and to help them. Signs are put up in the zoo to tell the story of each animal. Associated with several animal shelters, many cats and dogs are also available for adoption. Popcorn Park Zoo is an advancement in the promotion of a closer relationship between animals and humans.

Questions

No.17 What happened to Popcorn Park Zoo in 1977?
No.18 What is one thing we learn about Popcorn Park Zoo?

動物救助動物園

ニュージャージーのポップコーンパーク動物園は，動物にとって特別な場所である。非営利団体によって運営されているこのユニークな動物園は，1977年以来，けが，病気，その他の危険にさらされている動物と鳥を受け入れている。来園者は，野生動物と家畜だけでなく，トラやサル，カメといったアメリカに生息しない変わった動物を見ることができる。驚くべきことに，これらの動物の一部は人々によってペットとして飼われていたが，後に捨てられたか，虐待された状態で見つかったかである。

ポップコーンパーク動物園は，来園者がさまざまな種類の動物を見ることができる通常の動物園のような運営をする一方で，これらの動物の状況について学び，助ける機会を人々に提供するプログラムもある。動物園には各動物の背景を伝える看板が掲げられている。いくつかの動物保護施設と連携しており，里親を求める猫と犬もたくさんいる。ポップコーンパーク動物園は，動物と人間の間のより親密な関係の促進における進歩である。

No. 17 解答 **1**

「1977年，ポップコーンパーク動物園に何があったか」

1 助けが必要な動物と鳥を受け入れ始めた。 **2** 一時的にペットを飼い始めた。
3 野生動物と家畜を繁殖させ始めた。 **4** 絶滅危惧種の植物の保護を始めた。

解説 this unique zoo has been taking in injured, sick, or otherwise at-risk animals and birds since 1977 の部分から，**1** が正解。take in を選択肢では accept に，injured，sick，at-risk を in need に言い換えている。

No. 18 解答 **4**

「ポップコーンパーク動物園についてわかることの1つは何か」

1 来園者に良い物語が見つかる場所を教える。
2 野生生物の気配について人々を教育する。
3 ほかの動物園を助ける機会を提供する。
4 保護された猫と犬が住む新しい家を探す。

解説 動物保護施設との関係について述べられている部分がポイント。終盤の many cats and dogs are also available for adoption の部分から，**4** が正解。この adoption はペットの里親になることである。

(D)

Peter Norman

In the summer of 1968, the Olympic Games were held in Mexico City. Peter Norman, who ran the 200-meter race, won a silver medal for Australia. His time of 20.06 seconds remains an Australian record today. However, Peter Norman's name is better remembered for another reason. When Norman stood on the podium, the two other medalists, Americans Tommie Smith and John Carlos, each raised one arm. Their fists were covered with black gloves. This was a symbol calling for racial equality. Norman did not raise his arm or have a black glove, but he wore the badge of the Olympic Project for Human Rights to show support for the two Americans.

For a long time, Norman's silent action was unrecognized in his home country. When Norman died in 2006, the U.S. Track and Field Federation declared the day of his funeral Peter Norman Day. Two monuments were built on American soil to remember Norman along with Smith and Carlos. In contrast, it was only in 2012, six years after his death, when the Australian parliament offered an official apology and recognized his legacy.

Questions

No.19 What did Norman do during the 1968 Summer Olympics?

No.20 What happened after Norman's death?

ピーター・ノーマン

1968年の夏，メキシコシティーでオリンピックが開催された。200メートル競争を走ったピーター・ノーマンは，オーストラリアに銀メダルをもたらした。彼の20.06秒というタイムは今日でもオーストラリア記録である。しかし，ピーター・ノーマンの名前は別の理由でより記憶されている。ノーマンが表彰台に立ったとき，ほかの2人のメダリストであるアメリカ人のトミー・スミスとジョン・カーロスがそれぞれ片腕を上げた。彼らの拳は黒い手袋で覆われていた。これは人種的平等を求めるシンボルだった。ノーマンは腕を上げず黒い手袋もしなかったが，2人のアメリカ人への支持を示すために人権を求めるオリンピックプロジェクトのバッジを着けた。

長い間，ノーマンの暗黙の行動は彼の祖国で認められなかった。ノーマンが2006年に亡くなったとき，アメリカ陸上競技連盟は彼の葬儀の日をピーター・ノーマン・デーとした。スミスとカーロスとともにノーマンを記憶に残すため，2つの記念碑がアメリカの地に建てられた。対照的に，オーストラリア議会が公式に謝罪し彼の遺産を認めたのは，彼の死から6年も後の2012年だった。

No. 19　解答　2

「ノーマンは1968年の夏季オリンピックで何をしたか」

1 彼は両手に黒い手袋をはめた。　　　　　　　**2** 彼は人種的平等を支持する装飾品を着けた。

3 彼は勝者の表彰台に立つことを拒んだ。　　　**4** 彼は国籍を示すバッジを着けた。

解説　... he wore the badge of ... to show support for the two Americans から，ノーマンはほかの2人を支持するために badge を着けたことがわかる。その2人は人種的平等を求める行動をしていたので，ノーマンもそれに同調したことになる。badge を accessory と言い換えた**2**が正解。

No. 20　解答　3

「ノーマンの死後，何が起きたか」

1 オーストラリア議会がピーター・ノーマン・デーを宣言した。

2 オーストラリアに2つの記念碑が建てられた。

3 オーストラリア議会によって謝罪がなされた。

4 彼の行動がすぐにオーストラリアで認められた。

解説　終盤の the Australian parliament offered an official apology and recognized his legacy から，**3**が正解。**2**はオーストラリア→アメリカなら適切。**4**は，謝罪は死後6年後のことなので，immediately が不適。

(E)

Changes in Preferred News Sources

Newspapers have been a source of information for centuries. Over the years, as technological advancements resulted in lower prices, the number of newspapers and the number of people reading them increased dramatically. However, when radios and televisions became available to common households around the middle of the 20th century, they started taking over part of the role of providing people with news.

According to a research institute in the U.S., recent surveys revealed that television is currently the most preferred news source among Americans. In a survey conducted in 2016, nearly half of the total respondents reported television as their main source of information, while people who preferred print newspapers was merely 11%. A more recent survey, conducted in 2018, showed another interesting trend. Print newspapers have been outpaced by social media, which is the most preferred news source for younger generations.

Questions

No.21 What happened to newspapers around the middle of the 20th century?

No.22 What is one thing the 2018 survey indicated?

好みのニュースソースの変化

新聞は何世紀にもわたって情報源となってきた。長年にわたり，科学技術の進歩によって価格が下がるにつれ，新聞の数とそれを読む人の数は劇的に増加した。しかし，20世紀半ば前後にラジオとテレビが一般家庭に登場したとき，人々にニュースを提供する役割の一部を受け継ぎ始めた。

アメリカのある研究機関によると，最近の調査で，現在テレビがアメリカ人の間で最も好まれているニュースソースであることが明らかになった。2016年に実施された調査では，回答者の半数近くがテレビを主要な情報源として報告したが，紙の新聞の方を好む人は11%にすぎなかった。2018年に実施されたもっと最近の調査では，別の興味深い傾向が示された。紙の新聞が，若い世代に最も好まれるニュースソースであるソーシャルメディアに抜かれたのだ。

No. 21 解答 **4**

「20世紀半ば前後に新聞に何が起こったか」

1 生産が増加し続けた。　　　　　　　　　　**2** 一般家庭に現れ始めた。

3 より安い価格で売買された。　　　　　　　**4** ラジオとテレビに人気を奪われ始めた。

解説　20世紀半ばに登場したラジオとテレビが「ニュースを提供する役割の一部を受け継ぎ始めた」とはつまり，それまで情報源だった新聞が人気を奪われ始めたことを意味する。

No. 22 解答 **4**

「2018年の調査が示したことの1つは何か」

1 紙の新聞が最も好まれるニュースソースだった。

2 多くの人がテレビを見るのをやめた。

3 新聞読者の数が増えた。

4 ソーシャルメディアを介したニュースが新聞よりも人気がある。

解説　2018年の調査について，「新聞がソーシャルメディアに抜かれた」とはつまり，ニュースソースとして新聞よりもソーシャルメディアの方が人気が高くなったのである。

(F)

Babies Know Best

　　Researchers from Yale University have found that infants as young as six months old are able to tell the difference between nice and naughty playmates. In an experiment, researchers showed infants a wooden doll that was walking up and down small hills. Another doll would come up to the first doll and either help it climb up the hill or push it backward. The researchers then passed the dolls to the babies to see which one they wanted to play with. Almost all chose the helpful doll over the naughty one. The Yale researchers believe the experiment shows that humans have basic social skills even before they are taught the difference between right and wrong.

　　However, psychology professor David Lewkowicz of Florida Atlantic University criticized the researchers' conclusions. While finding the experiment and the results interesting, Lewkowicz argues that the research failed to prove that social skills are inherent. He believes that infants observe and learn acceptable social behaviors from parents and others.

Questions

No.23　What did the Yale researchers hope to find out about infants?

No.24　What did David Lewkowicz criticize about the Yale study?

赤ん坊が一番よく知っている

　　わずか６カ月の幼児が良い遊び相手とわんぱくな遊び相手を区別できることをエール大学の研究者が明らかにした。ある実験で，研究者が幼児に小さな丘を上ったり下りたりする木製の人形を見せた。別の人形が最初の人形のところにやって来て，丘を上るのを手伝うか，後ろに押し戻すかのどちらかをした。それから研究者はそれらの人形を赤ん坊に手渡し，どちらと遊びたがるかを確かめた。ほとんどすべてがわんぱくな人形よりも助けてくれる人形を選んだ。この実験は，善悪の区別を教わる以前でも，人間には基本的な社会的スキルが備わっていることを示している，とエール大学の研究者は考えている。

　　しかしながら，フロリダアトランティック大学心理学教授のデービッド・ルーコウィッツは，この研究者たちの結論を批判した。実験と結果は興味深いとしながらも，ルーコウィッツはこの研究は社会的スキルが生得のものであると証明できていないと主張する。彼は，幼児が両親や周りの人間から好ましい社会的行動を観察して学ぶ，と信じている。

No. 23　解答　1

「エール大学の研究者は幼児について何を知りたいと思ったのか」

1　幼児に善悪の概念があるかどうか。

2　幼児は何歳で人形と遊ぶ能力があるか。

3　幼児が人形の行動をまねるかどうか。

4　幼児は何歳で社会的スキルを習得することができるか。

解説　冒頭の ... infants as young as six months old are able to tell the difference between nice and naughty playmates と，The Yale researchers believe the experiment ... で述べられた研究者の考えから判断する。

No. 24　解答　4

「デービッド・ルーコウィッツはエール大学の研究について何を批判したのか」

1　実験の行われ方。　　　　　　　　**2**　それほどの幼い幼児を使用したこと。

3　研究の実際の結果。　　　　　　　**4**　研究者たちの結論。

解説　後半で ... criticized the researchers' conclusions. While finding the experiment and the results interesting と言っており，「実験」そのものや「結果」ではなく，「結論」を批判した。

(G) *No. 25* 解答 1

Well, your nose seems very congested. You say you don't have a cough or a sore throat, however, so that's good at least. Let me take a look at the inside of your nose again... hmm, this could be a seasonal allergy. The sudden temperature swings during this time of year can easily cause this condition. Let's try a different kind of medicine from the one we've been using. If you don't notice any improvement after a week with that, just give us a call. We'll schedule another appointment, and I'll check the inside of your nose again.

状況： あなたは１週間以上鼻水が出ている。あなたは医者に行き次のアドバイスを受ける。

質問： あなたはまず何をすべきか。

ええと，あなたの鼻はとても詰まっているようです。ただ，咳も喉の痛みもないとおっしゃっているので，少なくともそれはいいことです。もう一度鼻の中を見せてください…，うーん，これは季節性アレルギーかもしれません。この時期，気温の変化が激しいときにこの症状が出やすくなります。これまで使用してきたのとは違う種類の薬を試してみましょう。それで１週間経っても改善が見られなければ，お電話をください。また予約を入れて，あなたの鼻の中をもう一度検査します。

1 別の薬に切り替える。　　　　　　　　　**2** 鼻を検査してもらう。

3 アレルギー検査のために再来院する。　　　**4** アレルギーの薬を飲むのをやめる。

解説　医者のアドバイスの中で，Let's try a different kind of medicine from the one we've been using. の部分と**1**が一致する。「今服用している薬を別の薬に替える」を選択肢ではswitchで表している。

(H) *No. 26* 解答 2

First of all, you did the right thing by coming and asking a teacher for help. A lot of students don't bother to do that. Now, as I've mentioned to everyone in class, the writing resource center is a great place to get your writing checked over. Also, the library can help. Their computers have an application called "journal finder," which lets you find academic journals that normally cost money to view. However, if you visit the computer center, they can help you set up a personal account through the university. That way you can use the application from any computer, not just the library.

状況： あなたは大学生である。あなたは自分が書いている論文の研究資料を見つける手助けが必要である。あなたは自宅でも自分のコンピューターから作業をしたいと思っている。あなたは教授の１人に相談し，次のようなアドバイスを受ける。

質問： あなたはまずどこへ行くべきか。

第一に，教員に助けを求めて来たのは正しいことでした。多くの学生はわざわざそんなことはしません。さて，クラスの皆さんに言ったように，ライティング・リソース・センターは書いたものに問題がないかチェックしてもらうのに最適な場所です。また，図書館も役に立ちます。そこのコンピューターには「ジャーナル・ファインダー」というアプリケーションが入っており，それによって，普通なら閲覧するのにお金がかかる学術雑誌を見つけることができます。ただし，コンピューターセンターに行けば，大学を通して個人アカウントを設定する手助けをしてくれます。そうすれば，図書館だけでなく，どのコンピューターからでもそのアプリケーションを使用できます。

1 ライティング・リソース・センターへ。　　　**2** 大学のコンピューターセンターへ。

3 別の教授のオフィスへ。　　　　　　　　　**4** 大学の図書館へ。

解説　However以下がポイント。「コンピューターセンターに行って個人アカウントを設定すれば，（自宅のコンピューターを含め）どのコンピューターからでもアプリケーションが使える」という流れから，**2**が正解。

(I) *No. 27* 解答 4

Let's see, they just moved the cheeses. They used to be over by meats and poultry. Oh, I know where they are. OK, we're now in aisle 12. Go to the end of the aisle and turn right. Go all the way past aisle 1 to the dairy section. Close to the dairy section you'll see cold cuts, the delicatessen, and just to the other side of the delicatessen, you'll find our cheese selection. We have a sale on many of our cheeses today, so it's a good day to stock up. If you have any more questions, I'll be right here in aisle 12.

状況：あなたはスーパーで買い物をしており，チーズを探している。店員から次のような案内を聞く。

質問：チーズはどこで見つかるか。

えーと，チーズは場所を移したばかりなのです。以前はあそこの肉と鶏肉の近くにあったのですが。あ，わかりました。いいですか，私たちは今12番通路にいます。この通路の端まで行って，右に曲がってください。そのままずっと1番通路を通り過ぎ，乳製品売り場まで行ってください。乳製品売り場の近くにはコールド・カット（ハムやサラミなど）に総菜売り場，そして総菜売り場の反対側にチーズがそろっています。本日はチーズの多くがセールとなっておりますので，買い置きをなさるにはいい日ですよ。何かほかに質問がありましたら，私はここ12番通路におります。

1 1番通路。　　　　　　　　　　　　　**2** 12番通路。

3 乳製品売り場。　　　　　　　　　　　**4** 総菜売り場の隣。

解説　チーズの売り場の場所が聞き取るポイント。放送の中ほどで ... just to the other side of the delicatessen, you'll find our cheese selection と言っている。

(J) *No. 28* 解答 1

Hi, this is Wendy, and I'm calling from Tarryton Employment regarding an online application you filed with us on Tuesday. We just want to let you know that your résumé looks really good, although we were unable to reach you by the e-mail address you provided, which is the reason I'm calling. If you could send a brief e-mail to the address on our website, we can add it to your application and get you started with job offers. Just so you know, we do offer a premium service for a small monthly fee, which provides potential employers with paper copies of your résumé.

状況：あなたは人材紹介会社に履歴書を提出した。あなたは申し込みに関して次のボイスメールを受け取る。

質問：申し込みを完了させるにはあなたは何をすべきか。

もしもし，こちらはウェンディです。あなたが火曜日に弊社に提出されたオンライン申込書に関してタリートン人材紹介会社から電話をしています。あなたの履歴書はとても良さそうであることをお伝えしたいと思います。ただ，あなたが記入されたEメールアドレスではあなたと連絡がつかず，それが電話をしている理由です。弊社のウェブサイトのアドレスに手短なメールをお送りいただければ，弊社の方でそれをあなたの申込書に追加し，仕事のオファーに取り掛かることができます。ちなみに，弊社はあなたの履歴書のコピーを就職候補の会社に提供するプレミアムサービスを，少額の月額料金で提供しております。

1 タリートン人材紹介会社にEメールを送る。

2 別のオンライン申込書を提出する。

3 オンライン調査に記入する。

4 履歴書のコピーを提供する。

解説　although we were ... 以下で提出したEメール情報が無効であること，そして If you could send a brief e-mail to the address on our website, ... の部分から，会社にEメールを送れば申し込み手順が完了することがわかるので，**1**が正解。

(K) No. 29 解答 3

The National Oceanic Atmospheric Administration is forecasting 12 to 15 tropical storms to form during the season which runs from June 1st to November 30th. Six to eight storms are predicted to become hurricanes with two to four storms developing into major hurricanes ranked as Category 3 or higher. About two hurricanes are predicted to hit us here in the Miami area, so let's just hope they won't include one of those big ones. Be sure to purchase some boards and have them ready to board up your windows in case of a major blow. Those living in the islands of Key Largo or Key West are advised to listen to weather reports frequently and be prepared to evacuate at any time.

状況： あなたはフロリダ州マイアミに住んでいて，ラジオで天気の長期予報を聞く。あなたはハリケーンのシーズンに備えたいと思っている。

質問： あなたは何をすべきか。

米国海洋大気局は，6月1日から11月30日までのシーズン中に12から15の熱帯暴風雨が発生すると予想しています。6つから8つの暴風雨がハリケーンになると予想され，そのうち2つから4つがカテゴリー3もしくはそれ以上の大型ハリケーンに発達する見込みです。およそ2つのハリケーンがここマイアミ地域を襲うと思われますので，大型ハリケーンの1つにならないことを願いましょう。必ず板を何枚か購入し，大きな打撃に備えて窓を板で覆う準備をしておいてください。キーラーゴやキーウェストなどの島部にお住まいの方は頻繁に天気予報を聞き，いつでも避難できる心構えをしておくことが勧告されています。

1 この後の予報を聞く。　　　　　　　　**2** 避難の心構えをする。

3 板を何枚か用意する。　　　　　　　　**4** 特別な強度の窓を購入する。

解説　レポーターがいくつか警告している中で，「マイアミに住んでいる」という状況から，in the Miami area, so ... の聞き取りがポイント。Be sure to purchase some boards以下の内容から，**3**が適切。

Day
2

25

筆記試験
解答と解説

問題編 p.29〜40

1

問題	1	2	3	4	5	6	7	8	9	10	11	12	13	14	15	16	17	18
解答	2	2	2	3	2	4	1	1	4	4	1	4	1	4	3	4	3	2

2

問題	19	20	21	22	23	24
解答	2	3	1	4	4	1

3

問題	25	26	27	28	29	30	31
解答	2	2	4	3	4	1	3

4 解説内にある解答例を参照してください。

5 解説内にある解答例を参照してください。

1

(1) 解答 **2**

「その労働組合と会社が新しい協定を案出するには3週間にわたる激しい交渉を必要としたが，みんなが安心したことに，彼らは最終的にはそれに成功した」

解説 労働組合と会社が主語で，目的語がagreement「協定」なのでforge「案出する」が適切。admonish「諭す」，haunt「（考えなどが）付きまとう」，inhibit「（行動など）を抑制する」

(2) 解答 **2**

「スキャンダルにもかかわらず，その政治家は結局は人々の尊敬を勝ち得た。彼には自分の過ちを認める勇気があった」

解説 acknowledge one's mistake で「間違いを認める」という意味。retrieve「回収する」，browse「ざっと見る」，embellish「飾る」

(3) 解答 **2**

「その経済学者は，倒産を避けるために，さらに多くの銀行が合併しなければならなくなるだろうと論じた。競争の極めて激しい市場において，銀行の数が本当に

多過ぎるのだった」

解説 倒産を避けるためにすることで，銀行の数が多過ぎるのが問題なのだから，merge「合併する」である。circulate「循環する」，blend「溶け合う」，mingle「混ざる」

(4) 解答 **3**

「弁護士は依頼人に対する申し立てが誤っていたことを証明する確固たる証拠を提示したため，その訴訟は棄却された」

解説 訴訟が棄却された理由として何が誤っていたかを考えると，依頼人に対する「申し立て」である。allegationは法律用語で，立証しようとする事実についての「申し立て，主張」の意味。initiative「主導権」，expectation「予期，期待」，contemplation「熟考」

(5) 解答 **2**

「その客はパーティーでスピーチを頼まれたとき，何の準備もしていなかったので，即興でせざるを得なかった」

解説 スピーチの準備を何もしていなかったので，

26

improvise「即興でする」しかなかったのである。ascend「登る」，assume「仮定する」，inoculate「予防接種をする」

(6) 解答 **4**

「自動車の組み立てといった退屈な仕事でロボットが人間の代わりを果たしつつある。したがって，工場労働者は，もっと困難な作業を引き受けることができるよう，より高いレベルの技能を習得するために再訓練する必要がある」

解説 ロボットが人間の代わりにする仕事とはどんな仕事か。第2文のchallenging workと対照的な意味になるtedious「（仕事などが）退屈な」が適切。gratifying「満足させる」，reassuring「安心させる」，tender「優しい」

(7) 解答 **1**

A「私はたいてい，レポートはタイプする前に手書きで書きます」

B「それはとても非効率的だ。最初から入力すれば時間の浪費が少なくて済むのに」

解説 空所後の内容から，「タイプする前に手書きで書く」という行為は非効率的（inefficient）だと言える。unassuming「控えめな」，inevitable「避けられない」，unoriginal「独創性に欠ける」

(8) 解答 **1**

「大統領には，辞職させるとまではいかなくても，彼のあらゆる動きを阻止することに狙いを定めている厳しい批判者が議会に何人かいる」

解説 「あらゆる動きを阻止することに狙いを定めている批判者」を形容する語として，fierce「厳しい」が適切。sympathetic「同情する」，fraudulent「詐欺的な」，striking「著しい」

(9) 解答 **4**

「ギャングの一味は，富裕な実業家の息子を誘拐し，100万ドルの身代金を要求した」

解説 誘拐犯が要求するのはransom「身代金」である。revenue「歳入」，debt「借金」，bond「債券」

(10) 解答 **4**

「ロバートは，自分のやり方を押し通し，めったに意見を変えないので，同僚とよく言い争いになる。同僚とうまくやりたいのなら，彼は頑固な性格を抑える必要がある」

解説 「自分のやり方を押し通す」「意見を変えない」という性格を表したstubborn「頑固な」が正解。人のネガティブな性格を表す語が入るとわかれば**4**が選べるだろう。productive「生産的な」，startling「驚くべき」，portable「携帯用の」

(11) 解答 **1**

「その雑誌の最新号は選挙運動への啓発的な新しい洞察を提供している」

解説 雑誌が何を提供するかを考えると，insight「洞察」が適切だとわかる。advocate「唱道者」，telescope「望遠鏡」，revision「改訂」

(12) 解答 **4**

「新しい支社の事務所の提案が棚上げされたと知り，その重役は失望した。現在の振るわない市況では費用がかかり過ぎると見なされたのだ」

解説 市況が振るわないので，新しい提案はshelve「棚上げする」ことになった。floor「床を張る」，wall「壁で囲う」，book「予約する」

(13) 解答 **1**

「独裁者によって長く支配されてきたその国を民主化するためには，抜本的な変革が必要であると誰もが認めている」

解説 独裁国家を民主化するためにはdrastic「抜本的な」変革が必要だと考えられる。fragile「壊れやすい」，illiterate「読み書きのできない」，lethal「致命的な」

(14) 解答 **4**

「徹底した研究のおかげで，現在は新鮮なトマトを食べることでがんの危険性が低くなることを納得のいくように証明する十分なデータがある」

解説 研究のおかげで，convincingly「納得のいくように」証明するデータがある。intimately「親密に」，disdainfully「軽蔑して」，perversely「意地になって」

(15) 解答 **3**

「その環境会議は，オゾン層を破壊する気体を段階的に削減する決議案を採択して，先週閉幕した」

解説 目的語の「オゾン層を破壊する気体」に合うのはphase out「～を段階的に削減する」である。adhere to「～に固執する」，drag along「足を引きずるように歩く」，work out「（問題）を解決する」

(16) 解答 **4**

A「トムが学級委員長の選挙に３度目の立候補をする決心をしたんだ」

B「なんてこった。また落選すると思うよ」

解説 目的語が「学級委員長」なので, run for「〜に立候補する」が適切。think up「〜を考え出す」, feel for「〜を手探りで捜す」, make up「〜を組み立てる; 化粧する」

(17) 解答 **3**

「非常にショックなことに, われわれの会社は今後３カ月で従業員の半数を一時解雇しなければならないことがわかった」

解説 It came as quite a shock to *do*「〜するのは非常にショックであった」という内容から, lay off「〜を一時的に解雇する」が合う。break into「〜に侵入する」, fall through「失敗に終わる」, kick up「〜を蹴り上げる」

(18) 解答 **2**

「今日では世界中のほとんどの銀行は, 国際的な業務規約や協定に従うことが求められている」

解説 「規約や協定」という目的語に合う動詞は conform to「〜に従う」である。allude to「〜についてそれとなく言う」, testify for「〜に有利な証言をする」, substitute for「〜の代用になる」

2

全訳
サーフィン

　サーフィンは, 近年考案された, 勇気ある人間を自然と戦わせるエクストリームスポーツと見なされることが多い。しかし, その起源はまったく異なり, 多くの人が想像するよりもずっと昔までさかのぼる。サーフィンは, すべての人に開かれた, 現代的なアドレナリンを刺激する娯楽であるというよりも, 古代に貴族と上流階級を中心とした宗教的探求として誕生した。ポリネシア人は2,000年以上も何らかの形でサーフィンを行ってきたと考えられており, この古くからの習わしは特にハワイ文化の中に溶け込んでいる。

　当初のサーフボードは, 多くの場合, 非常に長く, 木でできていて, 35キロの重さになることもあった。これは今日の軽量炭素繊維のショートボードとはまったく異なるものであるが, 劇的に変わったことはこれだけではない。現在のサーファーには厳しいトレーニング法があり, 国際大会で競うために世界を旅する。トップにたどり着くサーファーには, プロサーフィンの発展による, ほかの近代プロスポーツ同様のすべての特典がもたらされる。元来のサーファーは実際の王族であったが, 現在のトップレベルのサーファーもよくそのような扱いを受けることがある。

　このスポーツの頂点に立つ者たちは, 世界的に有名になって, 賞金とスポンサー契約で何百万ドルも稼ぐことができる。11回世界チャンピオンに輝いたケリー・スレーターのように, 中には起業, 俳優業, 作家業, モデルなど多岐にわたる分野に手を広げる者も

いる。このレベルのプロにとっては, 近年の発展は彼らの注目度とこのスポーツの認知度を高めている。例として, オリンピック競技としてサーフィンが追加されたことは, 彼らの献身とライフスタイルに対する最高の評価だと多くの人に見なされている。

(19) 解答 **2**

解説 however と Rather than がポイント。冒頭の「勇気ある人間を自然と戦わせるエクストリームスポーツ」というサーフィンに対する誤った見方と同意で, かつ, 空所後の「古代に貴族や上流階級を中心とした宗教的探求」と相反する内容となる**2**が適切。

(20) 解答 **3**

解説 While があるので空所には後と対比的な内容が入る。ここでは**3**の original と空所後のtoday's が対比になっており, また as such が指す内容は**3**の royalty「王族」である。

(21) 解答 **1**

解説 recent developments「近年の発展」が注目度を高めたという空所前の内容と, オリンピック競技になったことは最高の評価だという空所後の内容を考えると, オリンピックは「近年の発展」の代表的な例として挙げられていることになる。

全訳

2つの島国

　日本と英国諸島は膨大な距離により隔てられ，それぞれが固有の文化を有している。表面的には両国はまったく異なっているように見えるが，表面を削り取ってみると，いくつかとても興味深いパターンが現れてくる。

　2つの島国の国土はほぼ同じ大きさであり，はるかに大きな大陸の沿岸からあまり離れていない所に位置している。長年にわたって行われた数々の戦争は，（両国よりも）ひどい戦禍を被った近隣諸国を荒廃させ，そこでは都市が全壊したり，いくつかの帝国が崩壊したりしたのだが，この地理的な孤立がこうした戦争から両国を守る上で役立ってきた。

　特にこの2つの小さな島国の住民は，多くの特徴を共有している。両国民ともその歴史をはるか遠い昔にたどることができる。彼らは家族と強固な道徳上の規律を基礎にして階級的な社会を作った。両国は貿易に秀でており，世界中の国々と強い商業的関係を結んできた。伝統に固執する人々はしばしば変化に抵抗するが，絶対に必要とあれば変化に対処することができるのは間違いないところだ。

　現在両国民が直面している1つの問題は，過去ほど輝かしくはないことが確実な未来にいかに対処するかということだ。彼らが現実を受け止め，この先も新しい世界秩序を受け入れる決心を持ち続けることがこの上なく重要だろう。両国は海図のない今日の海を着々と進む強い意志の力を見いださなければならない。この試練に対応する能力が自らの運命を決めるのである。

(22)　解答　4

解説　直前の文で，両国は島国であり，大陸と陸続きでないことを説明しているので，4「この地理的な孤立」が適切。

(23)　解答　4

解説　直前で人々が伝統に固執すると言っているので，変化には4「抵抗する」と考えられる。

(24)　解答　1

解説　最終段落は両国の今後の課題について述べており，空所にはこれからも受け入れていくべきものが入ると考えられるので，1「新しい世界秩序」が適切。ほかの選択肢は第3段落にあるように，すでに両国が昔から持っていたものである。

3

全訳

生物多様性の喪失

　生物多様性とは，地球上の生命の多様性と変動性を言う。それは，最大のものから微細なものまでのすべての種，およびそれらが形成する多くの生態系にかかわることである。われわれが呼吸する空気，食べる食物，飲む水はすべてそれに何らかの形で依存しているため，その重要性は計り知れない。しかし，都市のスプロール現象や気候変動，森林破壊などの問題が生物多様性を脅かしており，その結果は悲惨なものになりかねない。生物多様性の喪失は，食料生産や医療から，生態系の喪失や種の生存に至るまでのすべてに影響を及ぼす可能性がある。

　しかし，気候変動とは異なり，生物多様性の喪失をわれわれの日常生活で感じることは難しい。異常気象や山火事，干ばつ，洪水，そして気温の上昇はすべて，世界中の人々が直接経験している気候変動の兆候である。種の絶滅は，それほど目立つものではないかもしれないが，それが引き起こす連鎖反応は壊滅的な被害をもたらす可能性がある。生物多様性に変化があると，例えば，有害な細菌を殺すのに役に立つ微生物や昆虫が消えてしまうこともある。これは次に病気や食料不足，栄養不良につながることも考えられる。資源が乏しくなるにつれて，これらの一連の出来事が世界的な欠乏や，価格上昇，政治的混乱，さらには戦争にさえつながりかねない。

　その結果，生物多様性の喪失は「沈黙の殺し屋」と呼ばれているが，意識の高まりが解決につながり得る。重要なこととして，科学的関心および事業上の関心はこの領域に集約しており，この問題が金銭的な利益に支配されたり，単純に無視されたりしないようにすることに役立っている。われわれの命は，われわれがしばしば理解できない方法で生物多様性に依存しているため，それを守るための取り組みが国際的な政治的努力によって支えられることを多くの人が期待している。われわれはすでに厄介なほど大量の生物多様性を失い

つつあるが，楽観できる余地はある。地球上の生命の生存に不可欠であるとして，生物多様性を保護することの重要性を強調することを目的とするいくつかの協定が提案され，署名されている。

　少なくとも国際レベルでは，生物多様性を保護する取り組みは，これまで幸いなことに政治に関係がない傾向にある。問題が政治的に扱われるほどに，協定が批准され，繰り返される可能性が少なくなり得るため，これは重要なことである。国内レベルではこれらの争点が政治的な得点稼ぎに用いられるので，こうはいかないことが多い。政治的動機に基づいているかどうかはともかく，協力的な取り組みは，もしかするとわれわれが自らの絶滅を理解するだけではなく，それを目の当たりにすることにもなる最初の種となることが見込まれる運命から救ってくれるかもしれない。

(25)　解答　2

「この文章は生物多様性の重要性について何と言っているか」

1 生物多様性の重要性は，自然災害について議論するときに過大評価されてきたかもしれない。

2 あらゆる形態の生命は相互依存的であり，われわれが生み出すいかなる損害もわれわれ自身の生存を危うくする可能性がある。

3 生物多様性は，都市化や集中的な食料生産などの人的介入によって高めることができる。

4 生物多様性は，それを保護する新薬を開発するのに十分重要であると考えられている。

解説　biodiversity「生物多様性」について説明している第1段落を参照。**2**が正解で，前半のAll forms of life are interdependentは 本 文 のIt involves all species, ...，後 半 のany damage we create could imperil our own survivalは本文のHowever, ... の内容に合う。

(26)　解答　2

「生物多様性の喪失が「沈黙の殺し屋」と呼ばれることがあるのはなぜか」

1 栄養不良の方が社会にとってより大きな脅威となると見なされているため，生物多様性の喪失の影響は過小評価される傾向がある。

2 生物多様性の喪失の影響は深刻ではあるものの，直ちにそうと見て取れるものではないので，ほとんどの人に気付かれない傾向にある。

3 人々は虫と微生物が死に絶えていくのを見聞きしないため，その結果を気にかけない。

4 人々には火災や干ばつなど，もっと心配すべき重要事項があり，それは情報が不足していることを意味する。

解説　第3段落のAs a result, biodiversity has been referred to as a "silent killer," から，そう呼ばれる理由は第2段落にある。第1文のit is difficult to feel biodiversity loss in our everyday livesや中ほどの ... not be so noticeableから，**2**が正解。

(27)　解答　4

「どんな問題が生物多様性の喪失に対処する努力を弱める可能性があるか」

1 生物多様性の喪失の背後にある科学は理解するのが難しいため，政府は研究のための資金を引き付けることができない。

2 経済的利益と政治的利益との間の矛盾が，意味のある進歩がありそうもないことを示唆している。

3 私たちが理解していない状況を政治化しようと急ぐことが，問題を取り巻く無知さ加減を強調している。

4 国内レベルでの意見の不一致により，集団的な国際的努力が妨げられる可能性がある。

解説　第4段落の第1～2文で，生物多様性の問題は「政治的に扱われるほど合意されにくい」，「少なくとも国際レベルでは問題が非政治的に扱われる傾向にある」と書かれている。続くThat is often not the case at domestic levels, where the issues are used to score political points. から，国内レベルでは政治の争点として使われていることがわかる。これは国際的努力の妨げになり得ると考えられるので，**4**が正解。

全訳
チームワークに関する内なる真実

　労働者がより効率良く働くために良いチームワークを構築することの重要性は，1920年代から1930年代にかけて行われたホーソーン（工場）の実験にまでさかのぼることができる。これは，ハーバード・ビジネス・スクールのエルトン・メイヨー教授が行った一連の研究で，労働環境と生産性の関係を明らかにするというものであった。メイヨー教授は，例えば照明など，労働環境において変えることのできるいくつかの要素を実際に変えてみた。教授が発見したことは当初，相反するものであった。照明の明るさをどう変えようと，暗くなろうが明るくなろうが，研究対象となった労働者の生産性は向上したのである。同じことがほかの環境的な変化についても見られた。やがてメイヨー教授は，かなり重大なことに気付いた。すなわち，

職場における環境の変化は，チームワークと比べてずっと重要性が低いのである。メイヨー教授の研究対象となったグループは，研究者から注目されることで，また（環境的な）変化を強いられることで，より強いチームワークを発揮したようなのである。

　ホーソーンの実験は，労働環境における人間関係の重要性にスポットライトを当てることになった。この実験以降，企業はグループでの（仕事から離れての）修養やその他のさまざまなチーム訓練といった，チームワークを構築するさまざまな訓練に何十億ドルもの費用を費やしてきた。しかしながら，マサチューセッツ工科大学（MIT）のデボラ・アンコナ教授と欧州経営大学院（INSEAD）のヘンリック・ブレスマン准教授は，その共著『Xチーム——リードし，革新し，成功するチームの作り方』において，企業内でのチームワーク構築に時間と費用を費やすよりも，別のところに費やした方が実際には良いのではないかと主張している。なぜならば，2人が行った数十年にもわたる研究を通じてわかったことは，企業外の人間関係も企業内の結び付きと同じように重要であるということである。2人の著者は，上層の経営人にチームの有能性と価値を証明すること，顧客だけでなく，このチームが頼りにするほかの人々とより親密な絆を築くこと，そしてそのチームがうまく導入し実践できるような社外の考え方や提案を探すことなど，社外の人々との人間関係にもっと焦点を当てるべきであると主張している。

　アンコナ教授は，効果的なチームワークに関するより伝統的な考え方は，チーム・スピリットや明確な職場での役割分担などの特性に依存するものであったが，現実のビジネスの世界では，こういった特性が生産性や売上収益などといった成功を示す指標とはほとんど関係がないことを発見した。「内部モデルというものは私たちの脳裏に焼き付いているものですが，研究や多くの管理職の実際の体験が実証したのは，あるチームが社内的には非常にうまくその役割を果たしたとしても，それでもなお望まれるような結果を出せないことがあるということです。現実の世界において，良いチームは，私たちの定義によれば，往々にして失敗するものなのです」とアンコナ教授は語る。

　2人の著者が強調するのは，ホーソーン（工場で実験が行われた）時代以降，世界の実務社会は劇的に変化しているという点だ。今日の知識主導型の世界経済は，中央集権的な権限を持った人々に厳しく管理されるのではなく，もっと緩いヒエラルキー（階級制度）に依存するところが大きい。企業（組織）はより複雑なものになっており，情報や戦略がたびたび変化する

のに伴い，企業はもっと柔軟にならなければならない。世界的企業と顧客という，分散しながらも相互に関連し合う性質を持つ両者に必要なのは，社外の人々やグループとのさらなるネットワーク作りである。著者は，社内におけるチーム作りのモデルが完全に時代遅れだと主張しているのではない。というのも，チームを構成する人間同士の関係の重要性は率直に認めているのだ。しかしながら，チームがどのように効果的に社外の人々に手を差し伸べるかという状況下でこそ，こういった社内的な人間同士の結束は一番よく理解されると信じている。チームワークという社内的な結び付きは，方程式の評価され過ぎる半分でしかなく，より高い生産性を得て成功をするために社内のチームがどのようにしてチーム外部の人々との架け橋を構築するかを見なくては，社内的チームワークそのものだけでは有益な指標であるとは言えないのである。

(28)　解答　3

「ホーソーンの研究において，エルトン・メイヨーが最初に示し始めたのは，いかにして」

1 チームワークが組織の有効性にとって不可欠であるか。

2 チームワークが職場の環境変化にほとんど関係がないか。

3 職場の環境要因が生産性に影響を及ぼすか。

4 職場の環境変化がチームワークの構築に影響を与えるか。

解説　ホーソーンの研究におけるメイヨー教授の目的が書かれた第1段落第1文のto determine the relationship between the working environment and productivity の部分から，**3**が正解。

(29)　解答　4

「アンコナの引用は，基本的に～と述べることで要約することができる」

1 チームワークの内部モデルは時の試練を乗り越えてきたが，それは内部だけでなく外部的要因によっても評価されるべきだ

2 まずチームが強い内的結合を構築しようと努力しない限り，外的な成功は達成しそうにない

3 チームワークは相対的な用語であり，企業が成功するには実際さまざまな形でのチームワークが必要だ

4 内部における効率の良いチームワークは，実社会での成功達成の点から見るとそれほど効果的でないかもしれない

解説　アンコナ教授の発言は第3段落に引用を伴い紹

介されているが，その要点が書かれた第２文の a team can function very well internally and still not deliver the desired results から，**4**が適切。

(30)　解答　**1**

「アンコナとブレスマンは，現在のビジネス環境について何と言っているか」

1 ホーソーンの時代よりも複雑かつ流動的で，企業により柔軟性を求めている。

2 チームは，ビジネス環境がグローバルなコミュニティーでますます階層的になっていることを受け入れなければならない。

3 ホーソーンの時代よりも情報や戦略に依存しており，チームの構築を無意味にしている。

4 知識ベースの世界経済は，企業チームの負担を大きく変えてはいない。

解説　現在のビジネス環境の変化については，最終段落第１～３文に説明がある。第３文の Companies are more complex and ... they must be more flexible. の部分から，**1**が適切。

(31)　解答　**3**

「アンコナとブレスマンは，内部チーム構築について何を信じているか」

1 今日の現実的なビジネスの世界では，もはや関連性もないし有用な概念でもない。

2 概念には調整が必要だが，今でもホーソーンが最初に示したのと同じくらい重要である。

3 外部のグループとより良い関係を築くのに比べ，過大評価されている。

4 実際には現在の世界経済において逆効果であることが証明されている。

解説　内部チームの構築に対する２人の考えは最終段落第５～６文に紹介されている。第６文 The internal bonds of teamwork are the overrated half of the equation, ... の部分を言い換えた**3**が正解。

問題文の訳

　ビーガンのライフスタイルに従う人々は，肉，魚，卵，乳製品，蜂蜜などの動物由来の食品を一切摂取しない。彼らはまた，皮革や毛皮など動物由来の製品も避ける。このような制限にもかかわらず，さまざまな理由でビーガンになる人の数は増えている。

　ビーガニズムの支持者たちは，ビーガニズムは，野菜，全粒穀物，果物，植物性の油をベースにしているため，動物性食品を摂取するよりも健康的だと主張する。さらに，ビーガニズムは残虐行為を一切伴わず，傷つけられたり殺されたりする動物もまったくいないためにこのライフスタイルを選ぶ人も多い。

　それにもかかわらず，ビーガンのライフスタイルを実践している人の中には，バランスの取れた食事を摂れず，結果的に栄養不足につながる可能性がある人もいる。人間の体はたんぱく質や，鉄分や亜鉛のようなさまざまな種類のミネラルを必要とするが，それらは伝統的な人間の食生活では通常，動物性食品から得られる。しかし一部のビーガンは，これらの栄養を含んだ代替食物を十分に食べていない可能性がある。さらに，一部のビーガン食品は見つけにくく，また高価になり得るため，制限のあるビーガンの食事を維持するのは難しい場合がある。

解答例

　The number of vegan people who do not accept any foods or products of animal origin is increasing. Reasons for choosing a vegan lifestyle include the health benefits of plant-based foods along with its ethical concern of not harming or killing animals. On the other hand, veganism has the disadvantage of unbalanced diets leading to poor nutrition. Also, vegan foods may be difficult to obtain and expensive. (67語)

解答例の訳

　動物由来の食品や製品を一切受け入れないビーガンの人の数が増加している。ビーガンのライフスタイルを選ぶ理由には，植物性食品の健康上の利益のほか，動物を傷つけたり殺したりしないという倫理的な配慮が挙げられる。一方，ビーガニズムには偏った食事が栄養不足につながるという欠点がある。また，ビーガン食品は手に入れるのが難しく，高価な場合がある。

解説　まず，英文を読んで，各段落の要点を押さえる。各要点を1（～2）文でまとめて全体を3～4文で書こう。解答例は，第1文「トピックの導入（ビーガンの増加）」（第1段落），第2文「利点」（第2段落），第3～4文「欠点」（第3段落）の4文構成。第3段落のNonethelessは対比を表す印で，解答例ではOn the other handでつなげている。さらに，In additionをAlsoに置き換えて，欠点を2文に分けて表している。

　要点をまとめるポイントは，①重要な情報を見極め，細かい情報や具体例は省く，②具体的な情報を抽象化する，の2点。例えば，第1段落のA, such as BやA, including Bの表現ではAが重要な情報。それぞれのAの部分を解答例ではfoods or products of animal originと抽象的に表している。複数の文にわたってビーガンの利点を述べた第2段落は，解答例ではビーガンを選ぶ理由としてReasons for ～ include A along with B「～の理由にはAのほか，Bが挙げられる」という表現で1文にまとめている。このように，「文」の情報を「名詞句」に置き換えることが端的に言い換えるコツである。第3段落の<u>fail to</u> eat a balanced dietのような否定表現は，<u>un</u>balanced dietsのように否定の接頭辞を利用して短く表すこともできる。また，第2段落のno animals are harmed or killed（受動態）→not harming or killing animals（能動態）のような文法的な言い換えも有効である。

　そのほかの解答例の言い換えは以下のとおり。not consume[avoid]→not accept，rising→increasing，healthier→health benefits，based on vegetables ...→plant-based，result in→leading to，a lack of→poor

問題の訳
TOPIC：賛成か反対か：会社は年功序列よりも業績に応じて従業員を昇進させるべきである
POINTS：勤労意欲・忠誠心・経験・公正さ

解答例

　When it comes to promotions, I think that more emphasis should be placed on work performance rather than on seniority. There are two main reasons why I think this way.

　The first reason is connected to motivation to work. When people know they will be promoted just for staying in a company for a long time, they have little incentive to work hard. Focusing on achievement, rather than seniority, is an effective way to increase productivity.

　Another issue is unfairness. If workers see less productive colleagues being promoted over them, it is likely to make them feel unappreciated. In the worst case, companies may lose talented workers to other businesses.

　While it is obviously important to reward loyalty and long term commitment, promotion should be based on performance and ability.
(130語)

解答例の訳

　昇進に関して言えば，年功序列よりも業績が重視されるべきだと思う。私がこのように考える主な理由は2つある。

　1つ目の理由は勤労意欲に関連する。人々はある会社に長く勤めているだけで昇進するとわかっていれば，一生懸命に働く意欲がほとんどなくなる。年功序列ではなく業績に焦点を合わせることは，生産性を向上させる効果的な方法である。

　もう1つの問題は不公正である。従業員が自分よりも生産性の低い同僚が自分を追い越して昇進するのを見れば，自分は正当に評価されていないと感じる可能性がある。最悪の場合，会社は有能な労働者をほかの企業に奪われてしまうかもしれない。

　忠誠心と長期的な献身に報いることは明らかに重要だが，昇進は業績と能力に基づくべきである。

解説　「会社は年功序列よりも業績に応じて従業員を昇進させるべきだ」という考えに対し，解答例ではAgreeの立場を取っている。序論では，まずWhen it comes to ...「…に関して言えば」で始め，「年功序列よりも業績が重視されるべきだ」という賛成の立場を明らかにしている。続いて，There are two main reasons why I think this way. の部分で「理由が2つある」と前置きした後，第2段落ではThe first reason is ... の形でPOINTSのMotivation to work，第3段落ではAnother issue is ... の形でFairnessの観点を詳しく述べている。

　第2段落はMotivation to workの観点で，年功序列の問題点として「会社に長く勤めているだけで昇進すると知っていたら勤労意欲がなくなる」と述べた後，業績の利点として「業績が重視されれば従業員の生産性（productivity）が向上する」と説明している。第3段落はFairnessの観点で，年功序列によって自分より生産性の低い従業員が昇進することの問題点を説明している。

　POINTSのLoyaltyは最終段落でも登場しているが，Agreeの立場でほかに「最近の会社は従業員に意欲や生産性を求めており，会社への忠誠心や年齢は関係ない」などの意見も可能であろう。Experienceの観点では，Disagreeの立場で「年配の従業員の方が経験豊富である」，逆にAgreeの立場で「経験豊富な従業員が生産的だとは限らない」などの意見があり得る。

リスニングテスト
解答と解説

問題編 p.41〜46

Part 1	問題	1	2	3	4	5	6	7	8	9	10	11	12
	解答	3	2	2	3	3	3	4	3	1	4	3	3

Part 2	問題	13	14	15	16	17	18	19	20	21	22	23	24
	解答	4	1	4	2	3	4	2	1	4	1	3	1

Part 3	問題	25	26	27	28	29
	解答	3	3	3	2	2

Part 1   🔊 027〜039

No. 1   解答 3

☆：Have you got any plans for the weekend?
★：None at all, and that's fine. I need to rest. I had to work overtime every day this week.
☆：It sounds like you're not just tired.
★：You're right. The new boss makes a lot of paperwork mistakes and I constantly have to cover for him. He's my boss, so it's hard to speak up about it.
☆：I see what you mean, but on the other hand, if you don't say anything to anyone, it won't do anyone any good. Especially you.
★：True. Maybe I can bring it up to the Human Resources head.
Question：What does the man say about his job?

☆：週末の予定はあるの？
★：何もないけど，それでいいんだ。僕は休息する必要がある。今週は毎日残業しなければならなかったからね。
☆：疲れているだけじゃないみたいね。
★：そうなんだ。新しい上司が書類仕事でたくさんミスをするから，僕が絶えずカバーしないといけない。彼は僕の上司だから，この件で声を上げるのは難しいんだ。
☆：言いたいことはわかるけど，一方で，誰にも何も言わなかったら，誰のためにもならないわよ。特にあなたのためにね。
★：そうだね。人事部長に話を持ち掛けることはできるかもしれないな。
質問：男性は仕事について何と言っているか。

1 彼は同じミスを繰り返す傾向がある。
2 彼の上司は彼の意見を聞こうとしない。
3 彼は上司にいら立ちを感じている。
4 彼の上司はとても快く手を貸してくれる。

解説 男性は今週ずっと残業しているが，それは，The new boss makes ... から，自分が上司のミスをカバーしているからである。ミスが多いのは男性ではなく上司なので，**1**は不適。

Day
4

No. 2　解答　2

●：What is that, Gail? A test answer key?	●：それは何，ゲイル？　テストの解説？
☆：Um, yeah. It's from last year's test. I got it from a second-year student. Want a copy?	☆：あー，そうよ。昨年のテストの。2年生からもらったの。コピーいる？
●：No! I mean, no thanks. You're not seriously thinking of taking that to the test, are you?	●：駄目だよ！　ていうか，いらないよ。君はテストにそれを持ち込むなんて本気で考えていないよね？
☆：I know we aren't allowed to bring anything with us, but I thought it couldn't hurt, either.	☆：何も持ち込んじゃいけないことは知っているけど，支障がないとも思ったわ。
●：Gail, you're my friend, so I won't tell anyone, but not only is it wrong, it's dumb. How do you know the test hasn't changed? And couldn't you just study? Look, I'll even help you study.	●：ゲイル，君は友達だから僕は誰にも言わないけど，間違ったことだっていうだけでなく，ばかばかしいよ。テストが変わってないってどうしてわかるんだい？　それに勉強したらいいだけじゃないか。ねえ，僕も君の勉強を手伝うからさ。
☆：OK, Jim, you just talked some sense into me.	☆：わかったわ，ジム。あなたに言われて目が覚めたわ。
Question：Why is Jim upset with Gail?	**質問**：ジムはなぜゲイルに憤慨しているのか。

1　彼女が彼よりも高い点数を取った。　　2　彼女がテストでカンニングすることを計画していた。
3　彼女が彼に答えをコピーさせない。　　4　彼女が彼にテストが変わったことを教えなかった。

解説　男性が憤慨しているのは，女性が昨年のテストの解説を入手し，それをテストに持ち込もうとしていると知ったから。これを正解**2**ではcheat on a testと表している。

No. 3　解答　2

☆：Jack, you're totally not yourself today. What's wrong?	☆：ジャック，今日は全然あなたらしくないわね。どうしたの？
★：Oh, you haven't heard? Mary and I had a little fight last weekend. Well, not a little fight, a big one. We broke up.	★：ああ，聞いてない？　メアリーと僕は先週末にちょっとしたけんかをしたんだよ。えっと，ちょっとしたじゃなくて，大きなけんかだね。別れたんだよ。
☆：No way! You two have been together for, what, a year now?	☆：うそでしょ！　あなたたち2人は付き合ってもう1年になる？
★：Had been. But truth be told, it wasn't going as well as everyone around us thought it was. She has a short temper.	★：付き合っていた，だね。でも本当のことを言うと，周りのみんなが思うほどうまくいっていなかったんだ。彼女はかんしゃく持ちなんだよ。
☆：I'm sorry to hear that, Jack. I can't imagine someone as kind as you being yelled at. Let me know if you want to talk.	☆：それは気の毒ね，ジャック。あなたみたいな優しい人が怒鳴られるなんて想像できないわ。話がしたくなったら教えてね。
★：Thanks, Kay. I will.	★：ありがとう，ケイ。そうするよ。
Question：What does Kay think about Jack?	**質問**：ケイはジャックのことをどう思っているか。

1　彼はささいなことにすぐに憤慨する。　　2　彼は優しい性格である。
3　彼が問題の原因だった。　　4　彼は前の彼女と話をするべきだ。

解説　彼女と別れたばかりのジャックとケイとの会話。ケイはジャックの性格についてI can't imagine someone as kind as you being yelled at. と言っており，kindをgentleと言い換えた**2**が正解。

No. 4 　解答　3

●：Mmm ... something smells good! Is that salmon pie you're making for dinner, Jenny?

☆：Yes. I've just put it in the oven but it won't be ready for more than an hour.

●：I'm starving. What can I have right away?

☆：I can make some vegetable sticks with a cream cheese dip if you'd like. That should keep you going until dinner.

●：That would be great. Thanks.

Question：What will the woman do next?

●：うーん，何かいい匂いがする！ 夕飯に作っているのはサーモンパイなの，ジェニー？

☆：ええ。オーブンに入れたところだけど，あと1時間以上はかかるわね。

●：おなかがぺこぺこだよ。すぐに食べられるものは何？

☆：クリームチーズのディップを付けて食べる野菜スティックでよければできるわよ。それで夕飯まで持つでしょ。

●：それはいい。ありがとう。

質問：女性は次に何をするか。

1　夕食を食べ始める。
2　夕食をオーブンに入れる。
3　軽食を用意する。
4　野菜を買いに行く。

解説　女性のI can make some vegetable sticks with a cream cheese dip ... という発言に対し，男性がThat would be great. Thanks. と答えている。vegetable sticks ... dipを正解**3**ではsnacksと言い換えている。

No. 5 　解答　3

☆：How long have you been working in the sales department, George?

★：Too long. That's what it feels like sometimes.

☆：I see. So, do you think you would ever want to try doing something else?

★：I'm not sure. I like my co-workers, and I enjoy working with people. Recently, however, I've just gotten tired of the pressure to sell people things that they don't really need.

☆：Well, my department could really use someone with people skills and creativity like you. There's an opening, you know.

★：Advertising? I'd never considered that before.

Question：What does the woman encourage George to do?

☆：あなたは営業部でどのくらい働いているの，ジョージ？

★：長過ぎるくらい。時々そんなふうに感じるね。

☆：そうなんだ。じゃあ，いつか違うことをやってみたいと思う？

★：どうかな。僕は同僚が好きだし，人と一緒に働くことを楽しんでいる。でも最近，人々が本当に必要としているわけではない物を売るというプレッシャーにうんざりしてきたところなんだ。

☆：うーん，私の部署は，あなたのような対人スキルと創造性を持つ人がとても必要なの。つまり，空きがあるの。

★：宣伝部？ それは考えたことがなかったな。

質問：女性はジョージに何をするよう促しているか。

1　優れた対人スキルがある人を見つける。
2　営業担当者としてのスキルを向上させる。
3　彼女の部署の職に応募する。
4　別の会社で働くことを検討する。

解説　営業部の仕事を不満に思う男性に対し，女性はmy department could really use ... There's an opening ... の部分で自分の部署に空きがあると言うことで，遠回しに応募を促している。

No. 6 解答 **3**

●：I think I'll take Ray skiing this weekend.
☆：Skiing!? Don't you think it's a little early for that? Sledding and building snowmen are plenty for him at this age.
●：With skiing, the earlier the better, they say. If you start kids out too late, they get scared away from it too easily and never get good at it.
☆：I think there's plenty reason to be scared. I've seen kids get hurt on those slopes. He should wait another year at least.
Question：Why is the woman against letting her son ski?

●：今週末，レイをスキーに連れていこうと思うんだけど。
☆：スキーですって！？　ちょっと早いと思わない？　彼の年齢ではそりとか雪だるまを作るので十分よ。
●：スキーについては，早ければ早いほどいいらしいよ。もし始めさせるのが遅過ぎたら，子供は怖がって簡単に逃げてしまい，絶対うまくならないよ。
☆：怖がる理由は十分にあると思うわ。子供たちがああいう斜面でけがをするのを見たことがあるの。少なくとももう1年待った方がいいわ。
質問：女性はなぜ息子にスキーをさせることに反対しているのか。

1 彼がスキーを始めるのは遅過ぎるかもしれない。
2 夫が彼に対して厳し過ぎるかもしれない。
3 彼女はほかの子供たちがスキーでけがをするのを見たことがある。
4 彼女は彼がスキーを好きではないと言うのを聞いたことがある。
解説　女性が息子にスキーをしてほしくない理由を述べている中で，I've seen kids get hurt on those slopes. の部分と**3**が一致する。

No. 7 解答 **4**

☆：What do you think of the new dress I bought to wear to your parents' party this weekend?
★：Well, it's pretty, but ...
☆：What's wrong with it?
★：Nothing's wrong with it. It really is nice, but my parents are having a barbecue, and everyone will be wearing jeans and T-shirts.
☆：Oh, shoot! I spent a lot of money on this, but I guess I shouldn't wear it then.
Question：Why is the woman unhappy?

☆：この週末にあなたのご両親のパーティーに着ていくために買った新しいドレス，どう思う？
★：ああ，かわいいよ，だけど…
☆：何か問題ある？
★：問題は何もない。本当にすてきなんだけど，両親はバーベキューをするつもりだから，みんなジーンズとTシャツを着ると思う。
☆：あら，まあ！これにはだいぶお金をかけたのに，それじゃ着ていかない方がいいわね。
質問：女性はなぜ不満なのか。

1 男性が彼女のドレスは高過ぎると言った。
2 男性が彼女の新しいドレスを気に入らない。
3 ドレスのサイズが彼女にぴったり合わない。
4 パーティーに対してドレスがフォーマル過ぎる。
解説　女性はパーティー用にドレスを買ったのに，バーベキューをすると聞いてOh, shoot! ... I shouldn't wear it then. と残念がっている。つまりドレスはjeans and T-shirtsに対してフォーマル過ぎるのである。

No. 8　解答　3

☆：Do you want any lettuce in your sandwich, Bobby?
●：Um, my friend told me that we shouldn't eat lettuce.
☆：That sounds ridiculous. Where did he or she hear that?
●：Cindy said she saw it on TV. Supermarkets took lettuce off the shelves in 15 cities. Some kind of poisoning outbreak.
☆：Oh, I remember that. That's why the price of lettuce has gone up so much. Anyway, it was about two weeks ago and it was only a certain kind of lettuce.
●：Are you sure?
☆：Yes, and anyway I just bought this yesterday. I'm sure it's OK.

Question：What reason does Bobby give for not eating lettuce?

☆：サンドイッチにレタスはいる，ボビー？
●：うーん，友達がレタスは食べるべきじゃないと言ってた。
☆：ばかばかしいわ。その友達はどこでそれを聞いたのかしら。
●：シンディはテレビで見たって言ってた。15の都市でスーパーが棚からレタスを撤去したんだ。ある種の食中毒の発生だよ。
☆：ああ，覚えているわ。だからレタスの値段がこれほど上がったのよ。ともかく，それは2週間ほど前のことで，特定のレタスだけだったわ。
●：それは確かなの？
☆：ええ，とにかくこれは昨日買ったばかりよ。きっと大丈夫だと思うわ。

質問：ボビーはレタスを食べない理由として何を挙げているか。

1 1年のこの時期は高過ぎる。　　**2** 近くのスーパーで見つけるのが難しい。
3 彼はそれを食べると病気になるかもしれない。　　**4** 彼は違う種類のレタスの方が好きだ。

解説　my friend told me that we shouldn't eat lettuce の部分から，ボビーはレタスを食べることをちゅうちょしていることがわかる。その理由は後の Some kind of poisoning outbreak. から，**3** が正解。

No. 9　解答　1

☆：Hey, Pete. Have you finished all your classes for today?
★：Yeah, Cathy. I need to ask you a big favor. I've got a bit of a cash flow problem at the moment and I was wondering if...
☆：Sure, no problem. How much do you need?
★：Er, a hundred should cover it. I've got to buy some new textbooks this weekend.
☆：OK. Let's go over to the ATM at the Student Union. It will take just a minute.

Question：What does the man ask Cathy to do?

☆：ねえ，ピート。今日の授業は全部終わったの？
★：うん，キャシー。君に大きなお願いをしなければならないんだ。今，ちょっとお金がなくて，できたら…
☆：いいわよ，構わないわ。どのくらい必要なの？
★：ええと，100ドルあれば大丈夫なはず。この週末に新しい教科書を何冊か買わないといけなくてね。
☆：わかった。学生会館にある ATM に行きましょう。すぐに済むわ。

質問：男性はキャシーに何をするよう頼んでいるか。

1 彼にお金を貸す。　　**2** 彼女が借りたお金を彼に返す。
3 彼に教科書を何冊か貸す。　　**4** 彼を学生会館まで車に乗せていく。

解説　ask you a big favor から男性は女性に頼みたいことがあるとわかる。男性の a cash flow problem や女性の How much do you need? から，それが借金の申し込みであることを理解しよう。

No. 10 解答 4

☆：The word is that Mike quit his job as an accountant.
●：Really? Hmm. I'd heard his mother wasn't feeling well. His family lives out east, so maybe he wanted to be closer to them.
☆：Yeah, maybe, but I also happen to know his dad had been pressuring him to take over his real estate business.
●：Oh, I see. He always used to go around grumbling about his dad's business. In the end, he must've been convinced to do it somehow.
Question：Why does the woman think Mike quit his job?

☆：マイクが会計士の仕事を辞めたらしいわ。
●：本当に？　うーん。彼のお母さんの具合が悪いと聞いたことがある。彼の家族は町のずっと東の方に住んでいるから，もっと家族と近くにいたかったのかもしれない。
☆：うん，かもね，でも私，たまたま知っているんだけど，不動産業を継ぐようお父さんがずっと彼に圧力をかけていたの。
●：ああ，そうなんだ。彼はお父さんの仕事についていつもぼやき回っていたんだけどな。結局彼はそうするようううまいこと説得されたに違いない。
質問：女性はなぜマイクが仕事を辞めたと思っているか。

1 彼は体調が悪かった。
2 彼は同僚とうまくいかなかった。
3 彼は会計士に向いていなかった。
4 彼は父親の事業を継がなければならなかった。

解説　女性は，マイクが仕事を辞めた理由として，his dad had been pressuring him to take over his real estate business と言っていることから，**4**が正解。

No. 11 解答 3

★：You're in charge of marketing at Frontier Corporation now, aren't you, Reina?
☆：That's right. I'm the director of marketing.
★：So how are you finding your new position?
☆：Right now, it's pretty stressful. I have so much to learn. It's a lot more responsibility than my last job as sales manager.
★：Well, let me know if you have an opening at your company. I may want to change jobs soon.
☆：I will, Roger.
Question：What does the woman imply?

★：君は現在フロンティア・コーポレーションでマーケティングを担当しているよね，レイナ？
☆：そうよ。マーケティングの部長をしているわ。
★：それでその新しい役職はどうだい？
☆：今はかなりストレスが多いわ。学ばなければならないことがたくさんあるの。販売部長としての前の職よりもはるかに責任があるわ。
★：ねえ，君の会社で空きがあったら教えてよ。僕も近く転職してもいいと思っているんだ。
☆：わかったわ，ロジャー。
質問：女性は何をほのめかしているか。

1 彼女はマーケティングに興味がない。
2 彼女の上司の下で働くのは難しい。
3 彼女の新しい役職は難しい。
4 彼女は新しい仕事を探している。

解説　女性は新しい役職について，I have so much to learn. や It's a lot more responsibility ... と言っており，これを正解の**3**では challenging と表している。

No. 12 解答 **3**

☆ : Did Julie tell you she took first place in the high school sketching contest?

● : Whoa, that's fantastic! You know, just the other day she mentioned she was interested in going to a university of fine arts.

☆ : Yeah, well, hmm... she said the same thing to me, but honestly I'm not sure that's the best idea. I mean, you know the art world, right? Starving artists?

● : I know. Not the most stable career choice. Still, I think we need to respect her current dreams. They'll likely change, after all.

Question：What does the man recommend the woman do?

☆ : 高校の絵画コンテストで1位になったってジュリーはあなたに言った？

● : おお，それはすごいね！　ほら，つい先日，彼女は芸術大学に進学することに興味を持っているって言ってたよね。

☆ : ええ，まあ，うーん…，彼女は私にも同じことを言ったけど，正直なところ，それが最善策かどうかはわからない。つまり，芸術の世界を知っているでしょう？　飢えた芸術家とか？

● : 知ってるさ。最も安定した職業の選択ではないね。それでも，僕たちは彼女の今の夢を尊重しないといけないと思う。最終的にそれらの夢は変わる可能性があるし。

質問：男性は女性に何をするよう勧めているか。

1 娘に美術学校へ行かないように話す。

2 彼女の懸念を娘に話す。

3 娘が芸術への興味を持ち続けるかどうかを見守る。

4 娘に職業を変えるよう説得する。

解説　娘が芸術の道に進むことについて，男性は，「今の夢を尊重しよう」「夢は変わるかも知れない」→「今は様子を見よう」と言っている。それをWait and see ... と表した**3**が正解。

(A)

Robot Spiders

Spiders are known for their ability to move their legs flexibly and keep stable at the same time. A spider has eight legs, each leg with seven joints. Spiders also have an outer skeleton, rather than bones and muscles like humans. This means the legs are hard on the outside and hollow on the inside. These legs are moved by pumping fluid inside of them. A spider can also move steadily by keeping four of its legs on the ground while the other four are in motion.

Researchers at the Fraunhofer Institute in Germany were inspired by this mechanism of movement to develop an artificial spider that can get into places where people cannot. The robot spider that they invented moves on eight legs in the same way as its natural counterparts. In addition, the robot spider can be equipped with measuring devices and sensors. This invention can also be produced relatively easily with 3-D printers. Researchers anticipate robot spiders will be used for exploration or rescuing people in dangerous environments.

Questions

No.13 How do spiders move?

No.14 What do the researchers expect robot spiders to do?

ロボットスパイダー

クモは脚を柔軟に動かし，同時に安定を保つ能力で知られている。クモには8本の脚があり，それぞれの脚には7つの関節がある。クモにはまた，人間のような骨や筋肉ではなく，外骨格がある。これは，脚が，外側は硬く内側は空洞であることを意味する。これらの脚は，内側に流体を送り込むことによって動かされる。クモはまた，ほかの4本が動いている間にも，4本の脚を地面に置いて着実に動くことができる。

ドイツのフラウンホーファー研究機構の研究者たちは，この動きのメカニズムに触発され，人間が入り込めない場所に入ることができる人工のクモを開発した。彼らが発明したロボットスパイダーは，本物のクモと同じように8本の脚で動く。さらに，ロボットスパイダーには測定装置とセンサーを装備することができる。この発明は，3Dプリンターでも比較的容易に製造することができる。研究者たちは，ロボットスパイダーが危険な環境での探査や人々の救助に使用されることを期待している。

No. 13 解答 4

「クモはどのようにして動くか」

1 脚の関節を動かすことによって動く。

2 脚の骨と筋肉を使うことによって動く。

3 8本の脚がすべて同じように動かされる。

4 脚の半数がほかの半数と異なる動きをする。

解説 クモの8本の脚について「4本が動いている間にほかの4本は地面に置いて着実に動く」という説明を，「脚の半数がほかの半数と異なる動きをする」と言い換えた**4**が正解。

No. 14 解答 1

「研究者はロボットスパイダーが何をすることを期待しているか」

1 危険な場所で任務を遂行する。

2 3D印刷技術の開発を助ける。

3 人々が測定装置を使用するのを助ける。

4 センサーを使ってほかのロボットを検出する。

解説 研究者の期待については最後のResearchers anticipate robot spiders will be used ... in dangerous environments. の部分から，**1**が正解。

(B)

Norte Chico Civilization

The oldest civilization in the Americas is the Norte Chico in Peru. The civilization developed 5,000 to 6,000 years ago. There were about 20 communities that settled around the valleys along three rivers. Little is known about Norte Chico because almost no cultural evidence has been found. In fact, unlike other well-known civilizations, Norte Chico seems to have had no writing system, forms of art, pottery, or even crop farming, even though the people made irrigation systems to control the water flow.

Despite the lack of agriculture for food, a written language, and artwork, the Norte Chico civilization left behind large monuments made of stone. These monuments that still remain today include stepped stone pyramids and circular plazas. These constructions suggest organized workers and resources. After 1,200 years of settlement, the Norte Chico civilization vanished. Archaeologists have yet to discover the reason behind the people leaving this land.

Questions

No.15 Why is little known about the Norte Chico civilization?

No.16 What do the monuments in Norte Chico suggest?

ノルテ・チコ文明

南北アメリカで最も古い文明はペルーのノルテ・チコである。この文明は5,000年から6,000年前に発展した。3つの川に沿う谷の周りに定住したコミュニティーが20ほどあった。文化的証拠がほとんど見つかっていないため、ノルテ・チコについてはほとんど何もわかっていない。実際、ほかの有名な文明とは異なり、ノルテ・チコは、人々が水流を制御するために水利システムを作ったにもかかわらず、文字体系、芸術形式、陶器、さらには作物栽培さえもなかったようである。

食料を得る農業、書き言葉、芸術品がなかったにもかかわらず、ノルテ・チコ文明は石で作られた大きな記念碑を後世に残した。今日もなお現存しているこれらの記念碑は、階段状の石のピラミッドと円形の広場を含む。これらの建造物は組織的な労働者と資源があったことを示唆する。1,200年間の人の定住の後、ノルテ・チコ文明は消滅した。考古学者は、人々がこの土地を去った理由をいまだに解明していない。

No. 15 解答 **4**

「なぜノルテ・チコ文明についてほとんど知られていないのか」

1 コミュニティーがほんの少ししかなかった。 **2** 文字体系が複雑過ぎる。

3 数千年前に完全に消滅した。 **4** 文化的な情報を示す証拠が限られている。

解説 Little is known about Norte Chico because almost no cultural evidence has been found. の部分から、**4**が正解。almost no cultural evidenceを選択肢ではEvidence ... is limited. と言い換えている。コミュニティーは約20あったので**1**はonly a fewが不適。

No. 16 解答 **2**

「ノルテ・チコの記念碑は何を示唆しているか」

1 近辺の石造りのピラミッドを説明するのに役立つ。

2 互いに協力して働くシステムがあった。

3 ノルテ・チコ文明はペルーで始まった。

4 その時期のライフスタイルは非常に質素だった。

解説 記念碑についての説明の中で、These constructions suggest organized workers and resources. と**2**が一致する。organized workersを選択肢ではworking togetherと表している。

(C)

Sharing Coffee Cups

According to the UK Parliament, 5 billion coffee cups are thrown away every year. It is also estimated that only 0.25%, that is, one in 400 cups, are recycled. Single-use cups are one of the top thrown-away items that make up the world's waste. A team of technologists, designers, and engineers, led by entrepreneur Safia Qureshi, set out to make a difference. In April 2018, the team established a reusable cup subscription service. They named it the CupClub.

CupClub's cups are made of plant-based plastic and a radio-frequency identification tag is embedded in each cup and lid in order to track them. Stores that subscribe to the service serve coffee using these cups. Customers can return the cups at any participating location in the city for a reward. Once collected, these cups are washed and redistributed to the stores for reuse. CupClub's cups can be reused up to 132 times.

Questions

No.17 Why was the CupClub founded?

No.18 What is one thing the customers do with the cups?

コーヒーカップのシェアリング

イギリス議会によると，毎年50億個のコーヒーカップが捨てられている。また，0.25%，つまり400カップに1つの割合しかリサイクルされていないと推定されている。使い捨てカップは，世界のごみで最も多く捨てられる物の1つである。起業家サフィア・クレシが率いる科学技術者，デザイナー，エンジニアのチームが，状況を改善するために立ち上がった。2018年4月，チームは再利用可能なカップの会費制サービスを開始した。彼らはそれをカップ・クラブと名付けた。

カップ・クラブのカップは植物由来のプラスチック製で，それを追跡するために無線自動識別タグが各カップとふたに埋め込まれている。サービスに加入している店はこれらのカップを使ってコーヒーを提供する。客は報奨金と引き換えに市内の加入店ならどこでもそのカップを返すことができる。これらのカップはいったん回収したら，洗浄して再使用するために加入店に再分配される。カップ・クラブのカップは最大132回まで再利用できる。

No. 17 解答 **3**

「なぜカップ・クラブが設立されたか」

1 さまざまな素材でカップを作るため。

2 不要なカップを捨てるため。

3 ごみの量を減らすため。

4 コーヒーのサービスを契約するため。

解説 多くのコーヒーカップが捨てられる問題に対応すべく，再利用可能なカップの会員制サービスを始めたのがカップ・クラブ。この捨てられるカップを抽象的にwasteと表した**3**が正解。

No. 18 解答 **4**

「客がそのカップですることの1つは何か」

1 各カップとふたのタグを集める。

2 クラブに寄付するためにカップを提示する。

3 カップを自分で洗って再利用する。

4 サービスに参加している店にカップを持っていく。

解説 終盤のCustomers can return the cups at any participating location in the city for a reward.の部分を言い換えた**4**が正解。

(D)

Amsterdam Albatross

The Amsterdam albatross is an enormous seabird that can weigh 5 to 8 kilograms and have a total body length of 1.1 to 1.2 meters. When its wings are spread out, it can be as long as 3.5 meters. The Amsterdam albatross is named after Amsterdam Island, an island in the southern Indian Ocean, where it makes a nest and takes care of its young.

A pair of Amsterdam albatross produces only one egg every other year. Scientists have counted about 170 of these birds on Amsterdam Island. Due to its very small population and low reproduction rate, the Amsterdam albatross is listed as critically endangered. When the Amsterdam albatross was discovered in 1983, it was thought to be a wandering albatross subspecies. However, according to recent DNA testing by Canadian researchers, the Amsterdam albatross was found to be a unique species. Researchers hope that the fact that it is one-of-a-kind will help promote the conservation of these birds.

Questions

No.19 What is one thing the Amsterdam albatross does?

No.20 What is one reason for the Amsterdam albatross being endangered?

アムステルダムアホウドリ

アムステルダムアホウドリは，重さ5～8キログラム，全長1.1～1.2メートルになることもある巨大な海鳥である。翼が広がると3.5メートルにもなることがある。アムステルダムアホウドリは，インド洋南部の島であるアムステルダム島にちなんで名付けられている。アムステルダムアホウドリはそこで巣を作り，幼鳥の世話をする。

アムステルダムアホウドリのつがいは，1年おきに1個しか卵を産まない。科学者たちはアムステルダム島のこの鳥を170羽ほど数えた。その非常に少ない数と低い繁殖率のため，アムステルダムアホウドリは深刻な絶滅危惧種に分類されている。アムステルダムアホウドリが1983年に発見されたとき，それはワタリアホウドリの亜種だと見なされた。しかし，カナダの研究者による最近のDNA検査により，アムステルダムアホウドリは固有種であることがわかった。研究者たちは，それは比類のない種であるという事実がこの鳥の保護を促進するのに役立つことを望んでいる。

No. 19 解答 2

「アムステルダムアホウドリがすることの1つは何か」

1 次から次へと島を渡る。　　　　　　　　　**2** アムステルダム島でひなを世話する。

3 大きな翼幅を使って巣を作る。　　　　　　**4** 1年おきにカナダへ渡る。

解説　アムステルダム島について，where it makes a nest and takes care of its young と述べている部分から，**2** が正解。young を選択肢では babies と表している。

No. 20 解答 1

「アムステルダムアホウドリが絶滅の危機に瀕している理由の1つは何か」

1 1度に1個しか卵を産まない。　　　　　　　**2** すべての鳥が巣を作れる場所がない。

3 過去10年の間食料が不足している。　　　　　**4** 住む場所を見つけるのに苦労している。

解説　絶滅に瀕している理由は，A pair of Amsterdam albatross produces only one egg every other year. から，1年おきに1個しか卵を産まないからである。続く Due to its very small population and ... の部分もヒントになる。

(E)

Christmas Book Giving in Iceland

Many countries celebrate Christmas and the holiday season, but not necessarily in the same way. In Iceland, there is a tradition of giving books as Christmas gifts. It is part of a holiday season event called *jolabokaflod*, which means "Christmas book flood" in English. *Jolabokaflod* begins in mid-November, when a catalog of books that have been published throughout the year is sent to each household in Iceland. People use this catalog to select and buy books for family and friends. On the night of December 24th, people give books to each other and spend the rest of the night reading.

The tradition of *jolabokaflod* began during the Second World War, when the government restricted the import of certain types of goods. However, paper was one of the few items that was not limited by import restrictions, and so it was easier to obtain. Books became a common gift, since other items were in short supply. More than half a century later, books still remain Iceland's primary choice for a holiday gift.

Questions

No.21　What do people in Iceland use to find books for Christmas?

No.22　Why did books become popular gifts in Iceland?

クリスマスに本を贈るアイスランド

　多くの国がクリスマスと休暇シーズンを祝うが，必ずしも同じやり方で祝うわけではない。アイスランドでは，クリスマスの贈り物として本を贈る伝統がある。これは，英語で「クリスマスの本の洪水」を意味するヨーラボカフロードと呼ばれる休暇イベントの一環である。ヨーラボカフロードは11月中旬に始まり，そのとき，1年間に出版された本のカタログがアイスランドの各家庭に送られる。人々は，家族や友人のために本を選んで購入するのにこのカタログを利用する。12月24日の夜，人々はお互いに本を贈り，残りの夜を，読書をして過ごす。

　ヨーラボカフロードの伝統は，政府が特定の種類の品の輸入を制限していた第2次世界大戦中に始まった。しかし，紙は輸入規制によって制限されていない数少ない品目の1つだったので，ほかの品目より入手が容易だった。ほかの品が不足していたので，本は一般的な贈り物になった。半世紀以上たった今でも，本は，アイスランドのクリスマスギフトとしての主要な選択肢として残っている。

No. 21　解答　**4**

「アイスランドの人々はクリスマスのための本を見つけるのに何を利用するか」

1 年次出版物のオンラインカタログ。　　　　**2** 大手書店からの推薦。

3 地元の図書館に掲示された情報。　　　　**4** 1年間に出版された本の一覧。

解説　クリスマスに贈る本を選ぶ方法について，People use this catalog to select and buy books for family and friends. と言っている。この this catalog にはその前の内容から1年間に出版された本が載っているので，**4** が正解。カタログは家庭に送られるので，**1** の「オンラインカタログ」は誤り。

No. 22　解答　**1**

「アイスランドではなぜ本が人気のある贈り物になったのか」

1 本を作るのに紙は入手するのが容易だった。　　**2** 政府が本を推奨する法律を可決した。

3 本が大量に輸入された。　　　　**4** 配送サービスが不足していた。

解説　伝統の始まりを説明している部分の中で，However, paper was one of ... it was easier to obtain. の部分から，第2次世界大戦当時は紙が入手しやすかったことがわかる。

(F)

Bank Holidays

A British bank holiday is an official public holiday, that is not a Saturday or Sunday, when all banks and post offices are closed. Most factories, offices, and shops are also closed. Days such as New Year's Day, Good Friday, Easter Monday, the first Monday in May, the last Monday in May, the last Monday in August, Christmas Day, and Boxing Day are bank holidays in England, Wales, Scotland, and Northern Ireland. The first Monday in May is called the May Day Bank Holiday and the last Monday in August is known as the August Bank Holiday.

There is one additional bank holiday in both Scotland and Northern Ireland. In January, 2007, November 30th officially became the bank holiday of Saint Andrew's Day in Scotland. The 1903 Bank Holiday Act added March 17th, Saint Patrick's Day, to the Northern Irish calendar. Much as the British love their bank holidays, they have fewer of them than their European counterparts.

Questions

No.23　What does the speaker say about British bank holidays?

No.24　What does the speaker say about Scotland and Northern Ireland?

バンクホリデー（一般公休日）

　イギリスのバンクホリデーとは，土曜でも日曜でもない法定公休日で，その日はすべての銀行と郵便局が閉まる。ほとんどの工場と会社と店も休業する。元日，聖金曜日，復活祭の翌日の月曜日，5月の第1月曜日，5月の最終月曜日，8月の最終月曜日，クリスマス，ボクシングデーといった日が，イングランド，ウェールズ，スコットランドそして北アイルランドのバンクホリデーである。5月の第1月曜日はメーデー・バンクホリデーと呼ばれ，8月の最終月曜日は8月バンクホリデーとして知られている。

　スコットランドと北アイルランドにはほかにも1日バンクホリデーがある。2007年1月，スコットランドでは11月30日が正式に聖アンドリューの祭日というバンクホリデーになった。1903年のバンクホリデー法は，3月17日の聖パトリックの祭日を北アイルランドの暦に付け加えた。イギリス人はバンクホリデーが好きなのに，ヨーロッパの国々のバンクホリデーよりもその日数が少ないのだ。

No. 23　解答 **3**

「話者はイギリスのバンクホリデーについて何と言っているか」

1　そのときほとんどの工場と会社と店が営業している。

2　それはしばしば土曜日か日曜日である。

3　そのときすべての銀行と郵便局が閉まる。

4　イギリスはほかのヨーロッパの国々よりもバンクホリデーが多い。

解説　冒頭の when all banks and post offices are closed という説明から，**3**が正解。

No. 24　解答 **1**

「話者はスコットランドと北アイルランドについて何と言っているか」

1　イングランドよりもバンクホリデーが1日多い。

2　全体的にバンクホリデーが少ない。

3　イングランドと共有するバンクホリデーがほとんどない。

4　新たにバンクホリデーを追加することを望んでいる。

解説　イギリスのバンクホリデーの説明に続いて後半では，スコットランドと北アイルランドについて There is one additional bank holiday ... と言っている。

(G) No. 25 解答 3

As you may know, there are several routes you can take to Oceanview Peak, which has several shops and a breathtaking view of the sea. Unfortunately, Woodhaven Road is closed for maintenance. The Windhill Summit Trail has some challenging areas, so it's probably better for experienced hikers. There's the Seaview Trail, which is good for families. It's about 40 minutes to the peak. Lighthouse Walk is the easiest, so it's great for kids. Instead of the peak, it goes to Crane Lake. It's about a 20-minute walk one way. Please remember that eating and drinking is prohibited there.

状況：あなたはシカモアウッドランド公園に4歳の息子とハイキングに行きたいと思っている。あなたは道中でランチを食べたいと思っている。ガイドが公園のルートに関して次のようなアドバイスをする。

質問：あなたはどのルートを行くべきか。

ご存じかもしれませんが，お店がいくつかあって海の素晴らしい景色が臨めるオーシャンビュー・ピークに行くにはいくつかのルートがあります。あいにく，ウッドヘブン道は整備のため閉鎖されています。ウインドヒル山頂コースにはいくつかの険しい道なりがあるので，おそらく経験豊富なハイカーにとってより良いコースです。シービュー・コースがあって，こちらはファミリー向けです。山頂まで約40分です。ライトハウス・ウオークは最も簡単なので，お子さんに最適です。そちらは山頂へ行く代わりにクレーン湖に行きます。歩いて片道約20分です。そこは飲食禁止ですのでご注意ください。

1 ウッドヘブン道。　　　　　　　　　　　**2** ウインドヒル山頂コース。

3 シービュー・コース。　　　　　　　　　**4** ライトハウス・ウオーク。

解説　子供でも歩ける易しいルートは，ファミリー向けのSeaview Trailである。Lighthouse Walkも簡単で子供に最適だが，飲食が禁止されているので不適。

(H) No. 26 解答 3

This is Skyways Airlines. Your call is very important to us. Calls are answered in strict rotation, so please do not hang up if the line is busy. If you wish to contact reservations, please press 1; for departure and arrival information for today's flights, press 2; for reconfirmations of previously booked flights, press 3; for cancellations, press 4, and for all other information, press 5. While we will endeavor to answer your call within five minutes, sometimes due to circumstances beyond our control, or at times of peak demand, we may take a little longer. Thank you for calling Skyways.

状況：あなたは3日後にニューヨークの自宅に戻る予定でいる。帰りの予約を確認するためにスカイウェイズ航空に電話して，次のメッセージを聞く。

質問：あなたは何をすべきか。

こちらはスカイウェイズ航空でございます。お客さまのお電話は，私どもにとって大変重要でございます。厳正に順番を守って応対いたしますので，話し中でも，どうぞ電話をお切りにならないでください。予約係に連絡を取りたい場合は1を，本日の便の発着状況は2を，事前に予約された便の再確認は3を，キャンセルは4を，その他の情報は5を押してください。私どもでは5分以内にお電話にお応えするよう努めておりますが，時にはやむを得ない状況にある場合や電話のピーク時には，少々長引くこともございます。スカイウェイズ航空にお電話いただき，ありがとうございました。

1 1を押す。　　　　**2** 2を押す。　　　　**3** 3を押す。　　　　**4** 4を押す。

解説　状況のcheck your return reservation「帰りの予約を確認する」は，放送中のreconfirmations of previously booked flightsのこと。よって，3を押す。

(I) *No. 27*　解答 3

Hi, it's Roxanne. You're visiting Jasperson Printing this morning to pick up the pamphlets, right? I'm really looking forward to seeing the finished version. Anyway, the reason I'm calling is, if you have time, would you mind dropping by an office supply store and picking up some printer ink? There's one across the street from Jasperson. Just one black cartridge will do. The one in our printer is just about out, and we don't have any in the stockroom. I'd appreciate it. But only if you can make it in time for the 11 a.m. department meeting. Thanks!

状況：あなたは仕事に行く前に印刷会社に立ち寄ることになっている。午前10時30分ごろに職場に到着する予定である。あなたは同僚からボイスメールを受け取る。

質問：あなたは何をすべきか。

もしもし，ロクサーヌです。今朝，パンフレットを取りにジャスパーソン印刷会社に行くんですよね？　完成版を見るのが本当に楽しみです。ところで，私が電話をしているのは，もし時間があれば，事務用品店に立ち寄ってプリンターのインクを買ってきてもらってもいいですか。ジャスパーソン社から通りを渡った所に1軒あります。黒色のカートリッジ1つだけで大丈夫です。会社のプリンターの黒カートリッジがちょうど切れそうで，倉庫に1つもないのです。よろしくお願いします。でも，午前11時の部門会議に間に合う場合だけにしてください。ありがとう！

1 自分用にパンフレットを印刷する。　　　　2 印刷所からのEメールを読む。

3 途中で事務用品を買う。　　　　　　　　4 部門会議を延期する。

解説 would you mind dropping by an office supply store and picking up some printer ink? の部分から，**3**が正解。事務用品（＝カートリッジ）を買うのは印刷会社からオフィスに行く間にすることなので，on the way と表している。

(J) *No. 28*　解答 2

I'm sorry, but it looks like we only have yellow and red in the store right now. We'll be getting some new shoulder bags in stock next week, however, including navy blue and dark green. They are really popular colors for this bag. You can also buy these colors on the Internet, but it takes about two weeks. There might be some darker-colored ones available at our other locations. One of our other stores is right nearby, in Hemlick's Mall on the third floor. They usually have this brand of bags on hand in many colors. It's about a 10-minute walk from here. I can give you a map if you'd like.

状況：あなたはキャンプ用品店にいて，今週末の旅行用のショルダーバッグを見ている。あなたはすてきなデザインのバッグが展示されているのを見るが，濃い色のものを買いたい。店員が次のように言う。

質問：あなたは何をすべきか。

申し訳ありませんが，現在当店には黄色と赤しかないようです。でも，濃紺と深緑を含め，来週新しいショルダーバッグが入荷する予定です。それらはこのバッグでとても人気のある色です。それらの色はインターネットでも買えますが，2週間ほどかかります。ほかの店舗にもっと濃い色のバッグがあるかもしれません。ほかの店の1つはすぐ近くのヘムリックズ・モールの3階にあります。その店にはたいてい，このブランドのバッグはたくさんの色がそろっています。ここから歩いて10分ほどです。よろしければ地図をお渡しできます。

1 今手に入るバッグを選ぶ。　　　　　　　2 近くの別の店舗に行ってみる。

3 来週店に戻ってくる。　　　　　　　　　4 店のウェブサイトでバッグを注文する。

解説 この店には欲しい色のバッグがなく，店員は来週入荷すると言っているが，それでは今週末の旅行に間に合わない。There might be ... at our other locations. One of our other stores is ... の部分で近くにある他店舗を紹介していることから，**2**が正解。

(K) No. 29 解答 **2**

Attention, shoppers. A lost child has been brought to our service desk on the second floor. The child is a little girl, approximately four years old, and was found on the third floor in the confectionery section. She is wearing a red skirt with blue dots and a white hat. To reach the desk from the first or third floors, use the east escalator. After getting off the escalator, walk towards the wall with a black star on it. And for all our shoppers, be sure to stop by our information booth near the front door on the first floor to pick up your discount coupons for special savings. Thank you.

状況：あなたはデパートで買い物をしており，４歳の娘がいなくなってしまったことに気が付く。あなたは迷子に関する次のアナウンスを聞く。

質問：あなたは娘を引き取るのにどこへ行くべきか。

お客さまに申し上げます。ただいま迷子のお子さまが保護されて，２階のサービスデスクでお預かりしています。お子さまは小さな女の子で４歳ぐらい，３階のお菓子売場で保護されました。青の水玉模様のある赤いスカートに，白い帽子をかぶっています。１階もしくは３階からデスクへいらっしゃる場合，東側のエスカレーターをご利用ください。エスカレーターを降りたら，黒い星のマークがある壁の方へお進みください。またすべてのお客さまに申し上げます。１階正面玄関近くの案内所にぜひお立ち寄りになり，特別割引クーポンをお受け取りになってください。ありがとうございます。

1 １階の案内所。　　　　　　　　　　**2** ２階のサービスデスク。

3 ３階の遺失物取扱所。　　　　　　　　**4** ３階のお菓子売場。

解説　冒頭の A lost child has been brought to our service desk on the second floor. から，娘が保護されている場所は２階のサービスデスクなので，引き取り場所として**2**が正解。

筆記試験＆リスニングテスト
解答と解説

問題編 p.47〜63

筆記

1

問題	1	2	3	4	5	6	7	8	9	10	11	12	13	14	15	16	17	18
解答	3	2	3	1	2	2	4	1	3	3	3	3	2	2	3	2	4	3

2

問題	19	20	21	22	23	24
解答	3	4	2	3	1	2

3

問題	25	26	27	28	29	30	31
解答	3	2	3	2	3	4	3

4 解説内にある解答例を参照してください。

5 解説内にある解答例を参照してください。

リスニング

Part 1

問題	1	2	3	4	5	6	7	8	9	10	11	12
解答	3	2	2	2	1	2	2	4	3	4	4	1

Part 2

問題	13	14	15	16	17	18	19	20	21	22	23	24
解答	2	4	3	2	3	4	4	1	4	1	1	3

Part 3

問題	25	26	27	28	29
解答	4	1	1	1	2

Day 5

1

(1) **解答 3**

「最近のリストラの結果，その自動車会社では2千人以上の労働者が解雇された」

解説 リストラの結果労働者がどうなったかを考えると，be made redundant「解雇される」が適切。synthetic「統合的な」，optional「選択の」，potent「効力がある」

(2) **解答 2**

「そのがん患者は心臓に問題のあることがわかった。

この併発により医者は自分たちが望んでいたほど早くには手術ができなかった」

解説 がんと心臓の問題を併せ持つ患者の手術を阻む原因となるものだから，complication「併発，合併症」が入ると推測できる。abbreviation「略語」，application「申し込み」，contrivance「工夫」

(3) **解答 3**

「その大学の開校式はキャンパス・スタジアムで行われる予定だが，そこは2万5千人の収容能力がある」

解説 スタジアムについての説明の部分で, 25,000 という数字が出てくるので, seating capacity「座席収容能力」が適切。adversity「不運」, commission「委任」, redemption「救い」

(4) 解答 1

「マイクは高校時代に一生懸命勉強したので, 一流の大学への入学許可を手に入れることができた」

解説 目的語が admission「入学許可」なので, secure「手に入れる」が動詞としてふさわしい。surpass「しのぐ」, concede「認める」, reflect「反射する」

(5) 解答 2

「少年たちは, 庭を熊手で掃いた後, 葉の山を大きなビニールのごみ袋に入れた」

解説 庭を熊手で掃いて何を大きなごみ袋に入れたかを想像すると, 葉っぱの山（heap）である。clamp「締め具」, blaze「炎」, grave「墓」

(6) 解答 2

「エドワーズ夫人は, 夫が1年以上も彼女を欺いて浮気をしていたことがわかったとき, 離婚を要求し, 弁護士に相談した」

解説 cheat は口語で,「（～を欺いて）浮気をする」という意味。divorce「離婚」がふさわしい。retreat「撤退」, recess「休憩」, diversion「そらすこと」

(7) 解答 4

「休み一つ取らずに一日中懸命に働いた後, その建設技師は完全に疲れ切っていた」

解説 前半の内容から, feel drained「ひどい疲れを感じる」が自然。drain には「（液体）を流出させる」のほかに「（人）を疲れさせる」という意味がある。deplore「嘆き悲しむ」, crouch「かがむ」, immerse「浸す」

(8) 解答 1

A「君はまだいくつかの新聞に記事を書いているの？」
B「いいえ, 今はもっぱら『ニューズ・トゥデー』紙に書いています。それが常勤の仕事になりました」

解説 「今は複数の新聞では記事を書いていない」と答えていることから, exclusively「もっぱら～だけ」が適切。disdainfully「軽蔑して」, superficially「表面的に」, attentively「注意深く」

(9) 解答 3

「この報告書の中の大きな誤りは, 月曜日の社長とのミーティング前に修正しなければならないだろう」

解説 大きな誤りは rectify「修正する」必要がある。reclaim「改心させる」, exempt「免除する」, exceed「超える, 勝る」

(10) 解答 3

「子供は脆弱なので, 子供に対し罪を犯した大人は厳しく処罰されるべきだ。子供は大人の保護を必要とする」

解説 子供に対し罪を犯した大人が処罰されるべきなのは, 子供が脆弱（vulnerable）だから。後の require the protection がヒントになる。variable「変わりやすい」, fascinating「魅力的な」, filthy「不潔な」

(11) 解答 3

「顧客は支払いを済ませた後はレストランに長居すべきではない」

解説 支払いを済ませた客がすべきではないことを考えると, linger「長居する」が正解だとわかる。swindle「（金など）をだまし取る」, pluck「引っ張る」, flirt「（異性と）いちゃつく」

(12) 解答 3

「ジュリーは地方の古風で趣のあるホテルに泊まった。部屋は小さかったが, すてきな装飾が施され, とても快適だった」

解説 「快適なホテル」を修飾する形容詞として quaint「古風で趣のある」がふさわしい。vague「曖昧な」, dire「恐ろしい」, crucial「決定的な」

(13) 解答 2

A「カールがぶつかってきて, 彼のジュースを私の体中にこぼしたのよ。私のシャツを見てよ」
B「それは意図的だったに違いない。彼はいじめっ子だから」

解説 直後の bully「いじめっ子, 弱い者いじめをする人」から, Bはカールの行動が意図的な（deliberate）ものだと思った。watchful「用心深い」, functional「機能的な」, serene「穏やかな」

(14) 解答 2

「その2つの政党は連立政府を作るために一緒になることを決めた。さもなければ, 彼らがその国のリーダーシップを取る可能性はなかっただろう」

解説 2つの政党が一緒になって作るのは coalition

government「連立政府」である。collision「衝突」, compression「圧縮」, consolation「慰め」

(15) 解答 **3**

「情報筋によれば，その会社はとてもひどい1年を過ごした後，倒産に直面し，負債の返済を履行しない模様であった」

解説 倒産の状況から，default on a loan「負債の返済を履行しない」が文脈に合う。round off「～をしめくくる」, skim over「～をざっと見る」, scratch out「～を削除する」

(16) 解答 **2**

「その記者は目撃者たちが語ることをすべて書き留めようとしたが，それは不可能であった。彼らは早口であるばかりでなく，しばしば同時に話したのであった」

解説 早口のため何ができなかったかを考えると，jot down「～を書き留める」がふさわしい。write off「～を書き上げる」は文脈に合わない。make over「～を

譲る」, put up「～を泊める」

(17) 解答 **4**

「地元住民の度重なる苦情に応え，警察は道路や私設車道への違法駐車を厳しく取り締まることを約束した」

解説 違法駐車をどうするかを考えると，crack down on「～を厳しく取り締まる」がふさわしい。knock down「～を壊す」, strike out「三振する」, break out「勃発する」

(18) 解答 **3**

「両社の代表による長期の交渉の後，そのプロジェクトにおける協調関係を継続できるよう，主要な問題点が解決された」

解説 協調関係を継続するために，主要な問題点をiron out「解決する」必要があった。carry through「～を完遂する」, hang up「電話を切る」, wash up「～を洗う」

2

全訳
カシミヤ──見て，触る喜び

　カシミヤは魔力そのものである。その独特な柔らかさとビロードのような手触りで，ぜいたくと豊かさの最高の象徴になっている。スコットランドで作られるカシミヤの衣料が，丈夫さや色，そしてデザインによって，世界のニットウエア市場をリードしているのは誰もが認めるところである。デザイナーの中には，スコットランド製のカシミヤしか使うつもりはないという者もいる。

　高いかって？　もちろんである。価格が高い要因は，1つには原料を手に入れるのが難しいことにある。「カシミヤ」という言葉は，かつてカシミヤ・ウールの供給源であるヤギがいた，インドのカシミール州が英語化したものである。今日では，必要となる羊毛の下毛は中国やロシアのヤギから得ている。多大な費用がかかるのは，スコットランドから遠く離れた国々の高山をヤギが歩き回るからだけではなく，製造過程において多くの時間や技術を必要とするからである。製造作業中に行われるマッチングや縫合は，品質チェックを受けなければならない，熟練を要する工程なのである。頻繁にチェックをすることで，各段階において高い水

準を確実に満たすことができるのだ。製造作業の訓練にはおよそ1年から1年半かかる。

　カシミヤがどのようにして開発され，利用されてきたかは，ドーソン・インターナショナルとして知られる巨大複合企業の足跡をたどればわかる。1901年，ジョーゼフ・ドーソンはヤギの毛を分離できる機械を発明したが，この糸紡ぎのための下準備は，それまではすべて手で行われていた。その結果，同社は世界最大のカシミヤ加工会社の1つになった。しかし，カシミヤが今日のようにステータス・シンボルになったのは，1950年代になってからである。

(19) 解答 **3**

解説 カシミヤが高価である理由として，第2段落第3文と第6文に「原料入手の難しさ」と「製造過程において多くの時間や技術を必要とすること」が挙げられている。したがって，**3**を入れて「価格が高い要因は，1つには原料を手に入れるのが難しいことにある」とするのが適切。

(20) 解答 **4**

解説 熟練を要する工程なのでマッチングや縫合は，

品質チェックを **4**「受けなければならない」と考えるのが自然である。subject to には「〜を必要とする」という意味がある。

(21) 　解答 **2**

解説　前文の「それまで手作業だった工程を機械化した」という内容から、「同社はどこよりも大きなカシミヤ加工会社の1つになった」は「結果」である。よって、**2**が正解。

全訳

心の知能

　1996年、ダニエル・ゴールマンが『EQ こころの知能指数』という本を出版した。知能指数（IQ）テストといった従来の知能の測定法は、個人が人生において成功するか失敗するかを予言するのに用いられる場合、まったく正確さを欠くという見解をこの本は提示している。ゴールマンは、個人の感情的な性質の方がその人が現実世界でどの程度うまくやっていけるかを示す、はるかに信頼の置ける指標であると信じている。

　ゴールマンの考えは、私たちのほとんどにとって驚くべきことではない。私たちは皆、知的には優れていながら、仲間の人間と付き合うのに苦労しているような人物に出会ったことがある。人と付き合うのに苦労するというのは、社会と付き合うのに苦労するというのに等しい。そして、常識的に考えれば、社会と付き合うことができないというのは、個人的なあるいは仕事での成功を収めることにとって大きな障害である。

　従来の IQ テストに関する議論は、それが初めて考案されたときから激しく行われてきた。そもそも何らかの妥当性があるのか。あるとすれば、それは厳密には何を測り、またどんな意味を持つのか。ゴールマンは事実を正確にしたいと思っていたのだが、残念なこ

とに彼の本には心の知能を測定する方法がまったく示されていない。

　しかし、彼がこの問題を提示したという事実は、私たちを考えさせるのに十分である。人に好かれる人は、ほかの人も好きになる傾向がある。引っ込み思案で防御的な人は、家庭や職場で友人や協力者をほとんど見いだせない。ほかの人とうまく付き合うことのできる人ができない人と比べて、より大きな満足や成功を見いだすだろうというのは当然である。

　バランスは私たちの幸福にとって必要不可欠なものであり、ある意味で、これがゴールマンの主張していることの本質なのである。IQ は役に立つツールとなり得るが、バランスの取れたより人間的な観点がなければ、それは単に十分とは言えないのである。

(22) 　解答 **3**

解説　人生の成否を予見する上で「知能テストはまったく正確さを欠く」と議論を始め、知能テストと対照的な議論が展開していくので、感情的な性質は**3**「はるかに信頼の置ける」指標と考える。

(23) 　解答 **1**

解説　続く部分で、「われわれは皆会ったことがある」や「常識の示すところでは…」など、常識的な議論がなされている。よって、第2段落冒頭ではゴールマンの考えは**1**「驚くべきことではない」とするのが適切。

(24) 　解答 **2**

解説　前の段落には「残念なことに…示されていない」とあるが、空所のある文は「…させるのに十分である」という言葉で終わっている。この2つを結ぶ接続詞は逆接の**2**「しかし」が適切。

3

全訳

「Me Too」運動

　「Me Too」運動は2017年から広く注目を集め始めたが、このフレーズの使用とその背景にある理由は10年余り前に始まった。#MeTooというハッシュタグがソーシャルメディアで急速に広まる前、ニューヨークの公民権運動家が、女性が被った虐待に注目を集め被害者を助けるための彼女の活動の一環として、このフ

レーズを使っていた。ハリウッドでの性的虐待に対するいくつかの非難が世間の注目を集めた後、ある女優がこのハッシュタグを使って自分の経験を打ち明けるようほかの人たちに働き掛け、それをネットで急速に広めた。

　その結果はすぐに広範囲に表れ、影響力のある男性の手による搾取と虐待の話を多くの女性が打ち明けた。この運動を始めた女性によると、マイノリティー出身

の女性は依然として特に被害に遭いやすく，この事実は見落とされてきたと一部の批判者が主張している。当初の運動の背後にいた女性は，彼女の巻き起こした運動が広く注目される前に，何年も，特に有色人種の若い女性について，男女不平等を改善しようとしていた。しかし2017年以降，ハリウッド内部からの虐待の申し立てと，エンターテインメント産業を支配する人物たちに，メディアの注目の大半は集中してきた。

ハリウッドにはその生活が多大な注目を集めやすい多くの有名人がかかわっているため，ハリウッドへの注目は当然と言える。この注目は，当初の運動の注目度を上げ，今度は被害者を支援する取り組みへの資金援助に役立っている。これまで以上に，虐待を受けている人々の苦境が世間の目にさらされるようになり，それが以前は声が聞き届けられていないと感じていた人々にとって多くのプラスの結果をもたらしている。悲しいことに，それはまた，不公正の憂き目にあった女性と男性両方に関する相次ぐ虐待を明らかにした。

この運動はまた，ニューヨークとハリウッドをはるかに超えて拡大し，「Me Too」の翻訳が世界中のソーシャルメディアで使われている。この運動を巡る談義は，今では不平等と不公正を取り上げるいくつかの論点に広がっているが，その中核となる問題は依然として性的虐待とハラスメントである。この運動のおかげで多くの虐待者が法の裁きを受けたものの，多くの人がそれはまだ初期段階にあると信じている。この考えは，それがほかの形の虐待を浮き彫りにする同様の運動につながったという事実によって強化されている。しかし，ソーシャルメディアを通じて素早く広がる，評判を損なうことを目的とする偽りの主張によって，良い行いがむしばまれかねないことを警戒する者もいる。

(25)　解答　**3**

「『Me Too』運動はどのように始まり，その後どのように発展したか」

1 元々純粋にソーシャルメディアから始まり，そして福祉サービスの提供者となった。

2 少数民族の女性たちがソーシャルメディアで自分たちの話を打ち明け，そこから成長した。

3 ある活動家が虐待を受けた女性たちと協力し，それからソーシャルメディアで注目を集めた。

4 ニューヨーク出身の虐待を受けた女性たちが虐待者に対して行動を起こし，それが急速に広まった。

解説　第1段落のBefore the hashtag #MeToo ... の部分から，ある公民権活動家（a civil rights activist）が虐待を受けた女性たちを助ける活動を行い，その後にソーシャルメディアを通じて広まったことがわかる。よって，**3**が正解。

(26)　解答　**2**

「ソーシャルメディアでの注目度はどのような点でこの運動に影響を与えたか」

1 注目度がものすごく高いにもかかわらず，この運動は目に見える形で恩恵を受けることができていない。

2 この注目は虐待の被害者を支援するのに役立ったが，焦点が狭過ぎると感じている人もいる。

3 ソーシャルメディアの注目は，名乗り出て自分の話を語る意思がある犠牲者が減ることを意味する。

4 ソーシャルメディアの注目は，マイノリティー出身の男性がハリウッドで仕事が得にくくなっていることを意味した。

解説　第3段落のThis attention has helped to ... から，この注目は被害者を支援するのに役立ったことがわかる。また，第4段落第2文以降の，運動は広がりを見せてはいるが性的虐待とハラスメントが中心であり，まだ「初期段階」にあると考える人が多い，という内容を抽象的に「焦点が狭過ぎる」と表した**2**が正解。

(27)　解答　**3**

「『Me Too』運動やほかの同様の運動は将来的にどうなるか」

1 これらの運動は今や勢いを増しているのだから，社会の問題と戦う余地がかなりある。

2 これらの運動は，その背後にいる人々の悪い評判のため，局所的のままであることが確実視されている。

3 誤った告発には用心している人もいるが，これらの運動は広がっており，すでに結果を出している。

4 これらの運動は多くの注目を集めている一方で，公正さへの真剣な取り組みを徐々に弱めていることは，間もなく勢いを失うということである。

解説　第4段落から，「Me Too」運動がほかの同様の運動につながったことがわかる。howeverを含む最後の文Others, however, are wary that spurious claims aimed at destroying reputations, ... から，**3**が正解。

全訳

長生きのための減食

　数々の研究が，齧歯類と霊長類は非常に制限された食事，つまり通常消費されるカロリーから20～30％低い食事をすることで恩恵を受けてきたということを明らかにしている。十分に食料を与えられていない実

験用動物は, より長く, より健康的に生きた。現在, ますます多くの人たちがその研究結果を額面どおりに受け止めて, カロリーの摂取を20〜30％制限している。カロリー制限は一般的にCRと呼ばれ, 多くのほかのダイエットプランに比べると人気はないが, それは『長寿ダイエット』,『120歳超えダイエット』を含む数々の本を生み出した。

ほとんどのダイエットは体重を減らすことがすべてだが, CRは主により長く, より健康的な生活をすることに関するものである。CRダイエットの支持者は食べる量を減らしているので, 確実に十分な栄養を摂取できるように, 食べ物の品質に高い関心を持っていることが多い。飽和脂肪, 糖分, 乳製品はたいてい減らされるか, 食事から外される。こうした食事は通常, 体重減少とより低い代謝率につながるものであり, ひいてはより長い寿命につながるかもしれない。

だが, CRが実際に人の寿命を長くしたと証明する長期的研究はない。しかし, それが多分実際にそうするだろうと示す数々の研究がある。2007年の『アメリカ生理学ジャーナル——内分泌学とメタボリズム』において発表されたある研究が示した内容によると, 摂取カロリーを20％削減したCRダイエットを計画的な運動と組み合わせた結果, 燃焼するカロリーは20％増し, 悪玉コレステロール値を下げ, 善玉コレステロールの量を増やした。運動なしのCRでさえ心臓病のリスクを大きく下げるという結果をもたらした。

しかし, CRはいくつかの深刻な危険につながることもある。多くのCRダイエットをする者は急に体重を落とし, すでにほとんど体脂肪のない人にとっては, この体重減が危険なこともある。CRダイエットは, 拒食症などの摂食障害を持つ人たちを含む, それを適用すべきでない種類の人たちを引き付ける可能性がある。そしてCRダイエット中の多くの人たちは, いつも空腹感を感じると不満をもらし, 食べ物のことで頭がいっぱいになってしまうほどである。ある研究では, CRダイエットを1年間してきた人は運動だけで体重を落とした人たちと比べて筋肉量が少なく, 運動能力も低いということが示された。別の研究では, CRで体重を落とした人たちは, 運動で体重を落とした人たちとは対照的に, 腰と背中の骨の発達が弱いということが示された。そのほかのCRダイエットの影響は風邪と不妊の増大を含む。ワシントン大学医学部の研究者たちは大きなカロリー減少は, 栄養不良, 貧血, 筋肉減少, 衰弱, うつ病さえも含む多くの病気につながることを発見した。幸運なことに, 最近の研究はCRが記憶や注意の問題に悪影響を与える証拠はまったく示していない。

CRの支持者には, より健康的で, より長生きする軌道に乗っているとの確信があるものの, どれだけの速さでどこまでやるべきかについては医師の診察を受けることが大事である。食事のカロリーを1日当たり500カロリー以上減らすことは, 短期的に見て不健康なだけでなく, 長期的には寿命に影響を与える悪い結果をもたらし得るのだ。

(28) 解答 **2**

「CRの方法に従おうと決めたダイエットする人たちは,」

1 人間を対象とした長期的研究によって, CRダイエットが最も効果的だと納得した。

2 最初は動物に対するCRの研究結果に魅了された。

3 人数が急増し, その計画は最も人気のあるものの1つになっている。

4 ほかのダイエットプランが自分にとっては同様にうまくいかないと気付いた。

解説 CRダイエットをする人々について, 第1段落第2〜3文に「動物実験を額面どおり受け止めてカロリーを制限している」とあることから, **2**が正解。

(29) 解答 **3**

「この文章は, CRダイエットは〜人々にとって健康的でないかもしれないことを示唆している」

1 高コレステロール血症や心臓病の現在の状態を下げることを望む

2 ほかの種類のダイエットで一度も成功したことがない

3 すでに食物やダイエットに関する深刻な心理的問題を抱えている

4 明らかに肥満であるか, 体脂肪が多い

解説 CRダイエットに向かない人々については, 第4段落第2〜3文にthose who already have little body fatとthose with such eating disorders as anorexiaが挙げられており, この後者と, **3**が一致する。

(30) 解答 **4**

「次のうちどれがCRダイエットから起こりそうにない結果か」

1 絶望感を含む気分変動。

2 食べ物と食べ物の消費への執着。

3 より弱い骨と筋肉量の減少。

4 知能低下と集中力の欠如。

解説 CRダイエットの実践結果に該当しないものが問われている。第4段落最終文でFortunately, recent research shows no evidence that CR negatively affects memory or attention issues. と述べられているので，**4**「知能低下と集中力の欠如」の心配はないと言える。

(31) 解答 **3**

「筆者はCRダイエットについて何をほのめかしているか」

1 CRダイエットは基本的に人々が20～30％のカロリー制限を守って初めて成功する。

2 CRダイエットは多くの人にとって効果的であることが示されており，体重を減らすための非常に一般的な方法になるかもしれない。

3 研究によるとCRダイエットは健康的なものとなり得るが，憂慮すべき危険性もある。

4 研究によるとCRダイエットのリスクは利益をはるかに上回っているため，多くの人はこのダイエットを避けた方がよい。

解説 筆者は第2～3段落でCRダイエット法の良い点を，また第4段落においてはCRダイエットに伴うリスクを説明している。この相反する内容を抽象的に表した**3**が正解。

問題文の訳

　かつては，最新のファッショントレンドを追う唯一の方法は，主に高級店で買える有名ブランドの衣料品を買うことだった。しかし，20世紀後半になると，各社が似たようなデザインを素早く大量に生産し，それらを低価格で販売し始めた。このビジネスモデルはファストファッションとして知られるようになった。

　ファストファッションの支持者たちは，ファストファッションのおかげで，富裕層だけでなく誰もが最新のスタイリッシュな衣料品を買って着ることができるようになったと主張する。今やファストファッションブランドはデザイナーブランドとまさに同じくらい見映えが良くなっている。また，ファストファッションの成長は，衣料品のデザイン，生産，販売する人々を含め，世界中の人々に雇用を提供した。

　これにもかかわらず，ファストファッションは人々に，衣料品にお金を浪費し，すぐにそれを処分するよう促すと言う人もいる。その結果，衣料品の生産によって生じる廃棄物が環境に悪いと見なされている。それに加えて，衣料品を作るために雇われている人々が，しばしば有害な化学物質にさらされるなどの危険な環境で，低賃金で長時間労働しているという懸念もある。

解答例

　Fast fashion has established a business model of mass-producing clothing and selling it at affordable prices. The benefits of fast fashion include not only making it possible for anyone to buy fashionable, good-looking clothes but also creating jobs. However, this phenomenon has caused problems, such as an increase in waste as people throw away clothes easily and poor working conditions for those involved in clothing manufacturing. （66語）

解答例の訳

　ファストファッションは，衣類を大量生産して手頃な価格で販売するというビジネスモデルを確立した。ファストファッションの利点には，誰もがファッショナブルで見栄えの良い服を買えるようになったことだけでなく，雇用が創出されたことも挙げられる。しかし，この現象は，人々が簡単に衣服を捨てることによる廃棄物の増加や，衣料品製造に携わる人々の劣悪な労働環境などの問題を引き起こしている。

解説　各段落の要点を1（〜2）文でまとめて全体を3〜4文で書こう。解答例は，第1文「トピックの導入（ファストファッション）」（第1段落），第2文「利点」（第2段落），第3文「欠点」（第3段落）の3文構成。第1文は高級ブランドとの対比でFast fashion is gaining popularity in competition with traditional luxury brands.「従来の高級ブランドに対抗してファストファッションが人気を博している」のような導入も可能。第3段落のDespiteは対比を表す印で，解答例ではHoweverでつなげている。

　要点をまとめるポイントは，①重要な情報を見極め，細かい情報や具体例は省く，②具体的な情報を抽象化する，の2点。例えば，第2段落のincludingに続く具体的な情報は省く。また，複数の文にわたる情報を名詞化することも端的に言い換えるコツである。例えば第2段落の利点を解答例では，The benefits of fast fashion includeに続けてnot only A but also Bでまとめている。〈利点・欠点＋include 〜〉「（利点・欠点）には〜が挙げられる」はどんなトピックでも使える便利な表現だ。第3段落は「浪費→廃棄物の増加→環境に悪い」という展開と「労働環境」についてで，「問題を引き起こしている」と前置きした後，情報を名詞化してsuch as A and Bでまとめている。第3段落第3文の労働者の具体的な状況は「劣悪な労働環境」と抽象化できる。

　そのほかの解答例の言い換えも参考にしよう。in large quantities→mass-producing, low prices→affordable prices, stylish→fashionable, look just as good as designer brands→good-looking, provided employment→creating jobs, dispose of→throw away

問題の訳

TOPIC：子供は夏休みに宿題がある方がよいと思うか。
POINTS：子供の幸せ・教師の仕事量・準備・学業的競争力

解答例

I think giving children summer homework is a good thing as it helps them to prepare for the next semester, and also allows students from less wealthy backgrounds to stay competitive.

First of all, it is easy for children to forget the information they have learned during long summer vacations. Doing a certain amount of homework helps reinforce their studies and prepares children for the next semester.

The second reason is that doing summer homework helps students from less wealthy backgrounds stay academically competitive. If teachers do not give out summer homework, children who have other methods of studying, such as going to cram schools, will have a greater advantage.

Summer homework not only allows children to review and reinforce what they have learned, but also offers a safety net for those from less privileged backgrounds to keep up with other students. (142語)

解答例の訳

　子供たちに夏休みの宿題を与えることはいいことだと思う。次の学期に向けて準備するのに役立つし、あまり裕福でない家庭の生徒が競争力を保てるようにするからである。

　第1に、子供たちは学んだ情報を長い夏休みの間に忘れやすい。ある程度の宿題をすることは、子供たちの学習を強化するのに役立つし、子供たちにとって次の学期の準備となる。

　2つ目の理由は、夏休みの宿題をすることは、あまり裕福でない家庭の生徒が学業的な競争力を保つのに役立つことである。もし教師が夏休みの宿題を出さなければ、塾に通うなどほかの方法で勉強する子供たちの方がずっと有利になるだろう。

　夏休みの宿題は、子供たちが学んだことを復習したり強化したりできるようにするだけでなく、恵まれない家庭の子供にほかの生徒に遅れないための安全策も提供する。

解説　「子供は夏休みに宿題がある方がよいと思うか」という問いに対し、解答例はYesの立場である。序論では、「子供たちに夏休みの宿題を与えることはいいことだと思う」と始め、as it helps ..., and also allows ... の形でPOINTSのPreparationとAcademic competitivenessを用いて理由を簡潔に述べた後、第2段落ではFirst of all, ...、第3段落ではThe second reason is that ... の形でそれぞれ詳しく説明している。

　第2段落はPOINTSのPreparationの観点で、「子供たちは夏休み中に学んだことを忘れやすい」と宿題がないことの欠点を述べた後、宿題があることの利点として「勉強を強化するのに役立つ」「次の学期の準備になる」と述べている。第3段落はAcademic competitivenessの観点で、「夏休みの宿題はあまり裕福でない子供が学業的な競争力を保つのに役立つ」という宿題の利点を述べた後、If teachers ... の部分で詳しく説明している。結論となる最終段落では、not only A but also Bを用いて、「学んだことを復習したり強化したりできる」「恵まれない家庭の子供の安全策」という宿題の利点を2つ述べることで主張を再確認している。

　POINTSのChildren's happinessとTeacher's workloadはNoの立場で使えそうだ。「子供は宿題で忙しく自由時間がない。子供の幸せを優先すべき」「宿題を用意する教師に負担がかかる」などの意見が考えられるだろう。

Listening Test

Part 1 🔊 053〜065

No. 1   解答 3

☆：Did you finally buy a car? I know you've been wanting one for a while now.

★：Hi, Tracy. Yeah, well, unfortunately, it's not mine. This is one of my company's cars.

☆：It looks brand new.

★：It is, actually. It's one of several we just bought. The good news is, since I travel so often, it can also be for personal use. I just have to pay for gas.

☆：Well, that's almost like having your own car, I guess.

★：I suppose. Too bad I don't get to use it on the weekends, though.

Question：What do we learn from the conversation?

☆：ついに車を買ったの？　しばらく前から車を欲しがっていたわよね。

★：やあ，トレイシー。うん，ええと，残念ながら僕の車ではないんだ。これは社用車の1台だよ。

☆：新車みたいね。

★：そうなんだよ，実は。うちの会社が買ったばかりの車の1台なんだよ。良い点は，僕はしょっちゅう外回りに出るから，個人的にも使えること。ガソリン代を支払わなければならないだけ。

☆：へえ，自分の車を持っているのと同じようなものね。

★：そうだね。週末に乗れないのが残念だけど。

質問：会話から何がわかるか。

1 男性は女性に新車を買ってやった。　　**2** 男性は自分の車を売ったばかりである。
3 男性の会社は彼に車を貸した。　　**4** 男性の会社には車が1台しかない。

解説 男性の This is one of my company's cars. や it can also be for personal use という発言から，男性は社用車を借りていることがわかる。**4**は It's one of several we just bought. から，only one が不適。

No. 2   解答 2

☆：I heard Cynthia is being transferred to our office in Minneapolis, Minnesota next October.

●：Oh, I'm envious! I hear Minneapolis has a lively community of artists and lots of culture. Great night life, too.

☆：She doesn't seem too excited about it. It's not that she doesn't want to move, but I think she was hoping to be transferred somewhere else.

●：Oh? Why is that, I wonder?

☆：Well, for one thing, Minnesota has long cold winters. Half the year you're stuck indoors.

●：Ah, right. I've heard her complaining about the cold even here.

Question：What is implied about Cynthia?

☆：シンシアが今度の10月にミネソタのミネアポリスのオフィスに異動になるって聞いたわ。

●：ああ，うらやましい！　ミネアポリスには芸術家の活気あるコミュニティーと豊かな文化があるらしい。素晴らしいナイトライフもね。

☆：彼女はこのことにあまりうれしくない様子なの。異動したくないというわけではなくて，ほかの場所への異動を望んでいたんだと思うわ。

●：へ？　どうしてなんだろう？

☆：うーん，1つには，ミネソタの冬は長くて寒いわ。1年の半分は室内に閉じ込められるのよ。

●：ああ，そうだね。ここですら寒いと彼女がこぼすのを聞いたことがあるよ。

質問：シンシアについて何がほのめかされているか。

1 彼女は旅行を楽しまない。　　**2** 彼女は寒い気候が好きではない。
3 彼女は芸術と文化の愛好家である。　　**4** 彼女は今のオフィスにとどまりたい。

解説 シンシアがミネアポリスへの異動を喜んでいない理由として，女性は for one thing, ... の部分で寒い気候に言及し，男性もシンシアは寒がりだと言っている。**4**は It's not that she doesn't want to move の部分から，不適。

No. 3　解答 2

★：So, Kim, do you like to run? I always see you running around campus.

☆：Actually, no. We just have to. I'm on the cross-country ski team, but there's no snow yet this year. So, our coach makes us run instead of ski.

★：Must be hard. Do you like skiing, then?

☆：To be honest, I've never been into sports that much. I joined the cross-country team because my friend did, but with all this running, I've dropped 10 kilograms and I feel good.

★：So it's a workout routine for you?

☆：Kind of like that, yeah.

Question：What is one thing we learn about Kim?

★：ねえ，キム，君は走るのが好きなの？　いつも君がキャンパスの辺りを走っているのを見かけるけど。

☆：実を言うと，好きじゃないの。私たちはただ走らないといけないの。私はクロスカントリースキー部に所属しているのだけど，今年はまだ雪が降ってないでしょ。だから，コーチがスキーの代わりに私たちを走らせているの。

★：それは大変だろうね。それで，スキーは好きなの？

☆：正直なところ，それほどスポーツに興味を持ったことはないのよ。友達が入部したから私もクロスカントリー部に入ったんだけど，こうやってずっと走ってばかりいるから10キロ体重が落ちて，気分がいいわ。

★：じゃあ，それが君にとっての日課のトレーニングなんだね。

☆：まあ，そういうことね。

質問：キムについてわかることの1つは何か。

1 彼女はさまざまなスポーツにかかわってきた。　**2** 彼女は以前は体重がもっとあった。
3 彼女のスキー板は履き心地が悪い。　**4** 彼女の友人はマラソンで走るのを楽しんでいる。

解説　女性はI've dropped 10 kilograms and I feel goodと言っており，「体重が落ちた」を「以前は体重がもっとあった」と言い換えている**2**が正解。

No. 4　解答 2

☆：What did you think of the football game last night, George?

●：Dreadful! It was pretty boring. And I got all wet, too.

☆：I know. They'd hardly got on the field when it started to pour.

●：Our team is useless in the mud. They couldn't keep the ball for more than a few minutes at a time.

☆：Well, I think the referees should have just canceled it.

Question：What do we learn about the game?

☆：昨晩のフットボールの試合をどう思った，ジョージ？

●：ひどかったね！　かなり退屈だったよ。ずぶぬれにもなったしね。

☆：そうね。選手がフィールドに現れたとたんに，雨が激しく降り始めたわね。

●：うちのチームは泥の中では役立たずだね。一度にボールを数分しかキープできなかったし。

☆：まあ，審判が試合を中止にすべきだったと思うわ。

質問：試合について何がわかるか。

1 試合はわくわくするものだった。　**2** 試合の最中に雨が降った。
3 彼らのチームはうまくプレーした。　**4** 試合は中止になった。

解説　They'd hardly got on the field when it started to pour. は言い換えると，「試合中に雨が降った」ということ。〈hardly ... when 〜〉「…するとすぐに〜」の理解がポイント。

No. 5　解答　1

★：Sylvia, when are you going to stop buying diet products? I mean, you just have to move around more.

☆：What am I supposed to do in the winter, Victor? Go jogging in the snow?

★：Well, I don't think these diet foods are healthy. You would be better off just eating more fruits and vegetables. They cost less and do the same thing.

☆：Maybe you're right, but ...

★：Look, how about you and I do a 30-minute workout routine together in the living room every day?

☆：OK, but if it doesn't work, you're buying me an exercise bike.

Question：What does the man say to the woman?

★：シルビア，君はいつダイエット食品の購入をやめるつもりなの？　つまり，君はもっと運動しさえすればいいんだよ。

☆：冬に何をしろって言うの，ビクター？　雪の中をジョギングするの？

★：ええと，これらのダイエット食品が健康的だとは思えない。単にもっとたくさんの果物と野菜を食べた方がいいよ。その方が安いし，効果は同じだよ。

☆：あなたの言うとおりかもしれないけど…

★：ねえ，君と僕とで一緒に，毎日リビングで30分の運動を日課にするというのはどう？

☆：わかった。でも，うまくいかない場合は，私にエアロバイクを買うのよ。

質問：男性は女性に何と言っているか。

1 運動はダイエット食品より効果的である。　　**2** 屋外でジョギングすることは年中可能である。
3 ダイエットをするのにはお金がかかる。　　**4** 運動は長時間やるべきではない。

解説　男性は冒頭で女性に，ダイエット食品を買うのをやめて運動するよう言っていることから，**1**が正解。後の how about you and I do ...? の提案部分でも運動を勧めている。

No. 6　解答　2

●：Did you see the soccer match last night?

☆：No, I fell asleep on the couch. What happened?

●：United lost two-to-nothing. The referee was awful. He gave five of our players yellow cards and you should have seen the number of penalties he called against us.

☆：Really? I'm glad I didn't stay up to watch it.

●：You'd have been as upset as I was.

Question：Why was the man upset?

●：昨晩のサッカーの試合は見たかい？

☆：いいえ，ソファーで寝ちゃったの。何があったの？

●：ユナイテッドが2対0で負けたんだ。審判がひどくてね。こちらの選手の5人にイエローカードを出してね，君もユナイテッドに出したペナルティーの数を見るべきだったよ。

☆：そうだったの？　起きて見てなくてよかったわ。

●：僕と同じくらいに腹を立てたと思うよ。

質問：男性はなぜ腹を立てたのか。

1 女性が試合を見なかった。　　**2** 審判がユナイテッドに対し不公平だった。
3 数名のユナイテッドの選手が負傷した。　　**4** 彼は試合を全部見ることができなかった。

解説　男性は The referee was awful. という発言に続けて，ユナイテッドの選手に対する審判のイエローカードやペナルティーの出し方に不満を語っていることから，**2**が正解とわかる。

No. 7　解答　2

☆：Did you get the results from your annual checkup at work, honey?

★：I sure did. The doctor told me he hasn't seen someone my age with as healthy a stomach in a long time.

☆：Well, you have been watching what you eat recently. I'll give you credit for that.

★：You know, maybe you, uh, might want to think about ...

☆：What, are you saying I'm fat?

★：No, no! You look great. It's just that I know you like oily, greasy, fried things to eat. Even if you're slender, that kind of food can give you high cholesterol.

Question：Why is the man concerned about his wife's health?

☆：会社の年1回の健康診断の結果はもらった？

★：確かにもらったよ。医者は僕の年齢でこれほど健康的な胃を持つ人は長い間見ていないと言っていた。

☆：うーん，あなたは最近ずっと食べる物に注意を払っているものね。それは偉いと思うわ。

★：ねえ，君もさ，考えた方がいいかもしれない…

☆：何？　私が太ってるって言いたいの？

★：いや，違うよ！　君はすてきだよ。ただ君が油っこい揚げ物を食べるのが好きだって知っているから。たとえ痩せていても，そのような食べ物はコレステロールを上げることがあるからね。

質問：男性はなぜ妻の健康を心配しているのか。

1 彼女は最近急激に体重が増えた。

3 彼女はあまり運動をしない。

2 彼女は高コレステロール食品をたくさん食べる。

4 彼女は年1回の健康診断を受けていない。

解説　男性のyou like oily, greasy, fried things to eat. ..., that kind of food can give you high cholesterolという発言を短くまとめた**2**が正解。**1**は，are you saying I'm fat? と言う女性にNo, no! と答えているので不適。

No. 8　解答　4

●：Hello, my name is Andy Trent, calling from Trent Industries. Is Ms. Daniels available please? She's expecting a call from me.

☆：I'm sorry, but it looks like she'll be away from her desk until noon today.

●：I see. Could you have her contact me when she gets in?

☆：Of course, Mr. Trent. May I have your number please?

●：On second thought, I'll call her back this afternoon around 1:00. Would that be OK?

☆：Certainly. I'll tell her you called.

Question：What is one thing we learn from the conversation?

●：もしもし，私の名前はアンディ・トレントで，トレント・インダストリーズから電話をしています。ダニエルズさんはお手すきでしょうか。彼女は僕からの電話を待っています。

☆：あいにくですが，彼女は本日正午まで席を外しているようです。

●：そうですか。彼女が戻りましたら僕に連絡してもらっていいですか。

☆：かしこまりました，トレントさん。あなたの電話番号をお願いできますか。

●：やっぱり，今日の午後1時ごろに僕が彼女に電話をかけ直します。それでいいでしょうか。

☆：かしこまりました。彼女にはあなたから電話があったことを伝えます。

質問：会話からわかることの1つは何か。

1 男性は間違った人に連絡を取った。

2 男性は今日この後，ダニエルズさんのオフィスに立ち寄る。

3 ダニエルズさんは仕事の電話を持っていない。

4 ダニエルズさんは今日の午後，オフィスにいる。

解説　不在のダニエルズさんについて，女性はshe'll be away from her desk until noon todayと言っていることから，**4**が正解。男性のI'll call her back this afternoon around 1:00もヒントになる。

No. 9　解答　3

☆ : Why weren't you in French class yesterday, Sam?

★ : I'm afraid I'm losing my enthusiasm. I don't have a gift for languages.

☆ : That's not true. Have you given up?

★ : Well, no ... but my friends just laugh at me when I try to speak French.

☆ : It's just your accent. Let's get together and work on it. I actually lived in France for a year when I was a young girl, so my pronunciation is pretty good.

Question : What does the woman say to the man?

☆ : サム，どうして昨日フランス語の授業に出なかったの？

★ : あいにくやる気をなくしているんだ。僕には語学の才能がないんだよ。

☆ : そんなことないわ。諦めたの？

★ : いや，そうじゃないけど…，僕がフランス語を話そうとすると友達が笑うんだよ。

☆ : それは単に発音のせいよ。一緒に練習しましょう。実は私，小さいときに1年フランスに住んでいたから私の発音はかなりいいわよ。

質問 : 女性は男性に何と言っているか。

1 彼はフランス語の能力がまったくない。　　**2** 彼の発音は実際はかなり良い。

3 彼女は彼の発音において手伝うことができる。　　**4** 彼女のフランス語は実際は彼よりも下手である。

解説 「フランス語を話そうとすると友達が笑う」と言う男性に対し，女性はIt's just your accent. Let's get together and work on it. と言っている点から考える。

No. 10　解答　4

☆ : That'll be 57 dollars, 23 cents.

● : Oh. That's cheaper than I thought it would be.

☆ : You've got two shirts there, and today we have a buy-two-get-20-percent-off deal.

● : Is that so? I didn't know these were on sale.

☆ : Yes. Also, if you buy three or more items from this part of the store, the discount jumps to 30%. So, if there's anything else you'd like, please feel free to look around.

● : I'll do that, thanks.

Question : What is the man likely to do next?

☆ : 57ドル23セントになります。

● : ああ。思っていたよりも安いですね。

☆ : お客さまはシャツを2枚お求めになりましたが，本日，当店は2点買えば20%オフになります。

● : そうなんですか？ これらがセール品だとは知りませんでした。

☆ : そうなんです。それに，店のこちらのコーナーから3点以上の品をお求めの場合，割引は30%に上がります。ですから，ほかに何か欲しいものがございましたらお気軽にご覧ください。

● : そうします，ありがとう。

質問 : 男性は次に何をすると考えられるか。

1 2枚のシャツの代金を支払う。　　**2** 割引を求める。

3 別の店を探す。　　**4** さらに多くの品を買い足す。

解説 女性店員のSo, if there's anything else you'd like, please feel free to look around. という提案に男性はI'll do that と答えている。つまり，男性はこの後，3点以上の品を買うのに店内を見て回ると考えられる。

No. 11　解答　4

☆: Joe, one of our clients, Mr. Simpson from Pegasus Travel, is coming to the office at two o'clock to see me.

★: I know. He wants to see our company's ideas for the new advertising campaign. But Jane, are you OK? You look pale.

☆: I feel dizzy.

★: You'd better go home and take a rest. Don't worry about Mr. Simpson. I'll show him our ideas and get his feedback.

Question: What does the man offer to do?

☆: ジョー，私たちのクライアントの1人，ペガサス・トラベルのシンプソンさんが，私に会いに2時にオフィスに来るの。

★: そうだね。彼は新しい宣伝キャンペーンについてのわが社のアイデアを知りたいんだよね。でもジェーン，大丈夫？ 顔色が悪いよ。

☆: 目まいがするの。

★: 家に帰って休んだ方がいいよ。シンプソンさんのことは心配いらないよ。僕がアイデアを説明して，彼の意見を聞いておくから。

質問: 男性は何をすると申し出ているか。

1 会議の予定を変更する。
2 女性を家に連れていく。
3 新しいアイデアを考え出す。
4 女性に代わってクライアントに会う。

解説　男性の You'd better go home and take a rest. や I'll show him our ideas and get his feedback. という発言から，男性は女性の代わりにシンプソンさんと会うことを申し出ているとわかる。

No. 12　解答　1

☆: Excuse me, what seems to be going on over there on the other side of the street?

●: Oh, the crowd? Apparently there's a celebrity in Giovanni's restaurant. I think they're waiting to take photos.

☆: Who is it? Is it Maya Endo?

●: You know, I'm not sure. I didn't ask. It's a younger lady, a singer, I think.

☆: I have to know if it's Maya. I think I'll go talk to someone over there and find out. Thanks.

●: The only thing I know is that no one knows whether or not she's coming out of the building's front door.

Question: What will the woman do first?

☆: すみません，通りの向こう側のあそこで何が起こっているんでしょうか。

●: ああ，あの人だかりのこと？ どうやらジョバンニ・レストランに有名人がいるんです。彼らは写真を撮ろうと待っているんだと思います。

☆: それは誰ですか？ マヤ・エンドー？

●: さあ，わかりません。聞きませんでした。もっと若い女性，歌手だと思いますが。

☆: マヤかどうかどうしても知りたいです。あそこにいる誰かと話をして確かめようと思います。ありがとう。

●: 僕が知っているのは，彼女が建物の正面玄関から出てくるかどうかを誰も知らないということだけです。

質問: 女性は最初に何をするか。

1 有名人について誰かと話す。
2 建物の写真を撮る。
3 出入口の外で待つ。
4 人だかりにいる誰かに文句を言う。

解説　女性が見知らぬ男性に人だかりについて尋ねている場面。女性は I think I'll go talk to someone ... と言っており，「有名人」（celebrity）が話題なので，**1** が正解。

(A)

Mia Hamm

Mariel Margaret Hamm, nicknamed Mia, was born in 1972 in Selma, Alabama. As a young girl growing up, there were not many female athletes for her to look up to as role models. Despite the lack of predecessors, she worked her way up to become one of the greatest female soccer players. At the age of fifteen, she became the youngest ever to join the U.S. National Team. When the first Women's World Cup was held in China in 1991, Mia helped the U.S. team win the title. Her feats continued. Mia played in three Olympic Games, contributing to two gold medals and one silver medal.

During her years as a world-class athlete, Mia was also devoted to a good cause. She lost her older brother Garrett in 1997 to a bone marrow disease. Following that, Mia started the Mia Hamm Foundation to support people suffering from the same disease as her late brother as well as to provide more opportunities for young women in sports.

Questions

No.13 How did Mia Hamm become a soccer player?

No.14 What is one thing Mia Hamm did after she lost her brother?

ミア・ハム

ミアというニックネームのマリエル・マーガレット・ハムは，1972年にアラバマ州セルマで生まれた。成長中の少女のころ，ロールモデルとして尊敬する女性アスリートはあまりいなかった。前例がなかったにもかかわらず，彼女は苦労して偉大な女子サッカー選手の1人にまでなった。15歳のとき，彼女は史上最年少でアメリカ代表チームに加わった。1991年に中国で第1回女子ワールドカップが開催されたとき，ミアはアメリカチームが優勝するのに一役買った。彼女の偉業は続いた。ミアは3つのオリンピックでプレーし，2つの金メダルと1つの銀メダルの獲得に貢献した。

世界レベルのアスリートとして活躍する間に，ミアは慈善事業にも献身した。彼女は1997年に兄のギャレットを骨髄疾患で亡くした。その後，ミアはミア・ハム財団を設立し，亡き兄と同じ病気にかかっている人々を支援し，また，スポーツにおいて若い女性にもっと多くの機会を提供している。

No. 13 解答 2

「ミア・ハムはどうやってサッカー選手になったのか」

1 彼女はロールモデルを見つけた。 　　　　**2** 彼女は自分で道を切り開いた。

3 彼女はほかの女性選手を模範とした。 　　**4** 彼女は偉大なアスリートから刺激を受けた。

解説 　ミアは，尊敬するロールモデルや前例がないにもかかわらず，偉大な女子サッカー選手になった。she worked her way up to become one of ... の部分を言い換えた**2**が正解。

No. 14 解答 4

「ミア・ハムが兄を亡くした後にしたことの1つは何か」

1 彼女は教育に関する財団を設立した。 　　**2** 彼女は職場の男女平等のために闘った。

3 彼女は貧しい生まれの人々の支援を始めた。 　**4** 彼女は積極的に女子スポーツを促進した。

解説 　兄を亡くした後の活動については，Mia started the Mia Hamm Foundation ... to provide more opportunities for young women in sports の部分と**4**が一致する。

(B)

Joik

Joiking is a traditional way of singing that was created and practiced by the Sami people, who live in Norway, Sweden, Finland, and Russia. *Joik* is usually not sung with words. Rather, it is an expression of a person or thing in a musical form. By singing a *joik*, the singer tries to recreate or re-picture a person, animal, or a place.

While *joik* is believed by researchers to be one of the oldest musical traditions in Europe to have survived to this date, throughout history a number of events have threatened its continuation. When Christianity was introduced in Sami villages, for example, *joiking* was banned in churches, schools, and even in homes. Today, *joik* is appreciated by a large audience and has been brought back into the general popular culture.

Questions

No.15 What is true about *joik*?

No.16 What happened to *joiking* when Christianity was introduced?

ヨイク

ヨイキングは，ノルウェー，スウェーデン，フィンランド，ロシアに住むサーミ人によって作られ，実践された伝統的な歌唱方法である。ヨイクは通常，言葉を使って歌われない。むしろ，音楽という形を取った人や物の表現である。ヨイクを歌うことにより，歌い手は人，動物，あるいは場所を再現したり，再び心に描いたりしようとする。

ヨイクは今日まで生き残ったヨーロッパで最も古い音楽伝統の１つだと研究者によって信じられているが，歴史を通していくつかの出来事がその存続を脅かしてきた。例えば，サーミの村々にキリスト教が伝わったとき，教会，学校，そして家庭でさえもヨイキングは禁止された。今日，ヨイクは多くの聴衆から高く評価され，一般的な大衆文化によみがえっている。

No. 15 解答 3

「ヨイクについて正しいことは何か」

1 現代的な歌唱形式である。

2 伝統的にほとんどの北欧人によって歌われている。

3 言葉を使わずに歌われる音楽形式である。

4 ロシアで発明された楽器である。

解説 ヨイクの説明の中で，冒頭の *Joiking* is a traditional way of singing や，not sung with words，it is an expression ... in a musical form などの表現から総合して考える。

No. 16 解答 2

「キリスト教が伝わったとき，ヨイキングに何が起こったか」

1 大衆文化の一部となった。　　　　　　**2** 多くの場所で禁止された。

3 年配のサーミ人だけが行うことができた。　　**4** サーミ人以外に広がった。

解説 When Christianity was introduced in Sami villages ... の部分に「教会，学校，家庭でヨイキングが禁止された」とある。banned を not allowed と言い換えた **2** が正解。

(C)

Teach Less, Learn More

Singapore has been among the top-ranking countries in the OECD's PISA survey, which is an examination that evaluates children's performance in math, reading, and science. Under Singapore's educational policy, students were taught with a lot of textbooks and worksheets to prepare for higher education. Classes were led by teachers with the focus on passing on facts and knowledge to students. However, this approach came to be doubted recently, as it does not seem to prepare students for a globalized real world.

Today, the Singaporean government promotes the "Teach Less, Learn More" scheme, where students take more control over their own learning. The school curriculum was made more flexible so that students have a greater choice of subjects and can learn what they are interested in in addition to academic skills. Teachers are encouraged to help students learn according to their different needs. Recent studies have shown that students are finding learning more exciting and interesting.

Questions

No.17 How were classes previously taught in Singapore?

No.18 What is true about the "Teach Less, Learn More" scheme?

教えることを減らしてもっと学ぼう

シンガポールは，子供の数学，読解力，科学の成績を評価する試験である，OECDのPISA調査において上位国の１つである。シンガポールの教育方針の下，生徒は高等教育に備えて多くの教科書とワークシートを用いて教えられた。授業は，事実と知識を学生に伝えることに重点を置いて教師主導で行われた。しかし，グローバル化した現実世界への備えを生徒にさせていないように思えるため，このアプローチは最近疑われるようになった。

今日，シンガポール政府は，生徒が自分の学習をよりコントロールする，「教えることを減らしてもっと学ぼう」構想を推進している。生徒がより幅広く科目を選択でき，学力に加えて興味のあることを学ぶことができるように，学校のカリキュラムがより柔軟になった。教師は，生徒それぞれのニーズに合わせて学習を支援するよう奨励されている。最近の研究によると，生徒は学習がより楽しく興味深いものだと感じていることがわかった。

No. 17　解答　3

「シンガポールでは以前，授業はどのように教えられたか」

1 実践的スキルに焦点を当てて。　　**2** 技術的知識を持つ教師によって。

3 多くの学習教材を使うことによって。　　**4** 多くの教師がいる大きな教室で。

解説　改革以前の教育について述べている中で，students were taught with a lot of textbooks and worksheets の部分を言い換えた**3**が正解。

No. 18　解答　4

「『教えることを減らしてもっと学ぼう』構想について正しいことは何か」

1 生徒は決まったプログラムを通して指導される。　**2** 教師が各生徒に同じ方法で注意を払う。

3 生徒は学校教育が厳しくなったと感じている。　**4** 教師は個別化された学習で生徒を支援する。

解説　新しい教育構想において教師に求められることが Teachers are encouraged to help students learn according to their different needs. の部分で述べられている。**4**が正解で，according to their different needs を with their individualized learning と言い換えている。

(D)

Airline Meals

Today, serving meals on airplanes has become the norm for long flights. The first airplane meal on record was served during a flight from London to Paris in 1919, and it included fruit and a sandwich. This custom took off in the U.S., Europe, and Australia during the 1920s. However, due to the limitations of weight and energy on board, only cold food that did not need to be heated was served in lightweight containers.

Hot meals were first served by United Airlines in 1936, on airplanes with kitchens where cooked food could be prepared for passengers. Other airlines followed this trend until frozen food was introduced in the 1940s. Frozen food made way for more variety because it allowed warm food to be prepared in minutes. The varieties and quality of airline meals flourished during the 1950s when air travel was a luxury. Passengers dined with tablecloths and silver cutlery. This high-grade cuisine experience came to an end in the 1960s when air travel became more affordable for middle-class people.

Questions

No.19 Why was only cold food served on flights when airline meals started?

No.20 What happened when frozen food was introduced as an airline meal?

機内食

今日，飛行機内で食事を提供することは，長距離路線では当たり前になっている。記録に残る最初の機内食は，1919年にロンドンからパリへ行くフライトで出され，果物とサンドイッチが含まれていた。この習慣は1920年代にアメリカ，ヨーロッパ，オーストラリアに広まった。しかし，機内に搭載する重量とエネルギーの制限のため，加熱する必要のない冷たい食べ物だけが軽量の容器に入れて提供された。

温かい食事は，1936年にユナイテッド航空によって，調理された食べ物が乗客に用意できるキッチンが付いた飛行機で最初に提供された。ほかの航空会社は，冷凍食品が1940年代に取り入れられるまでこの流れに沿った。冷凍食品は，温かい食べ物を数分で用意することができたため，バラエティーが豊かになった。機内食の種類と質は，飛行機旅行がぜいたくだった1950年代に発展した。乗客はテーブルクロスと銀食器で食事をした。この高級料理の経験は，飛行機旅行が中流階級の人々の手に届きやすくなった1960年代に終わりを迎えた。

No. 19 解答 **4**

「機内食が始まったとき，なぜ冷たい食べ物だけが飛行機で提供されたのか」

1 長距離路線では一般的だった。

2 人々は旅行中に冷たい食べ物だけを持ち歩いていた。

3 搭乗員は食の安全のため冷たい食べ物しか扱えなかった。

4 飛行機には加熱する十分なエネルギーがなかった。

解説 However, due to ...「機内の重量とエネルギーに制限があったから冷たい食べ物だけが出された」とはつまり，「加熱する十分なエネルギーがなかった」と言える。

No. 20 解答 **1**

「冷凍食品が機内食に取り入れられたとき，何が起こったか」

1 より多くの種類の食べ物がメニューに登場した。　**2** 食べ物を温めるのにより多くの時間がかかった。

3 食べ物の質が低下した。　　　　　　　　　　　　**4** 乗客は食べるのに銀食器が必要になり始めた。

解説 冷凍食品の導入後についてはuntil frozen food was introduced in the 1940s の後に説明がある。Frozen food made way for more variety ... の部分を言い換えた **1** が正解。

(E)

Wildlife Tourism

Wildlife tourism provides animal lovers with exotic experiences with animals in the wild. It has created a big market in developing countries in Africa and parts of Asia. Not only can wildlife tourism be entertaining and educational for visitors, it also brings in significant revenue for governments and other operators. Part of the earnings can also be used to protect the local environment and the natural habitats of the animals.

However, wildlife tourism can have negative aspects as well. Because it brings people close to natural environments, littering and pollution can be caused by careless tourists. Additionally, the animals' exposure to human beings may affect their behavior. In some cases, such as when wild animals are captured and presented to tourists, they may be overworked or otherwise mistreated. To make sure that wildlife tourism is sustainable, regulations and good planning are needed to prevent these problems.

Questions

No.21　What is one benefit of wildlife tourism?

No.22　What is one impact of tourism on wildlife?

野生生物観光

　野生生物観光は，動物愛好家に野生の動物との異国体験を提供する。それはアフリカとアジアの一部の途上国で大きな市場を築いてきた。野生生物観光は観光客にとって楽しくかつ教育的になり得るだけでなく，政府やほかの事業者にも多大な収入をもたらす。また，収益の一部はその地域の環境と動物の自然生息地を保護するためにも使用することができる。

　しかし，野生生物観光はマイナス面も持ち合わせている。それは人々を自然環境に近づけるため，不注意な観光客によってポイ捨てと汚染が引き起こされる可能性がある。さらに，動物が人間にさらされると，動物の行動に影響を与えることがある。野生動物が捕獲されて観光客に公開されるときなど，その動物たちが過重労働を強いられたり虐待を受けたりする場合もある。野生生物観光を確実に持続可能にするには，これらの問題を防ぐために規制と適切な計画が必要である。

No. 21　解答　**4**

「野生生物観光の利点の1つは何か」

1 野生動物に餌を提供する。
2 ほとんどの先進国において大きな市場である。
3 荒野での生活体験を提供する。
4 ビジネスとしてお金を稼ぐ。

解説　野生生物観光の利点を述べているit also brings in significant revenue for governments and other operatorsの部分から，**4**が正解。続くPart of the earnings can also be ... の部分もヒントになる。

No. 22　解答　**1**

「観光が野生生物に与える影響の1つは何か」

1 野生動物が観光客に見せられるときに良い扱いを受けないことがある。
2 宿泊施設の開発のために自然環境が失われる可能性がある。
3 動物が人間に対して暴力的になり得る。
4 観光業が持続可能な野生生物の保全を保証する。

解説　the animals' exposure to human beings may affect their behaviorの部分から，**1**が正解。本文の動詞affectを質問文では名詞impactで表している。

(F)

The V-Sign

Everyone is familiar with the V-sign. We see it everywhere, on TV and in photographs, people posing for the camera with their first two fingers held up in a V shape, palm facing outward. This has become an almost universal sign of peace and goodwill. However, the origins of the V-sign, palm facing inward, are darker, dating from hundreds of years ago during the many wars fought between the English and the French.

The English were renowned for their archers, who turned the tide of many battles. To fire an arrow from a bow, the index and middle fingers are needed to draw back the bowstring. Sometimes, when the French managed to capture English archers, they would simply cut off their index and middle fingers and send the men back to England. Before a battle, as the opposing armies drew close, English archers would raise their hands to give the V-sign to the French to show they had all their fingers and would shoot to kill. So, whenever you make the V-sign, make sure you face your hand the right way!

Questions

No.23 When did the V-sign made with the palm facing inward first originate?

No.24 Why did the English first use the V-sign with the palm facing inward?

Vサイン

　誰でもVサインをよく知っている。テレビや写真など，あらゆるところで人々が人差し指と中指をVの形にし，手のひらを外側に向け，カメラに向かってポーズをしているのを見かける。これは平和と友好を表すほとんど普遍的な印となっている。しかし，手のひらを内側に向けるVサインの元々の形にはもっと暗い意味があり，何百年も前にイギリス人とフランス人の間で戦われた多くの戦争中にさかのぼる。

　イギリス人は弓の射手で有名で，彼らは多くの戦いで流れを変えた。弓から矢を放つには，弓のつるを引くために人差し指と中指が必要である。イギリスの射手をどうにか捕らえると，時にフランス人はただ射手の人差し指と中指を切り落とし，その者たちをイギリスに送り返した。戦いの前，対立する両軍が接近すると，イギリスの射手たちは手を挙げてフランス人に向かってVサインを作り，指は全部そろっていて弓で射殺してやると示すのが常だった。だから，Vサインを作るときはいつでも，間違いなく正しい方向に手を向けよう！

Day 5

No. 23　解答　1

「手のひらを内側に向けて作るVサインが最初に生まれたのはいつか」

1 何世紀も前の戦争中。　　　　　　　　**2** 写真技術の初期の間。

3 平和条約の締結中。　　　　　　　　　**4** 何百年も前のアーチェリー大会の間。

解説　放送の中ほどで ... the origins of the V-sign, palm facing inward, are darker, dating from hundreds of years ago during the many wars ... と言っている。

No. 24　解答　3

「なぜイギリス人は手のひらを内側に向けるVサインを最初に使ったのか」

1 戦いの前に幸運の合図を作るため。　　**2** 仲間の兵士たちにやる気を起こさせるため。

3 自分たちは矢を射ることができると示すため。　　**4** フランス人と和解するため。

解説　イギリス人が手のひらを内側に向けるVサインをフランス人に示した目的として，後半で to show they had all their fingers and would shoot to kill と述べており，**3** がこの内容を短くまとめている。

(G) *No. 25* 解答 4

> Well, from the looks of your transcript, you've been pretty busy! Many students feel tired after their second year. That's normal. However, I understand you've talked to a number of teachers in the Psychology Department, and it seems to me like that major would better suit you. Both majors require the same basic-level classes, so it wouldn't be hard to transfer departments. You might have to take a couple of extra classes, though. What you'd need to do right now is fill out a transfer request and bring it to me. I'll sign and give it to the Humanities head.

状況：あなたは大学生で，アカデミック・アドバイザーと話している。あなたは成績は良いが，専攻を変更したいと思っている。

質問：あなたはまず何をすべきか。

ええと，あなたの成績表を見ますと，かなり忙しかったですね。多くの学生は2年目が終わると疲れを感じます。それは普通です。しかし，あなたが心理学部の何人かの教員と話をしたと聞いていますし，その専攻の方があなたに合っているように私には思えます。どちらの専攻も同じ基礎科目の授業が必須なので，転部は大変ではないでしょう。ただし，いくつか追加の授業を受ける必要があるかもしれませんが，あなたが今やらなければならないことは，転部申請書に記入して私に持ってくることです。私がそれに署名して人文科学の責任者に渡します。

1 追加でいくつかの基礎科目の授業を受ける。　　**2** 人文科学の責任者と話す。
3 成績表のコピー代金を支払う。　　**4** 記入済みの書類をアドバイザーに持ってくる。

解説　専攻の変更手続きとしてまずすべきことは，What you'd need to do right now is fill out a transfer request and bring it to me. の部分にある。**4** が正解で，transfer request を選択肢では paperwork と表している。

(H) *No. 26* 解答 1

> And now for the traffic around San Francisco. Conditions at the moment are pretty bad. As is usual for a holiday weekend, all major routes leading in and out of the city are heavily congested. There has been an accident on Highway 280 into the city. A seven-car pileup has caused traffic to be backed up for three miles. Only one lane is open right now. The police expect the highway to be cleared in the next couple of hours, although the work is going slowly due to heavy rain. Those heading into the city on the highway are advised to take the off ramp to Highway 101 from the 280. Meanwhile, traffic on Highway 1, the Bay Bridge, and Market Street are all congested.

状況：あなたは車でハイウエー280号線を走行しており，およそ20分でサンフランシスコに着く。あなたはラジオで次の情報を聞く。

質問：あなたは何をするよう助言されているか。

さて，ここでサンフランシスコ周辺の交通状況です。現在はかなりひどい状況です。連休ではいつものことですが，当市につながるすべての主要な幹線道路は，上り下りとも大変混雑しています。市内につながるハイウエー280号線では事故が発生しています。7台の車の玉突き衝突が，3マイルにわたる交通渋滞を引き起こしています。ただ今1車線のみ通行可能です。大雨のため作業は遅れていますが，警察は2時間後に道路が片付くと予想しています。この道で市内に向かう方々は，ハイウエー280号線から101号線への出口ランプで降りることをお勧めします。一方，ハイウエー1号線，ベイブリッジおよびマーケット通りの交通はすべて渋滞しています。

1 ハイウエー101号線への出口ランプで降りる。　　**2** ハイウエー1号線への出口ランプで降りる。
3 マーケット通りのハイウエー280号線で降りる。　　**4** ハイウエー280号線を注意して進む。

解説　今走行中のハイウエー280号線に注意して放送を聞くと，... are advised to take the off ramp to Highway 101 from the 280 という情報が入ってくる。

(I) *No. 27* 解答 1

Hello, this message is for Jim Stevenson. My name is Alex Rice, calling from Carry Card Services. As you indicated, there appears to have been some fraudulent activity on your card, and so we have placed a hold on any further purchases. Please be assured that you are not liable for any of these charges because you are enrolled in our fraud protection plan. If you can call our office back at your convenience, we'll be happy to reset your account and issue you a new card. Our toll-free number is 1-800-555-3132, again, my name is Alex, and I am at extension 313. Thank you.

状況：あなたはクレジットカードに問題がある。会社の担当者があなたに次のボイスメールを残す。
質問：あなたは次に何をすべきか。

もしもし，これはジム・スティーブンソンさんへのメッセージです。私の名前はアレックス・ライスで，キャリー・カードサービスから電話をしています。お客さまが指摘されたように，お客さまのカードには何らかの詐欺的行為があったように思われるため，以降のご購入を停止いたしました。お客さまは弊社の詐欺防止プランに加入されているので，これらの請求のいずれに対しても責任を負うことはありませんのでご安心ください。ご都合の良いときに当事務所に折り返しお電話を頂きましたら，お客さまのアカウントをリセットし，新しいカードを発行させていただきます。弊社のフリーダイヤルは1-800-555-3132です。改めまして，私の名前はアレックス，内線313番です。ありがとうございます。

1 フリーダイヤルに電話をする。　　**2** 新しいカードの申請書を送る。
3 カードのパスワードをリセットする。　　**4** クレジットカード会社の事務所を訪れる。

解説　If you can call our office back at your convenience, we'll be happy to ... と指示があり，その後にフリーダイヤルの番号を伝えていることから，**1**が正解。

(J) *No. 28* 解答 1

I think I know what you're going through. When I moved here 10 years ago, I bought an old house that needed a lot of plumbing work. After that, I had to call in a repairman to deal with a leaky roof. Your bank will send inspectors to check those things before they approve any loans. Plumbing, roof, and ... also the foundation, to make sure there are no cracks. You've found a bank already, I assume? I can recommend one if you like. You'll need to find out how much money you can borrow before you can do anything else.

状況：あなたはアメリカに引っ越したばかりで，中古戸建てを買いたいと思っている。友人があなたに次のようなアドバイスをする。
質問：あなたはまず何をすべきか。

私にはあなたがどんな大変なことをしようとしているかわかると思います。私が10年前にここに引っ越したとき，たくさんの配管工事を必要とする中古戸建てを買いました。その後，雨漏りする屋根を何とかするのに修理工を呼ぶ必要がありました。あなたの銀行はローンを承認する前にそういったことを点検する検査官を派遣するでしょう。配管，屋根，そして…土台も，ひび割れがないことを確認するために。たぶんもう銀行は見つけましたよね？　よければ，1つお薦めの銀行があります。何はさておき，いくらお金を借りることができるか知る必要があります。

1 銀行で専門家に相談する。　　**2** 家の土台にひび割れがないかを検査する。
3 配管に水漏れがあれば修理する。　　**4** 屋根の検査官を雇う。

解説　銀行は見つけたかと尋ねた後，You'll need to find out ... before you can do anything else. と言っていることから，まずすべきこととして**1**が適切。このanything elseは前の部分で述べた点検や修理のことである。

(K) No. 29　解答 2

The Health Center wishes to warn all consumers of an E. coli outbreak in the town of Littlecreek. The source of the bacteria is believed to be a certain batch of ground beef packaged by the Greenfield Packers under the label First Rate. The batch in question is marked "Best used before March 3rd." Chicken under the same First Rate label is not affected. All potentially contaminated packages of First Rate ground beef must be returned to the place of purchase by consumers. The purchase price will be refunded. Do not throw this meat out in your regular garbage. Symptoms to watch for are stomachaches, diarrhea, and possibly vomiting. See your physician immediately if you suspect infection.

状況：あなたは3月3日が賞味期限の「1級」の牛ひき肉を購入したが，まだ消費していない。あなたはテレビで次のような警告を聞く。

質問：あなたは何をするよう忠告されているか。

保健所では，消費者すべての皆さんにリトルクリークにおける大腸菌の発生について警戒をお願いしたいと思います。病原菌の発生源は，グリーンフィールド梱包により包装された「1級」のラベルが付いた牛ひき肉のひとまとまりと思われます。問題のひとまとまりの製品には「賞味期限3月3日」と記されています。同じ「1級」のラベルの付いた鶏肉には影響はありません。感染の可能性がある「1級」のラベルが付いた牛ひき肉のすべてのパッケージは，消費者が購入先に返品してください。代金は返金されます。この肉をご自宅の通常のごみの中に捨てないでください。注意すべき症状は腹痛と下痢，そして吐き気もあるようです。感染の疑いがある場合は，すぐに医者に行ってください。

1 すぐに医者に診てもらう。　　　　　**2** 返金してもらうため牛肉を返品する。

3 牛肉を十分に加熱する。　　　　　　**4** 牛肉を捨てる。

解説　... must be returned to the place of purchase by consumers. The purchase price will be refunded. という指示から，**2**が正解。状況に「購入したが，まだ消費していない」とあることから，**1**は不適。

筆記試験＆リスニングテスト
解答と解説

問題編 p.64〜82

筆記

1

問題	1	2	3	4	5	6	7	8	9	10	11	12	13	14	15	16	17	18
解答	3	1	2	4	4	3	3	1	4	2	1	3	2	1	3	2	4	2

2

問題	19	20	21	22	23	24
解答	3	4	3	3	2	1

3

問題	25	26	27	28	29	30	31
解答	1	1	1	4	1	3	2

4　解説内にある解答例を参照してください。

5　解説内にある解答例を参照してください。

リスニング

Part 1

問題	1	2	3	4	5	6	7	8	9	10	11	12
解答	1	2	1	3	2	4	4	3	1	1	4	4

Part 2

問題	13	14	15	16	17	18	19	20	21	22	23	24
解答	3	2	3	2	3	4	3	2	1	4	2	4

Part 3

問題	25	26	27	28	29
解答	4	4	1	3	4

1

(1) 解答 **3**

「トムは電力会社から，支払いが2週間遅れているので至急支払うようにと伝える手紙を受け取った」

解説 電力会社から支払いの督促状が届いた状況から，overdue「（支払いの）期限が過ぎた」が適切。unbalanced「不均衡な」，underdone「生煮えの」，premature「時期尚早の」

(2) 解答 **1**

「交通情報によれば，濃い霧のために高速道路で30台以上の車が衝突した」

解説 濃い霧の状態で，主語が「車」であることから，collide「衝突する」が自然。diverge「分岐する」，dispute「議論する」，violate「違反する」

(3) 解答 **2**

「その女性は台所の火事を消そうとしたが，無駄だった。彼女はついに家から走り出て，消防署に電話をしなければならなかった」

解説 extinguish the fire で「消火する」という意味。

ambush「待ち伏せする」, encounter「出会う」, stimulate「刺激する」

(4)　解答　4

「そのサッカーチームが大喜びしたのは, シーズン始めのひどいスタートの後, 最近5連勝したからだ」

解説　大喜びした原因を考えると, five consecutive wins「5連勝」がふさわしい。dubious「疑わしい」, crippling「ひどい打撃となる」, secluded「隠遁した」

(5)　解答　4

A「先生, 指が腫れているんです」

B「ええ, 痛そうですね。折れているかどうか調べるために, レントゲンを撮る必要がありそうですね」

解説　「痛そうですね」とBが答えているので, 指の状態としてswollen「腫れた」が適切。flimsy「もろい」, stale「腐りかけた」, invalid「病弱な」

(6)　解答　3

「公園管理者は, オオカミを再導入した後に公園の生息地が大きく変化したことに気付いた。シカの個体数は減少したが, 特定の種の植物と木がよみがえった」

解説　オオカミの再導入によって変化したものは, 第2文の内容から, 公園の生息地（habitat）である。reintroduceは動植物をかつての生息地に再移入させること。format「判, 型」, proposal「提案」, theory「理論」

(7)　解答　3

「もし家に2階を建て増したいのなら, 加わった重さに耐えられるように1階の壁を強化しなければならない」

解説　2階を建て増すには1階の壁をreinforce「強化する」必要があると考えられる。prearrange「事前に手はずを整える」, reinterpret「解釈し直す」, predetermine「前もって決める」

(8)　解答　1

「政情不安のため, その国は何年にもわたる無秩序と経済崩壊に陥った。その結果, 多くの国民がより良い機会を見つけるために近隣諸国に移住した」

解説　political unrest「政情不安」の結果として当てはまるもので, economic collapseと並列になるのはdisorder「無秩序」である。evasion「回避」, intention「意図」, clamor「叫び声」

(9)　解答　4

「ほとんどどんな点から見ても, ロジャー・モートンの作家人生は大成功だった。彼は15冊を超えるベストセラーを書き, 数多くの文学賞を受賞した」

解説　「作家人生は大成功」「多くのベストセラーと文学賞受賞」という内容から, 「ほとんどどんな尺度（measure）から見ても」とするのが適切。censure「非難」, ratio「比率」, felony「重罪」

(10)　解答　2

「ジョン, 君のレポートにはいくつか興味深い点がありましたが, ちょっとまとまりが悪かったですね。もっと一貫性を持つように書き直すべきでしょう」

解説　まとまりが悪いレポートを書き直して, coherent「一貫性のある」ものにすると考えれば意味を成す。awkward「不器用な」, contradictory「矛盾した」, rebellious「反乱の」

(11)　解答　1

「麻薬密売の容疑者たちは, 警察による市中心部の徹底的な捜索の一環で夜明けに逮捕されたと, 警察は語った」

解説　sweep「掃くこと」には「徹底した捜索」という意味もある。brush「ブラシ」, pat「軽くたたくこと」, rub「こすること」

(12)　解答　3

「ある消費者のグループは, 欠陥品の製造者を訴えるのを助けてもらうのに弁護士を雇った」

解説　弁護士を雇って「欠陥品の製造業者」をどうするかを考えると, sue「告訴する」がふさわしい。deed「譲渡する」, cue「合図をする」, hail「歓迎する」

(13)　解答　2

「その研究者たちの最新の発見は重要で, がん治療の大きな進展になると期待されている」

解説　がん治療で期待されているのはbreakthrough「（科学などの）顕著な進歩, 大躍進」である。bundle「束」, condolence「哀悼」, dropout「落後（者）」

(14)　解答　1

「エンジニアは, その組み立てラインがきちんと動作するように, 一日中定期的に点検する」

解説　組み立てラインの点検という話題に合う副詞はperiodically「定期的に」。annually「毎年」, impulsively「衝動的に」, erratically「気まぐれに」

Day
6

(15) 解答 3

A「くたくたです。私はまともな休暇なしで1年以上働いています」

B「君は自分のためにいくらか時間を確保する必要があるよ，カイル。それほど一生懸命に働くのは君の健康に良くない」

解説 働き過ぎるカイルに対し，Bは自分のために時間を確保する（set aside）べきだと助言している。give off「〜を発する」，hand out「〜を配る」，set off「出発する」

(16) 解答 2

「用紙のお名前やご住所が間違っていたら，赤いペンを使って線を引いて消し，下に正しい内容を活字体で書いてください」

解説 間違っている文字をどうするかを考えると，cross out「〜に線を引いて消す」が適切。check out「〜を調べる」，hold up「〜を持ち上げる」，make up

「〜を組み立てる」

(17) 解答 4

「『物価が上昇し続ける中で，こんなわずかな年金では暮らせない』とその退役将校は不平を言った」

解説 a small pension「わずかな年金」が目的語だから，live on「（年金など）をよりどころに暮らす」が適切。see through「〜を最後まで見る」，give in「〜を提出する」，try out「〜を試す」

(18) 解答 2

「その走者はレースの大半で前の方を走っていたが，ゴールが近づくにつれ，ほかのランナーが彼に近づいてきた。彼は辛うじてレースに勝った」

解説 辛うじて勝ったとあるので，ほかの走者がgain on「〜に近づく」。benefit from「〜から利益を得る」，stir up「〜をかき混ぜる」。grow over は受け身（be grown over）で「（草木に）覆われている」という意味。

2

全訳

思考の糧

南アフリカ共和国のクワズールー・ナタール大学の研究者ラージ・パテルは，その著書『飽食と飢餓』の中で，世界の食の不均衡についての概観を提供してくれている。彼は，主に先進国に住む10億人もの人々がカロリーの取り過ぎであるのに対して，世界で8億人もの人々が空腹のまま毎晩床に就いているという問題の複雑に絡み合う原因について，徹底的に調べ上げている。これは，このひどい不均衡がなぜ起きたのかということに関して，私たちがさらに幅広く理解しなければ解くことができない解決至難な問題なのである。

しかし，この難問について理解することこそ，飽食にふけっている人々にその行動を改めようという気にさせる鍵である，とパテルは確信している。彼は，西欧諸国に商品を輸出する巨大食品企業の搾取を受けている国々が債務免除を受けられるよう闘うために，また正当な賃金の支払いに対する労働者の権利を守るために，読者たちを説いているのである。さらに，彼は，有機農法で育てられ環境的にも存続可能な農産物の重要性を説きつつ，地元で栽培された農産物にもっと頼ることを主張している。

今日の食品取引システムは，（食物の）生まれ持った

性質や育つ環境を守ることよりも強欲さに駆られて行動している大企業に依存しており，パテルはこの制度に疑問を呈している。彼は，アメリカと韓国の農民が借金と絶望に苦しむ経緯と理由を示し，インドに多発している悲惨な農民の自殺についても分析している。さらに彼は，貿易関税を低く抑え，農産物市場を開放することで世界の農民が公平な条件下で競争できるようにしようという，世界銀行や世界貿易機関（WTO）などといった組織の取り組みが，実は正反対の結果を生んできた経緯を詳細に調べ上げている。大企業や政府の官僚は，数多くの小規模農家を犠牲にして，こういった政策の変化から利益を得ているのである。

(19) 解答 3

解説 『飽食と飢餓』という本のタイトル，その内容を紹介する第2文，また第3文のthis gross inequity「このひどい不均衡」という表現から，この本は**3**「世界の食の不均衡」について概略を示していると推測できる。

(20) 解答 4

解説 第2段落はパテルの主張をまとめている。空所の前の文は巨大企業に搾取される国や労働者を守るこ

と，空所の文は地元の農産物を推奨することで，どちらも食の不均衡の問題解決のために必要だとパテルが読者に説いている内容なので，2つをつなぐ接続表現は**4**「さらに，加えて」が適切である。

(21)　解答　**3**

解説　後続する部分で，農民を犠牲にして大企業や官僚がもうけているという結果が語られているので，公平な条件下で競争できるようにしようとした世界銀行やWTOの努力は**3**「正反対の結果を生んできた」と推測できる。

全訳
人間のユーモア

今日「ユーモア」という言葉はほとんどジョークや笑いと結び付けて考えられているが，過去においては必ずしもそうではなかった。中世の生理学では，ユーモアは人間の体液や性格とより関係があった。人間には4つのユーモア，つまり血液，粘液，胆汁，黒胆汁という4つの体液があると考えられていた。人に備わる身体的・精神的な特質や性質は，体中を流れる4つの体液の相対的な割合で決定されると考えられた。

エリザベス朝の劇作家，ベン・ジョンソンは『人それぞれ（人間は皆自分の体液を持っている）』という劇を書いた。「自分の体液を持っている」というフレーズは，その人がどの体液を最も多く持っていて，どんな人間なのかを表している。もし，ある男性が太っていて陽気であれば，その人はほかの3つの体液よりも血液を多く持っていると見なされた。対照的に，ある人が痩せて陰気であれば，その人は非常に多くの黒胆汁の体液を持っていると考えられた。そして当然，健全な心と体を持つ人は4つの体液を適切な割合で有していると信じられていたのである。

それでは体液と関連した笑いの機能とは何であったのか。愚かな人々は，笑いを生む源と考えられていた。笑われる人は，4つの体液のうちの1つの影響をあまりにも多く受ける中で，風変わりな行動を示したと考えられた。笑っている人たちは，体液のバランスがよく取れているので，そのような度を越した異常な行動を正しく判断できると見なされていた。今日，ユーモアは体液と結び付けて考えられることはめったにない。その代わり，ユーモアの感覚を意味することの方が多い。しかし，バランスの取れた精神を維持する助けになる笑いの機能は，決して変わらない。世界中の多くの人々は，ユーモアの感覚は健康で楽しい生活に不可欠であり，体液と同じくらい欠かせないものだと信じているのである。

(22)　解答　**3**

解説　第1段落で4つの体液について触れ，第2段落ではその4つの体液でどのように人の性格が決まるかを具体的に述べている。その具体例を参考にすると，人の特質や気質は4つの体液の**3**「相対的な割合」によって決定されると考えられる。

(23)　解答　**2**

解説　前文で太って陽気な人の例を挙げているのに対し，空所以下では痩せて陰気な人の例が挙げられている。したがって，接続詞は**2**「対照的に」が適切。

(24)　解答　**1**

解説　現在の「ユーモア」については第1段落第1文に書いてあるとおり，ジョークや笑いと結び付けて考えられていて，Insteadから始まる空所の次の文にも同じ内容が続く。したがって**1**を入れて「体液と結び付けて考えられることはめったにない」とするのが適切。

3

全訳
音楽好きは生まれつき

圧倒的大多数の人にとって，音楽は生活の中で重要な役割を果たしている。楽しませてくれ，真の連帯感を呼び起こすばかりでなく，音楽は多くの感情をかき立てることが明らかにされている。昔のある特定の歌を聞けば，過ぎ去った日々の鮮明なイメージと感情が思い出される。お気に入りの曲は絶望を一瞬にして幸

福に変えることができる。音楽は私たちの存在の重要な一部であり，私たちの日々の生活の至る所で私たちとともにある。

私たちの音楽好きは，私たちがまだ子宮の中にいるときに始まると研究者たちは結論付けている。母親の心臓の規則的な鼓動が，私たちの聞く最初の音である。私たちの多くにとって，この世界に入るときからこの世界を離れるときまで，私たちは増え続ける装いと場

所の中で，音楽にさらされる。近年の社会変革は，技術の進歩と相まって，21世紀に私たちが聴く音楽にどのようにして強い影響を及ぼしてきたのだろうか。

　前世紀における全世界的な文化の一層の統合は，以前には地球の一隅に限られていた音楽が今やはるかに広範囲な聴衆によって楽しまれることを意味した。さらにこれらの集団がより緊密にまとまるにつれ，音楽家たちは数多くの芸術的な影響を得ることがますます可能になっている。文化の異なるスタイルは今や，混ざり合って刺激的で新しい融合体になることが可能であり，大衆に選択可能な一層多くのジャンルを提供している。1つの著名な例はアフリカ系アメリカ人のポピュラー音楽とヨーロッパ起源の音楽との融合であり，1950年代にはアメリカでロックンロールの誕生を見た。さらに，常に拡大を続ける街や都市は，創造的な才能をさらにはるかに大きな数で引き合わせた。ニューオーリンズはジャズの誕生の地であり，ソウルミュージックはデトロイトに由来することを歴史は教えてくれる。

　音楽が私たちの家に入り込む媒体は20世紀に広く利用可能となり，遠く離れ孤立した社会に住む人を除くすべての人に達した。これはラジオとともに始まった。人々は音楽を楽しむのに，もはや家を離れる必要がなくなった。ダイヤルを合わせさえすればよくなった。テレビは映像を付け加えることによってこの段階をさらに一歩押し進め，視聴者がさまざまな人気アーティストを快適なアームチェアに座りながらにしていつも見ることを可能にした。1970年代および1980年代における携帯機器の出現は，ある場所から別の場所へと移動する際に音楽を聞く自由を私たちに与えた。

(25)　解答　1
「調査によると，人間はいつ最初に音楽を認識するか」
1 私たちが母親の中で育っているとき。
2 生まれて周りのさまざまな音にさらされたとき。
3 両親によって特定の音を音楽と関連付けるように教えられたとき。
4 日常生活の中で最初に歌に触れた後。
　解説　音楽を理解・認識する時期については，第2段落第1文に our love of music begins while we are still in the womb とある。「子宮の中にいるとき」を「母親の中で育っているとき」と言い換えた1が正解。

(26)　解答　1
「筆者は，何が音楽のスタイルの新たな融合体への統合を加速化させたと述べているか」

1 音楽家を新しい音に触れさせる，文化的に多様な集団の一層の統合。
2 ジャズを生み出したアフリカ系アメリカ人の音楽とヨーロッパの音楽の融合。
3 農村に音楽をもたらしたラジオの発明。
4 世界中の新しいスタイルの音楽を聴きたいという1950年代の人々の願望。
　解説　音楽のスタイルの新たな融合体（new fusions）について第3段落第3文に出てくるが，段落冒頭から読むとそれが文化的統合（cultural integration）から起きていると読み取れるので，1が正解。第2文の as these groups are pulled closer together を選択肢では Greater integration of culturally diverse groups と表している。

(27)　解答　1
「文章によると，20世紀の技術は私たちの音楽体験をどのように変えたか」
1 人々が音楽に触れる機会を増やした。
2 音楽に対する認識を変えた。
3 現代音楽を孤立したコミュニティーにさえも届くようにした。
4 一般の人々が自分たち自身の音楽を作り出せるようにした。
　解説　20世紀の音楽体験の変化については，最終段落に記載がある。音楽はラジオの出現により家で楽しむことができるようになり，テレビの出現で映像も楽しめ，携帯機器の出現により場所の移動中にも楽しめるようになった。つまり人々は音楽に触れる機会が増えたということなので，1が正解。

全訳
よりクリーンな診断
　テクネチウム99m（Tc-99m）は放射性同位体であり，崩壊する際にエネルギーを放出するテクネチウムという化学元素の一形態である。発見が難しいがんも含め，がんの診断のための医用画像に広く使用されている。患者は，ガンマ線を発する Tc-99m の注射を受ける。これらのガンマ線は特殊なガンマカメラで検出され，これがその後画像を作成するが，ガンマ線の密度の高い所が腫瘍の位置を示している。年間4千万回を超える処置が Tc-99m を使用しており，世界中で最も診断に使用されている放射性同位体となっている。これは，Tc-99m が比較的安全な放射性同位体だからである。Tc-99m の半減期は約6時間と短く，つまり放射能が元の値の半分に減少するのにこれぐらいの長

さしかかからないことを意味する。そのため，患者の体から早く放射能がなくなるだけではなく，その周りの人々が間接的にさらされる放射線量もわずかであり，さらに環境を害する放射性廃棄物もない。しかしTc-99mの生産については，話が異なる。

モリブデン99（Mo-99）は，Tc-99mを生産するのに必要な基礎原料であり，高濃縮ウラン235（U-235）を使用して原子炉で作らなければならない。この工程の放射性副産物の半減期は非常に長く，廃棄処理は環境に有害で，かつ非常にコストがかかる。現在，世界でわずか4基の原子炉がMo-99を生産しているが，このうちの何基かは不安定で，一時に突然数カ月も閉鎖しており，放射性同位体の不足を引き起こしている。幸いにもアメリカのウィスコンシン州ベロイトに本社のあるノーススター・メディカル・ラジオアイソトープ（ノーススター）社がこれの呈する課題を認識し，2006年に，国産で信頼でき，環境に優しい医用放射性同位体の供給の確保に乗り出した。

ノーススター社は，自然界に存在する鉱物で，地殻にあるモリブデナイトからMo-99を生産する方法を開発した。これは，生産工程から放射性副産物だけでなくU-235も除去する。さらに，Tc-99mの半減期が病院への搬送を非常に高額にしたり，または場合によっては不可能にしたりする一方で，Mo-99の半減期は66時間で，これは国内または国際的な搬送にもはるかに便利な期間である。ノーススター社はRadioGenixシステムという機械を発明し，病院はこれを購入して院内で容易にMo-99をTc-99mに変換することができる。この方法により，世界中の病院が診断ニーズのすべてに即応できるTc-99mの供給を得ることができる。

ノーススター社の新技術は，ほかの放射性同位体の生産に取り組み始めることも可能にしている。例えば，アクチニウム225（Ac-225）とビスマス213（Bi-213）は，患者の体の中のがん細胞と結合して殺すことがわかっており，その後体から老廃物として排出される。残念なことに，これらの放射性同位体の供給量は非常に限られており，年間ほんのわずかの患者の需要しか満たせていない。ノーススター社は現在，臨床研究と臨床治療のためのこれらの放射性同位体を大量生産する工程を開発している。これらの開発により，ノーススター社の取り組みは，患者のニーズを満たすとともに環境をうまくクリーンに保てる方法で医用画像と治療の歴史を変えているようである。

(28) 解答 4

「テクネチウム99m（Tc-99m）はなぜ安全な放射性同位体と見なされるのか」

1 ほかの一般的に使用されている放射性同位体よりも，医用画像を成功させるのに必要な量が少ない。

2 それが放出するガンマ線は患者の腫瘍に直接届くが，外科的に腫瘍が摘出された後に痕跡を残さない。

3 それは害を及ぼし得る深部組織ではなく，患者の皮膚の上層に注入される。

4 その放射能は急速に消え，患者やほかの人々，そして地球にほとんどあるいはまったく害を及ぼさない。

解説　Tc-99mが安全であることは第1段落のThis is because it is a relatively safe radioisotope. に言及があり，その後のTherefore, not only are ... の部分から，**4**が正解。

(29) 解答 1

「原子炉の1基が閉鎖したときどんな問題が起こるか」

1 適切な治療に必要な画像診断を適時に受けることができる世界中の患者が減る。

2 ウラン235（U-235）よりも安定性の低い放射性同位体を使用しなければならず，より低品質のMo-99を作り出す。

3 生産を再開するために，Mo-99を生産する特別な装置が別の原子炉に輸送される。

4 放射性副産物が原子炉から漏れるため，周囲の環境を浄化するために多大な時間と労力を要する。

解説　第2段落のNow, only 4 nuclear reactors ... の文から，原子炉が閉鎖すると放射性同位体が不足することがわかる。第1段落から，放射性同位体はがんの診断のための医用画像に広く使用されているのだから，**1**が正解。

(30) 解答 3

「ノーススター社が生産するMo-99はどんな点が特別なのか」

1 それはTc-99mに似た特性があるため，病院が2つの放射性同位体を互換的に使用することができる。

2 それは半減期が非常に長いため，施設が時々それを大量に購入し，長期保存することができる。

3 その生産にはU-235も原子炉も使う必要がないため，環境に優しいものになる。

4 それは放射性ではないため，安全に輸送するための特別な容器や機器を必要としない。

解説　第2段落の最後から，ノーススター社は環境に優しい医用放射性同位体を取り扱っていることがわか

る。第3段落第2文にThis eliminates U-235 from the process as well as the radioactive byproducts. とあり，このThisは同社が生産するMo-99のことなので，**3**が正解。

(31) 解答 **2**

「この文章によると，将来的にノーススター社が行う可能性が高いことは，」

1 天然に存在する放射性同位体のある新しい地域を探し出して，医療分野での使用のためにそれを抽出するべく鉱業に拡大することである。

2 要求を満たすのに十分な量の重要な放射性同位体を

世界の医療産業に提供する方法を開発することである。

3 自社製品を適合させ治療法をもたらす手助けをすることができることを期待して，ほかの致命的な病気の研究を始めることである。

4 遠方に住む患者が放射性同位体を用いた医療検査に参加できる研究施設に行く手助けをすることである。

解説 ノーススター社の将来性について書かれた第4段落を参照。「放射性同位体の供給量が限られていて患者の需要が満たせていない」「現在それらの放射性同位体を大量生産する工程を開発している」という流れから，**2**が正解。

問題文の訳

　1983年，中国は，ヨーロッパの同様の学校を参考にして，初の高齢者向けの大学を開校した。それ以来，そのような大学が何千校も開設され，スキルベースのコースと合わせて従来の学術コースを提供している。それらの大学は60歳以上の学生が対象で，中国は世界最速で高齢化が進んでいることもあり，極めて人気が高いことを証明した。

　さまざまな授業を通して学生が得られる利点には，新しいスキルの習得や記憶力の向上が挙げられるが，そのどちらも脳の衰えを遅らせるのに役立つ。また，大学は，学生に人と出会ったり，コミュニティーの一員になったりする機会を提供し，それによって孤独を感じるリスクを軽減する。

　一方で，大学に通いたい人が誰でも通えるわけではない。入学したいと思う志願者の数があまりに多いため，今では抽選入学や受験競争が生じている。さらに，大学の資金は主に政府から提供されているため，大学増設を求めるとなるとさらに多額の資金が必要となり，福祉制度を圧迫することになるだろう。

解答例

　China has a growing population of elderly people, and many universities for them have been opened. These universities may provide students with the benefits of slowing down brain aging and decreasing loneliness by giving them the opportunity to be part of a community. However, competitions for admission are heating up because there are too many applicants. Additionally, it would cost the government a lot to establish more universities. (68語)

解答例の訳

　中国では，高齢者の人口が増加しており，彼ら向けの大学が多く開校している。これらの大学は，学生に脳の高齢化を遅らせたり彼らにコミュニティーの一員となる機会を与えることで孤独感を減らしたりするという利点を提供するだろう。しかし，入学希望者が多過ぎるために入学の競争が過熱している。また，大学を増設することは政府にとって多額の費用がかかるだろう。

解説　各段落の要点を1（～2）文でまとめて全体を3～4文で書こう。解答例は，第1文「トピックの導入（中国の高齢者向け大学）」（第1段落），第2文「利点」（第2段落），第3～4文「欠点」（第3段落）の4文構成。第3段落の On the other hand を解答例では However に，In addition を解答例では Additionally に置き換えている。

　要点をまとめるポイントは，①重要な情報を見極め，細かい情報や具体例は省く，②具体的な情報を抽象化する，の2点。例えば，英文冒頭の In 1983 や over the age of 60 のような具体的な数字は解答に含めない。利点を述べた第2段落は，解答例では provide students with the benefits「学生に利点を提供している」と前置きした後，同格の of を用い，どのような利点であるかという問題文の第1文と第2文の内容を〈名詞句+and+名詞句〉の形で盛り込んで，1文にまとめている。第2文については，thereby「それによって」で示されている原因→結果の構造を，解答例では by *do*ing「～することで」に置き換えている。なお，この giving them the opportunity to be part of a community は第2段落の give students a chance to be part of a community の言い換えである。また，第3段落の With such a high ..., there is now ～の文を因果関係と捉え，解答例では because を用いて表している。

　そのほかの解答例の言い換えは以下のとおり。aging population→a growing population of elderly people, slow the decline of the brain→slowing down brain aging, lowering the risk of loneliness→decreasing loneliness, require further amounts of money→cost ～ a lot

問題の訳
TOPIC：賛成か反対か：日本政府は若者を地方に住むよう促す必要がある
POINTS：生活様式・教育・経済・高齢者介護

解答例

　The government needs to encourage young people to reside in rural areas in order to provide elderly care and stimulate their economies.

　First, there are too many elderly people requiring care in rural villages. This is because most of the villages are aging and their populations are decreasing. In order to solve this problem, the government needs to bring young people from the cities and encourage them to help the elderly.

　Second, the economies of these places need improvement. The local governments need to provide jobs to the young people who move to the villages so that they will learn beneficial skills. Over time, they will become independent and productive, which will help these areas to grow.

　By encouraging young people to live in rural areas, the government can provide the care the older generations need and halt the economic decline. (141語)

解答例の訳

　高齢者介護を提供し地方の経済を刺激するために，政府は若者を地方に住むよう促す必要がある。

　第1に，農村には介護を必要とする高齢者があまりにも多い。これは大半の農村で高齢化が進み，人口が減少しているからである。この問題を解決するため，政府は都市から若者を連れてきて高齢者を手助けするよう促す必要がある。

　第2に，これらの地域の経済は改善が必要である。地方政府は，村にやって来る若者が役立つ技術を習得できるよう，働き口を提供する必要がある。やがて，彼らは自立した生産力のある働き手となり，そうした地域の発展の役に立つだろう。

　若者を地方に住むよう促すことによって，政府は高齢世代が必要な介護を提供でき，経済的衰退を食い止めることができる。

解説 「日本政府は若者を地方に住むよう促すべきか」という問いに対して，解答例ではAgreeの立場を取っている。その根拠として第1段落で，POINTSのElderly careとThe economyの観点を取り上げている。実際にこれらについて詳しく述べるのは本論ではあるが，このように序論であらかじめ2つの観点に触れておくと，論の展開が伝わりやすい。

　1つ目として，地方では高齢化が進んでいるため，介護の助けが必要である点を述べている。こうした問題背景を述べた上で，解答例はIn order to solve this problem, ... と解決策を提案している。また2つ目として，経済の活性化のためにも新しくやって来る若者の雇用が必要だと述べている。

　Disagreeの立場で書くとしたらどうだろうか。都市部に住む若者は，すでに確立したライフスタイル（Lifestyle）を持っており，それを変えることは難しく，政府が介入できることではないかもしれない。また，学生に至っては教育（Education）が優先であり，進学のため都市部に移ることを妨げるべきではないという意見もあるだろう。

Listening Test

Part 1 🔊 079〜091

No. 1 解答 1

★：The weather is supposed to be gorgeous this weekend. You're not thinking of spending it indoors, are you?

☆：What do you mean? It'll be perfect afternoon nap weather.

★：Are you kidding? How long has it been since we've been to the beach? How about we go camping?

☆：But it gets cold at night, and there are bugs.

★：That's what tents and blankets and campfires are for.

☆：Well ... OK, I'll go along, but you have to do most of the work.

Question：What do we learn about the woman?

★：今週末は天気がすごくいいみたいだよ。君は室内で過ごすなんて考えていないだろうね。

☆：どういう意味？　午後の昼寝にうってつけの天気になりそうだわ。

★：冗談だろう？　僕たちがビーチに行ってからどれくらいたつ？　キャンプに行くのはどう？

☆：でも夜は寒くなるし，虫もいるわ。

★：そのためにテントと毛布とキャンプファイヤーがあるんじゃないか。

☆：うーん…わかった，行くわ。でも，作業のほとんどをあなたがやってね。

質問：女性について何がわかるか。

1 彼女は室内で過ごす方がいい。
2 彼女は男性が仕事に行くのを許す。
3 彼女は一度もキャンプに行ったことがない。
4 彼女はビーチで昼寝をするのが好きだ。

解説　男性は冒頭で You're not thinking of spending it indoors, are you? と言っており，後のやり取りからも女性はキャンプがあまり好きではない様子なので，**1** が正解。

No. 2 解答 2

○：I'd like a medium seafood pizza, please.

★：Sure. Do you have something to carry it in?

○：No, I don't. Why?

★：Well, the theme of this food bazaar is "eco-friendliness," so we're asking everyone to bring their own plates, cups, and utensils.

○：Oh, I see. I'm afraid I didn't know that. I just stopped by.

★：That's fine. We don't have them at this booth, but for a small fee you can buy paper plates and cups at the bazaar entrance. They're made from recycled material.

Question：What is the woman's problem?

○：Mサイズのシーフードピザをください。

★：はい。何か入れるものをお持ちですか。

○：いいえ，持っていないです。どうしてですか。

★：ええと，このフードバザーのテーマは「環境への優しさ」ですので，皆さんにはご自身のお皿やカップ，カトラリーを持ってくるようお願いしているんです。

○：へえ，そうなんですか。あいにく知りませんでした。ちょっと立ち寄っただけでしたので。

★：大丈夫です。このブースにはないのですが，少しお金を出せば，バザー入り口で紙皿と紙コップが買えます。それらは再生材でできています。

質問：女性の問題は何か。

1 彼女には入場券がない。
2 彼女はポリシーを知らなかった。
3 彼女はカトラリーをリサイクルすることを怠った。
4 給仕係が協力的でなかった。

解説　フードバザーに立ち寄った女性は，ピザのブースで自分の食器を持参しなければならないと言われ，I didn't know that と言っている。つまり，バザーのポリシーを知らなかったことになる。

Day
6

No. 3　解答　1

★：Did you hear about Colin?	★：コリンのことは聞いた？
☆：No. What about him?	☆：いいえ。彼がどうかしたの？
★：He's just bought a new motorcycle, a 1500 cc. He's going to hurt himself badly one day.	★：1500ccの新しいオートバイを買ったばかりなんだ。いつかひどいけがをすることになるよ。
☆：What do you mean?	☆：どういう意味？
★：He becomes a different person on his bike. He's usually a very cautious person, but when he's on a bike he likes to do jumps and other stunts.	★：彼はオートバイに乗ると人が変わるんだよ。いつもはとても慎重な人だけど，オートバイに乗るとジャンプをしたり，ほかのスタントをしたりするんだよ。
Question：What does the man say about Colin?	質問：男性はコリンについて何と言っているか。

1 彼はオートバイで危ないことをする。　　　　**2** 彼は重大事故に遭った。
3 彼は新しいオートバイを買う計画を立てている。　**4** 彼はオートバイにお金を払い過ぎた。

解説　男性がコリンの行動や性格について説明している中で，when he's on a bike he likes to do jumps and other stunts を takes risks on motorcycles と言い換えている **1** が正解。

No. 4　解答　3

★：Deborah, are you taking Dr. Ryan's English History class too?	★：デボラ，君もライアン博士のイングランド史の授業を受けるの？
○：Hey, Matt. Yeah, I signed up a while ago. I just need the credits. Why? Is it really hard?	○：あら，マット。ええ，しばらく前に申し込んだわよ。私にはただ単位が必要なの。どうして？すごく大変なの？
★：It's really hard to get into! You did the right thing to sign up early. It's one of the most popular classes at the university.	★：授業を取るのがすごく難しいんだよ！　君は早めに申し込んで正解だったよ。大学で最も人気のある授業の1つだからね。
○：I thought history classes were supposed to be boring.	○：歴史の授業は退屈なものだと思っていたわ。
★：Dr. Ryan isn't. The word all around is he's dynamic and easy to understand. He totally changes people's perception about being in a history class. They say his lectures are hilarious.	★：ライアン博士は違う。みんなが言うには，彼は精力的で理解しやすい。彼は歴史の授業を受けるとはどういうことかという認識を完全に変えてくれる。彼の講義は素晴らしく面白いという話だよ。
○：Well then, I'll look forward to it.	○：それなら，楽しみだわ。
Question：What do we learn about the class?	質問：その授業について何がわかるか。

1 講師が平凡な講義をする。　　　　**2** 教科書が理解しにくい。
3 講師の評判が良い。　　　　　　　**4** 題材が豊富である。

解説　男性がイングランド史の授業について「人気なので取りにくい」と言った後，Dr. Ryan isn't. 以下でその講師（Dr. Ryan）がいかに良いかを説明している。

No. 5　解答　2

★：I'm sorry, but I can't take that. You need the exact change to ride this bus.
☆：But a five dollar bill is all I have.
★：This is a bus, not a bank. Either you have the correct change, or you have to get off. I have a schedule to keep, so can you decide right away?
☆：OK. I'll go to the bank then and take the next bus.
Question：What will the woman do next?

★：すみません。それは受け取れません。このバスに乗るには釣り銭がないようにしてもらわないと。
☆：でも，５ドル札しか持ち合わせがないんです。
★：ここはバスで，銀行ではないんです。小銭がちょうどないのなら，降りてください。僕はダイヤを守らないといけないので，今すぐ決めてもらえますか。
☆：わかりました。では，銀行に行って，次のバスに乗ります。
質問：女性は次に何をするか。

1 運転手にぴったりの運賃を渡す。
2 小銭を入手しに行く。
3 運転手に５ドルを渡す。
4 別の交通機関を利用する。

解説　女性はバスの運転手とのやり取りの末に I'll go to the bank then と言っている。銀行に行く理由は，バスに乗るのに必要な小銭を用意するためなので，**2**が正解。**1**はその後の行動なので，「次にすること」として不適。

No. 6　解答　4

○：Neil, this brochure draft needs some pictures. Could you add some?
★：I'd be happy to, Marcy, but can it wait until tomorrow? I have a meeting to go to in an hour.
○：Could you do it by noon tomorrow?
★：If I took it home, I could. Can you give it to me on a memory stick?
○：Yes, of course. I'll go do that now. I really appreciate your help.
★：OK. I'll give you my revised draft file when I get here tomorrow morning.
Question：What will the man do tomorrow morning?

○：ニール，このパンフレットの原稿に写真が必要なの。何枚か加えてもらえない？
★：喜んでやるけど，マーシー，明日まで待てるかな。行かなければならない会議が１時間後にあるんだ。
○：明日の正午までにやってもらえる？
★：家に持ち帰ればできるかな。メモリースティックに入れてそれをもらえる？
○：ええ，もちろん。今からそうする。助けてくれて本当にありがたいわ。
★：大丈夫だよ。明日の朝出社したら修正済みの原稿ファイルを君に渡すね。
質問：男性は明日の朝何をするか。

1 会議に出席する。
2 女性からパンフレットを返してもらう。
3 女性からメモリースティックをもらう。
4 更新したファイルを女性に渡す。

解説　原稿の修正を依頼された男性が，最後に I'll give you my revised draft file when I get here tomorrow morning. と言っていることから，**4**が正解。my revised draft file を選択肢では an updated file と言い換えている。**3**は今からすることであって，明日の朝することではない。

No. 7　解答　4

☆：Mr. Hendricks? I'm sorry, but I'm afraid we can't process your loan application.

★：You can't? Why not?

☆：There seems to be a problem with your credit rating.

★：How can that be? I almost never use my credit card.

☆：I see. All we can tell you is that your score was too low. What you could do is contact your credit card issuer and see if there isn't some kind of unseen trouble. Perhaps your identity got stolen. In the meanwhile, we'll keep your loan application on hold.

★：Well, OK, thanks. I'll do that right away.

Question：What does the woman suggest the man do?

☆：ヘンドリックスさん？　申し訳ありませんが，ローン申請の手続きを進められません。

★：できない？　どうして？

☆：お客さまの信用格付けに問題があるようです。

★：そんなことあり得るのかな。僕はほとんどクレジットカードを使わないんだけど。

☆：そうですか。お伝えできるのは，お客さまの格付けが低過ぎたということだけです。お客さまができることとしましては，クレジットカードの発行会社に連絡して，何らかの目に見えない問題がないかどうか調べることです。お客さまの個人情報が盗まれたのかもしれません。その間，私どもはお客さまのローン申請を保留にします。

★：うーん，わかりました，ありがとう。すぐにそうします。

質問：女性は男性が何をすることを提案しているか。

1 クレジットカードを見つけ出す。　　**2** 申請書を提出する。

3 より高い格付けを獲得する。　　**4** 彼のクレジット会社に連絡をする。

解説　男性はクレジットカードに問題があるためローンの申し込みができない，という状況を理解する。女性が提案を述べている What you could do is contact your credit card issuer ... の部分から，**4** が正解。

No. 8　解答　3

○：Good morning, Mr. Smith. Please sit down. Did you find us all right?

★：Yes, I had no problems.

○：Good. I've been reviewing your résumé and I have some questions I'd like to ask you.

★：Sure, that's fine.

○：First, before we discuss employment possibilities here, I'd like to ask you about your present position. You're in charge of the advertising for Roberts and Little, right?

★：Yes. I've held that position for three years.

Question：What is the man doing?

○：おはようございます，スミスさん。おかけください。すぐにここがわかりましたか。

★：はい，問題ありませんでした。

○：よかった。あなたの履歴書を拝見しているのですが，尋ねたいことがいくつかあります。

★：はい，どうぞ。

○：まず，当社での採用の可能性を議論する前に，あなたの現在の役職についてお尋ねしたいと思います。あなたはロバーツ・アンド・リトルで宣伝広告を担当されているのですよね？

★：はい，私は 3 年間その仕事をしています。

質問：男性は何をしているのか。

1 クライアントと打ち合わせをしている。　　**2** 広告計画を準備している。

3 仕事の面接を受けている。　　**4** 自分の会社経営者に報告している。

解説　女性の I've been reviewing your résumé や I'd like to ask you about your present position. という発言から，男性が転職のための面接を受けていることがわかる。

No. 9 解答 **1**

☆：Steve, did you invite everyone over for Sunday?

★：Do we have to have Uncle Ned over? He's always so quiet when he comes over, like he doesn't want to be here. He's been that way for years now.

☆：Oh, Steve, it's like you don't even know your own uncle.

★：What do you mean?

☆：I mean, it's obvious he's still heartbroken over Aunt Irene's passing. They used to argue a lot, but actually he adored his wife. He needs to be with people.

★：Wow, Jill. I am reminded why I married you: your kindness.

Question：What does the woman say about Uncle Ned?

☆：スティーブ，日曜日にみんなを招待した？

★：ネッド叔父さんは呼ばないといけないかな。彼は来てもいつも無口で，ここにいたくないみたいだ。もう何年もそんな感じだ。

☆：まあ，スティーブ，あなたは自分の叔父さんのことすらわかっていないようね。

★：どういう意味？

☆：つまり，アイリーン叔母さんが亡くなって彼がまだ悲しみに暮れていることは明らかよ。彼らはよく言い争いをしたけど，本当は彼は奥さんを心から愛していたのよ。彼は人と接している必要があるわ。

★：ああ，ジル。僕がなぜ君と結婚したのかを思い出すよ。君の優しさだ。

質問：女性はネッド叔父さんについて何と言っているか。

1 彼は妻を失ったことを悲しんでいる。

2 彼は社交の場を好んだことがない。

3 彼は人と口論するのが好きだ。

4 彼はなぜ結婚したのかをスティーブから思い出させられた。

解説　女性がネッド叔父さんについて説明している it's obvious he's still heartbroken over Aunt Irene's passing の部分から，**1**が正解。passing と選択肢の loss は「死」の遠回しな表現。

No. 10 解答 **1**

★：Sally! What's wrong? Why are you crying?

○：It's about Jeremy. He doesn't want to see me anymore, and I'm so upset.

★：Oh, Sally—I'm sorry. You guys have been going out such a long time. Is there anything I can do?

○：No. It was so sudden. Things were going fine until last week, but then he suddenly told me he wanted to break things off. I can't believe it.

★：Look. Let's go get a cup of coffee and you can tell me all about it.

Question：What is wrong with Sally?

★：サリー！　どうしたの？　なぜ泣いてるの？

○：ジェレミーのことなの。彼はもう私に会いたくなくて，私すごく動揺しているの。

★：おお，サリー，かわいそうに。君たちはずいぶんと長く付き合っていたからね。僕にできることが何かある？

○：ううん。あまりに突然だったから。先週まではうまくいっていたのに，それが突然私に別れたいと言ったのよ。信じられないわ。

★：ほら，コーヒーでも飲みに行こう。僕にすべて話してごらん。

質問：サリーに何があったのか。

Day **6**

1 彼女のボーイフレンドが関係を絶った。

2 彼女は友人が脚を骨折したと聞いたばかりである。

3 彼女はもうジェレミーと付き合いたくないと思っている。

4 彼女は最近体調が悪い。

解説　女性は会話中で He doesn't want to see me anymore や he wanted to break things off と言っている。これを正解の**1**では end one's relationship と言い換えている。

No. 11 解答 **4**

☆ : Hello, this is Tracy calling from Nandia Hotel. Is this Mr. Jim Rivers' office?

★ : Yes, it is. It must be about my smartphone, right? In a black case?

☆ : Yes, that's correct. We found it in your room after you checked out. You're welcome to come and pick it up any time.

★ : Couldn't you just mail it to me? It's an hour's drive out there.

☆ : Unfortunately, there's a law that prohibits us from sending smartphones through the mail.

★ : Alright, well, thanks. I'll be out there by 8 p.m. tonight.

Question : What does the man have to do?

☆ : もしもし，こちらナンディア・ホテルのトレーシーです。ジム・リバーズさんの事務所でしょうか。

★ : はい，そうです。僕のスマートフォンについてのお電話でしょう？　黒いケースに入っていますね？

☆ : はい，そのとおりです。お客さまがチェックアウトされた後，お部屋で見つけました。いつでも取りに来てくださればと思います。

★ : こちらに郵送していただくことはできませんか。そちらへは車で１時間かかるのです。

☆ : あいにくですが，郵便でスマートフォンを送ることを禁止する法律があります。

★ : わかりました，ありがとう。今夜，午後8時までにそちらへ行きます。

質問：男性は何をしなければならないか。

1 ホテルへ荷物を取りに戻る。 **2** ホテルに電話をかけ直す。

3 郵便で自分のスマートフォンを送る。 **4** 直接ホテルを訪ねる。

解説　男性はホテルにスマートフォンを忘れたが，郵便で送ってもらうことはできない。男性は最後に，I'll be out there ... と言っていることから，自分がホテルに取りに行くと考えられる。

No. 12 解答 **4**

○ : Well, it's been really nice meeting you, Masashi.

★ : It was very nice to meet you, too. And thank you for looking after me so well here in Los Angeles.

○ : It was my pleasure. Have a nice flight.

★ : Thanks. And see you in Osaka in July.

○ : Yeah, that's just three months away. I'm looking forward to that. Good-bye.

★ : Bye! Thanks again!

Question : What is the woman looking forward to?

○ : いや，マサシさん，お会いできて本当によかったです。

★ : 私もあなたにお会いできて本当によかったです。それから，ここロサンゼルスではとてもよく面倒を見ていただき，ありがとうございました。

○ : どういたしまして。楽しい空の旅をなさってください。

★ : ありがとう。それでは，7月に大阪でお会いしましょう。

○ : ええ，わずか3カ月先のことですよね。楽しみにしています。さようなら。

★ : さようなら！ありがとうございました！

質問：女性は何を楽しみにしているか。

1 楽しい空の旅をすること。 **2** ロサンゼルスに戻ること。

3 3カ月の休暇を取ること。 **4** 7月にまた男性に会うこと。

解説　女性の言う I'm looking forward to that. の that は，直前の男性の see you in Osaka in July という内容を指す。

(A)

Curupira

In Brazil, one of the most talked-about mythical forest creatures is the Curupira. While there are variations by region about its appearance, one feature is common: its feet are turned backwards. Generally, a Curupira is considered to look like a wild little boy with fiery hair and its characteristic feet. A Curupira is also commonly described to have magical powers or extraordinary physical abilities.

A Curupira is believed to use its special abilities to confuse or punish hunters and other wrongdoers who harm the forest and its inhabitants. A Curupira's backward feet also help it deceive humans as they leave footprints leading the opposite way. It may mislead those who enter the forest so that they get lost. The legend of Curupira may have been developed to remind people not to mistreat the natural environment.

Questions

No.13 How do Brazilians describe Curupira?

No.14 What is one thing that a Curupira does to people?

クルピラ

ブラジルで最も話題になる神話の森の生き物の1つはクルピラである。その外見に関しては地域によって違いがあるものの，特徴の1つは共通している。それは両足が後ろ向きになっていること。一般的に，クルピラは炎のような髪とその特徴的な足を持つ野生の少年のような外見をしていると考えられている。クルピラはまた，魔法の力や並外れた身体的能力を持つと一般的に言われている。

クルピラは，森と森の住民に害を与える狩人やその他の悪者を混乱させたり懲らしめたりするのにその特別な能力を使うと信じられている。また，クルピラの後ろ向きの足は逆の方向に向かう足跡を残すため，人間をだますのに役立つ。それは道に迷うよう，森に入ってきた人々を誤った方向に導く可能性がある。クルピラの伝説は，人々に自然環境を破壊しないよう留意させるために発展したのかもしれない。

No. 13 解答 **3**

「ブラジル人はクルピラをどのように説明しているか」

1 森に住む巨大な怪物。 **2** 赤い動物を連れた神話の精霊。

3 奇妙な足を持つ子供のような生き物。 **4** とても体力のある狩人。

解説 冒頭の mythical forest creatures, its feet are turned backwards, look like a wild little boy などのクルピラの特徴から，**3**が正解。並外れた身体的能力があるが，狩人ではないので**4**は不適。

No. 14 解答 **2**

「クルピラが人々にすることの1つは何か」

1 道に迷った人を家まで案内するために足跡を残す。

2 人間による被害から森を守る。

3 森の住民を混乱させるために特別な能力を使う。

4 狩猟場に関する情報を人々に知らせる。

解説 A Curupira is believed to use its special abilities to confuse or punish hunters and other wrongdoers who harm the forest and its inhabitants. の「森に害を与える人を懲らしめる」という内容を，「人間による被害から森を守る」と言い換えた**2**が正解。

Day
6

91

(B)

Tsodilo

   A large collection of ancient paintings can be found in Tsodilo, Botswana. More than 4,500 pieces of rock art have been discovered in an area as small as 10 square kilometers. The pictures on the rocks depict humans, animals, and various symbols, mostly painted in red, but some in white. What makes this site particularly interesting is that the pictures are not from the same age. They were in fact left by different human settlements over thousands of years.

   Together with the rock paintings, archaeologists have found various artifacts in Tsodilo. These artifacts were excavated from different layers in the ground, each representing a different age. For example, old jewelry pieces were found in the top layers, while stone tools and pottery were found in the deeper layers. Tsodilo offers a rich source of historical information about human activities throughout the ages.

Questions

No.15　What is one thing that makes Tsodilo unique?

No.16　What did archaeologists discover in Tsodilo?

ツォディロ

　ボツワナのツォディロには，数多くの古代の絵が見られる。10平方キロメートルという小さな地域に4,500点を超える岩絵が発見されている。岩面の絵は，人間，動物，そしてさまざまな象徴を描写しており，大部分は赤色で描かれているが，白色の絵もある。この場所を特に興味深くしているのは，絵が同じ時代に描かれたものではないという点である。絵は実際，何千年もかけてさまざまな集団の定住によって残された。

　岩絵と一緒に，考古学者はツォディロでさまざまな工芸品を発見した。これらの工芸品は地面の異なる層から発掘され，それぞれが異なる時代を表している。例えば，上層部からは古い宝石が見つかり，深層部からは石器と陶器が見つかった。ツォディロは，遠い昔から時代を超えて人間の活動に関する豊富な歴史的情報を提供している。

No. 15　解答　**3**

「ツォディロを独特なものにしている点の1つは何か」

1　広い地域に散らばった岩絵がある。　　　　**2**　岩面の絵がすべて赤く塗られていた。

3　絵がさまざまな時代に作られた。　　　　**4**　ほとんどの絵が地下で発見された。

　解説　ツォディロが独特である理由は，What makes this site particularly interesting is that ... にある。the pictures are not from the same age を言い換えた**3**が正解。ツォディロの広さは as small as 10 square kilometers と言っており，**1**は wide が不適。

No. 16　解答　**2**

「考古学者はツォディロで何を発見したか」

1　さまざまな時代に書かれた歴史文書。　　　　**2**　さまざまな層にあった工芸品。

3　深層にあった宝石類。　　　　**4**　人間の居留地の完全な遺跡。

　解説　Together with the rock paintings, archaeologists have found various artifacts ... や These artifacts were excavated from different layers から，**2**が正解。宝石は上層部から発見されたので**3**は不適。

(C)

Arabian Oryx Sanctuary

The Arabian oryx is a deer-like animal that became extinct in the wild. However, people managed to reintroduce the Arabian oryx into protected areas. One of those protected areas is the Arabian Oryx Sanctuary in Oman. The sanctuary is known for a unique desert ecosystem that has a rich variety of plants. Since the Arabian Oryx Sanctuary was named a World Heritage site in 1994, it has been home to other endangered species of animals as well.

However, in 2007, UNESCO removed the Arabian Oryx Sanctuary from their list of World Heritage sites. One of the reasons was that a number of Arabian oryx had been hunted and killed. To make matters worse for the oryx, the government of Oman had also decided to reduce the size of the sanctuary by 90% to drill for oil. This decision has led the Arabian oryx to lose their protection and the site to lose its status as a Natural Heritage site.

Questions
No.17　What is one thing the Arabian Oryx Sanctuary is known for?

No.18　What happened to the sanctuary after the government of Oman scaled down the site?

アラビアオリックス保護区

　アラビアオリックスは野生では絶滅した，シカのような動物である。しかし，人々はアラビアオリックスを保護地域に再導入することに成功した。これらの保護地域の1つは，オマーンのアラビアオリックス保護区である。その保護区は，豊かな種類の植物がある独特な砂漠生態系で知られている。1994年にアラビアオリックス保護区が世界遺産に指定されて以来，ほかの絶滅危惧種の動物もここに生息している。

　しかし，2007年，ユネスコはアラビアオリックス保護区を世界遺産のリストから抹消した。その理由の1つは，多くのアラビアオリックスが狩られて殺されたからである。アラビアオリックスにとってさらに悪いことに，オマーン政府はまた，石油採掘のためにその保護区の面積を90％縮小することにしたのだ。この決定により，アラビアオリックスは保護されなくなり，その場所は世界自然遺産としての地位を失うことになった。

No. 17　解答　3

「アラビアオリックス保護区が知られていることの1つは何か」

1 そこで絶滅した動物がいること。　　　　**2** アラビアオリックスの唯一の保護地域であること。

3 多様な植物を持つ生態系があること。　　**4** 狩猟動物のための保護地帯であること。

解説　質問文と同じ表現を含む The sanctuary is known for ... has a rich variety of plants. の部分から，**3**が正解。variety を diverse に言い換えている。One of those protected areas is ... から，唯一の保護区ではないので**2**は不適。

No. 18　解答　4

「オマーン政府がその場所を縮小した後，保護区に何が起こったか」

1 狩人が保護区に近づくようになった。　　**2** アラビアオリックスの数が増えた。

3 オマーンの石油掘削収入が大幅に減少した。　**4** 間もなくして世界遺産のリストから除かれた。

解説　However, ... の部分がポイント。UNESCO removed the Arabian Oryx Sanctuary from their list of World Heritage sites から，**4**が正解。〈remove A from B〉の能動態を〈take A off from B〉の受動態に言い換えている。

(D)

Gladys West

Sometimes it takes many years for a person to be recognized for an important contribution. Gladys West, an African-American woman whose work led to the later development of the GPS technology, was one of them. The GPS, or the global positioning system, is used in navigation systems in cars, smartphones, and numerous other electronic tools to determine the location of the user. Despite its broad use we see today, little was known about her role.

Gladys West was born in 1930 to a farming family. She earned a scholarship to go to Virginia State College, where she studied mathematics. In 1956, she was employed by the U.S. Naval Weapons Laboratory. There, she began to collect data from satellites and programmed a computer that produced accurate calculations of the Earth's shape and dimensions. Several decades later, this became known as the GPS. Her great work was finally discovered and eventually she was given one of the highest honors by the U.S. Air Force in 2018.

Questions

No.19 What is one thing we learn about Gladys West?
No.20 What did Gladys West do at the U.S. Naval Weapons Laboratory?

グラディス・ウェスト

　人が重要な貢献をしたと認められるまでに何年もかかることがある。後のGPS技術の開発につながる仕事をしたアフリカ系アメリカ人女性のグラディス・ウェストもその1人である。GPS，すなわち全地球測位システムは，自動車のナビゲーションシステム，スマートフォン，およびほかの多数の電子ツールにおいて，ユーザーの位置を特定するために使用されている。私たちが今日見ているその幅広い用途にもかかわらず，彼女の役割についてはほとんど知られていなかった。

　グラディス・ウェストは1930年に農家で生まれた。彼女は奨学金を得てバージニア州立大学に行き，そこで数学を学んだ。1956年，彼女はアメリカ海軍兵器研究所に雇われた。そこで彼女は衛星からデータを収集し始め，地球の形状と寸法を正確に計算するコンピューターをプログラムした。数十年後，これはGPSとして知られるようになった。ついに彼女の偉業が見いだされ，最終的に彼女は2018年にアメリカ空軍によって最も高い名誉の1つを与えられた。

No. 19 解答 3

「グラディス・ウェストについてわかることの1つは何か」
1 彼女はナビゲーションシステムを車に取り入れた。
2 彼女はスマートフォンの初期モデルを考案した。
3 彼女は最近までほとんど知られていなかった。
4 彼女はアフリカ系アメリカ人の活動家であることが知られている。
解説 「重要な貢献が認められるまでに何年もかかることがある」という出だしの後，「グラディス・ウェストもその1人」と続く。また，little was known about her role の部分からも，**3**が正解。

No. 20 解答 2

「グラディス・ウェストはアメリカ海軍兵器研究所で何をしたか」
1 彼女はコンピューターについて学ぶために奨学金を得た。
2 彼女は地球を研究するために衛星データを集めた。
3 彼女は既存のコンピューターシステムを改良した。
4 彼女は数学の新しい理論を発見した。
解説 研究所でしたことは There, she began to collect data from satellites and ... that produced accurate calculations of the Earth's shape and dimensions. にあり，「地球を研究するために」と表した**2**が正解。

(E)

Digital Nomads

Nomads are peoples who move from one place to another, herding and grazing their animals, or alongside seasonal animal migrations. Nowadays, some people choose to be digital nomads, a type of work style and lifestyle where people change locations as they see fit or simply work out of office. Digital nomads may work at temporary residences, local cafés, or in co-working spaces. With only a laptop computer and Wi-Fi, digital nomads work anywhere, anytime.

While this remote working style provides freedom from the constraints of traditional working in offices, it also has its own restrictions. Not all jobs are suitable for a digital nomad, because work must be done with only a computer and the Internet. Traveling digital nomads who change homes frequently must minimize their belongings. And while they can enjoy independence, they lack opportunities for close teamwork or physical community activities.

Questions

No.21 What is one characteristic of a digital nomad work style?

No.22 What type of jobs are suitable for digital nomads?

デジタルノマド

遊牧民（ノマド）とは，飼っている動物を移動させて草を食べさせながら，もしくは季節的な動物の移動に合わせて，ある場所から別の場所に移動する民族のことである。最近では，デジタルノマド，つまり自分の都合に合わせて場所を変えたり，単にオフィスの外で作業したりするような仕事スタイルとライフスタイルを選択する人もいる。デジタルノマドは，一時的な住居，地元のカフェ，もしくは共同作業スペースで働くことがある。ノートパソコンとWi-Fiさえあれば，デジタルノマドはいつでもどこでも仕事をする。

この遠隔勤務スタイルは，従来のオフィス勤務の制約から逃れられるが，特有の制限もある。仕事はコンピューターとインターネットだけでできるものでなければならないため，あらゆる仕事がデジタルノマドに適しているとは限らない。住まいを頻繁に変える移動デジタルノマドは，所持品を最小限に抑える必要がある。そして彼らは独立を享受することができる一方で，密接なチームワークや物理的なコミュニティー活動の機会に欠ける。

No. 21 [解答] 1

「デジタルノマドの仕事スタイルの特徴の1つは何か」

1 さまざまな場所で仕事ができること。

2 一時的な契約しか受けないこと。

3 同僚と一緒にさまざまなオフィスに移動すること。

4 永住用の実住居で働くこと。

[解説] Nowadays, ... で述べられるデジタルノマドの特徴を短くまとめた**1**が正解。「一時的な住居，地元のカフェ，共同作業スペース」を抽象的にvarious locationsと表している。

No. 22 [解答] 4

「デジタルノマドにはどのような職種が適しているか」

1 創造性とチームワークを必要とする仕事。　　**2** オフィスに多くの制限がある仕事。

3 コミュニケーション能力に依存する仕事。　　**4** コンピューターだけでできる仕事。

[解説] Not all jobs are suitable for a digital nomad, because work must be done with only a computer and the Internet. の部分から，**4**が正解。その前の「ノートパソコンとWi-Fiさえあれば仕事ができる」もヒントになる。

(F)

Mass Extinctions of the Past

　　From the beginning of life on Earth to the present day, many species have evolved and become extinct, sometimes in huge numbers at one time. What has caused these mass extinctions? Giant asteroids or comets smashing into the Earth are believed by scientists to be the main cause. The explosions from these impacts would have destroyed everything around them for hundreds and even thousands of kilometers. But the most catastrophic destruction from past impacts would have come from the resulting dust, which would have been sent high into the atmosphere. The dust from the explosion would have traveled around the world, which means that sunlight could not penetrate the atmosphere and temperatures would have plummeted, leaving animal and plant life to perish.

　　We have long known of these dangers, but very little is being done to detect such objects in space. For the first time in history, a species has the technology to prevent its own extinction, but it appears to be sorely lacking the willpower to do so.

Questions

No.23 According to the speaker, what was behind the extinction of many species?

No.24 What does the speaker imply about humans?

過去の大量絶滅

　　地球上に生命が生まれてから今日に至るまで，多くの種が進化しては絶滅し，時には膨大な数の種が一度に死滅したこともあった。これらの大量絶滅は，何が原因だったのだろうか。地球に衝突する巨大な小惑星や彗星が主な原因であると科学者たちに信じられている。これらの衝突による爆発は，周囲の数百キロ，さらには数千キロにわたるすべてのものを破壊したことだろう。しかし，過去の衝突による最も壊滅的な破壊は，衝突の結果発生したちりによるものだっただろう。このちりは，大気圏の高い層まで運ばれたことだろう。爆発のちりは世界中に広がっただろうし，そうなると太陽光線は大気圏を貫通できず，気温が急激に下がっただろうし，動植物の生命は滅びるままとなってしまった。

　　われわれはこのような危険の存在をずっと前から知っていたが，宇宙空間のそのような物体を検出するために実行されていることはほとんどない。歴史上初めて，1つの生物種が自らの絶滅を防ぐための科学技術を手にしているが，そうしようとする意欲にひどく欠けているようである。

No. 23　解答　**2**

「話者によると，多くの種の絶滅の背後には何があったか」

1 人間の破壊的な性質。　　　　　　　　　　**2** 太陽を遮った空中のちり。

3 地球と衝突しかけた小惑星と彗星。　　　　**4** 地震と火山噴火。

解説　放送の中ほどのButで始まる文で，小惑星などが地球に衝突したことで発生したちりが最も壊滅的な破壊を生んだと述べている。

No. 24　解答　**4**

「話者は人類について何をほのめかしているか」

1 人類は実際には絶滅の危機に瀕していない。　　**2** 人類は宇宙の物体を注意深く観察している。

3 人類は科学技術を最大限に活用している。　　　**4** 人類は身を守る動機に欠けている。

解説　放送の最後でa species has ...，but it appears to be sorely lacking the willpower to do soと言っている。a species ＝ it は「人類」のことで，willpowerを正解の**4**ではmotivationに言い換えている。

(G) No. 25   解答 4

It looks like there's an entire house for rent on Bixby Road, which runs right alongside campus. You could afford it if you found some other people to rent it with. Or there's a gorgeous studio apartment on the same road nearby, although for one person it's a little expensive. Alternatively, there's a low-priced private room in a house on Exeter Way, just a 5-minute walk to campus, if you don't mind sharing a bathroom and kitchen. Finally, if you're willing to walk 10 minutes, we have a very reasonably priced one-bedroom apartment on Molton Avenue. It's a little older, but it's spacious.

状況：あなたは大学近くの住居について住居相談員と話している大学生である。あなたは大学から徒歩圏内で１人暮らしをしたいと思っているが，お金はあまりない。

質問：あなたはどの住居先を選ぶべきか。

キャンパスのすぐそばにあるビクスビー通りに借りられる一軒家があります。一緒に借りる人がほかに何人か見つかれば，家賃を払えるでしょう。あるいは，１人だと少し高めですが，同じ通りの近くに豪華なワンルームアパートがあります。もしくは，バスルームとキッチンを共用しても構わないなら，エクセター通りにある一軒家に低料金の個室があり，キャンパスまで歩いてわずか５分です。最後に，10分歩いても構わないなら，モルトン通りにとても手頃な料金の１ベッドルームのアパートがあります。少し古いですが，広々としています。

1 ビクスビー通りの一軒家。

2 ビクスビー通りのアパート。

3 エクセター通りの一軒家。

4 モルトン通りのアパート。

解説 「大学の徒歩圏内」「１人暮らし」「低料金」の条件をすべて満たすのはモルトン通りのアパートである。ビクスビー通りの一軒家は他人と共同で借りるので不適。エクセター通りにある一軒家もバスルームとキッチンが共用なので不適。

(H) No. 26   解答 4

For a lot of younger people like yourself, who buy inexpensive used cars, our Basic Liability plan is popular. At $59 a month it's our cheapest. It only covers damage caused to other vehicles. Our Comprehensive Collision plan covers most kinds of auto damage, and runs about $170 monthly. We also have a Family Coverage plan if you want to enroll with other family members. It covers multiple cars at $240 a month. Finally there's our Economy Plus plan. It covers collision damage to your auto as well as other vehicles involved for just $129 per month.

状況：あなたは新しい車を買うつもりである。あなたは月額150ドル未満で自分の車への損害を補償する保険プランを希望している。あなたは自動車保険代理店に相談する。

質問：あなたはどのプランを選ぶべきか。

お客さまのような，安めの中古車をお求めになる多くの若い方々には，基本賠償プランが人気です。月額59ドルで，当社では最も安いです。そちらはほかの車両に加えた損害だけを補償します。総合衝突プランはほとんどの種類の自動車の損傷を補償し，毎月約170ドルです。お客さまがご家族の方と一緒に加入されたい場合，家族補償プランというものもございます。そちらは月額240ドルで複数の車両を補償します。最後に，エコノミープラスプランがございます。そちらは月々たった129ドルでお客さまの車だけでなく関連するほかの車両への衝突損害も補償します。

1 基本賠償プラン。

2 総合衝突プラン。

3 家族補償プラン。

4 エコノミープラスプラン。

解説 「月額150ドル未満」「自分の車への損害を補償する」の２つの条件を満たすのは，Economy Plus plan である。ほかの車両に加えた損害だけを補償する基本賠償プランは不適。

Day
6

(I) No. 27 解答 1

We will be arriving at London, King's Cross in a few minutes. Would passengers traveling on to Norwich on the 12:25 express please proceed to platform 17? The next train for Heathrow Airport will be leaving at 12:45 from platform 26. For destinations around London, please proceed through the ticket gate and take the escalator down to the Tube. Taxis into the city are located to the left of the main exit. Please make sure that you have all of your belongings with you before leaving the train. Don't forget to check the overhead racks. British Railways would like to thank you for traveling with us. We look forward to serving you again.

状況：あなたは間もなくロンドンのキングズ・クロス駅に到着し，それからヒースロー空港に行きたいと思っている。あなたは列車の中で次の放送を聞く。

質問：あなたは空港に行くのに何を利用するよう勧められているか。

この列車は間もなくロンドン，キングズ・クロス駅に到着いたします。ノリッジ方面，12時25分発の急行にお乗りのお客さまは，17番ホームにお進みください。ヒースロー空港行きの次の列車は，26番ホームから12時45分に出発いたします。ロンドン周辺の目的地へは，改札を出て，エスカレーターを降りて地下鉄へお進みください。市内へのタクシー乗り場は，正面玄関を出て左にございます。列車を降りられる前にお手持ちの荷物をすべてご確認いただきますようお願い申し上げます。忘れずに棚の荷物もご確認ください。ブリティッシュ鉄道は皆さまのご乗車に感謝申し上げます。またのご利用をお待ちしております。

1 26番ホームの列車。　　　　　　　　　　**2** 地下鉄。
3 タクシー乗り場のタクシー。　　　　　　**4** 17番ホームの急行列車。

解説　空港方面への交通手段に注意して聞こう。放送前半に The next train for Heathrow Airport will be leaving at 12:45 from platform 26. と案内がある。

(J) No. 28 解答 3

Thank you for calling Danworth Furniture Outlet customer care center. Your time is as important to us as it is to you. To better assist your call, please choose from the following four options. For store locations and hours, press one. For home delivery services, or for questions about scheduling a delivery, press two. If you need help with a purchase, or to report a problem with an item you have already purchased, press three. For inquiries about online services and accounts, press four. For all other inquiries, please stay on the line and the next available operator will assist you.

状況：あなたは家具店で新品のテーブルを購入したが，箱から取り出すと上部に大きな傷があるのに気付く。あなたは店の顧客サービスセンターに電話をする。

質問：あなたは何番を押すべきか。

ダンウォース家具直販店の顧客ケアセンターにお電話いただきありがとうございます。お客さまのお時間はお客さまにとってと同じくらい弊社にとっても重要です。お客さまのお電話により適切な対応をすべく，次の4つのオプションから選択してください。店舗の場所および営業時間については，1を押してください。宅配サービス，あるいは配達スケジュールに関するご質問は，2を押してください。ご購入にお手伝いが必要な場合，あるいはご購入済みの品物に関する問題を報告される場合は，3を押してください。オンラインサービスとアカウントに関するお問い合わせは，4を押してください。その他すべてのお問い合わせは電話を切らずにお待ちください。次に空いたオペレーターが対応いたします。

1 1番。　　　　**2** 2番。　　　　**3** 3番。　　　　**4** 4番。

解説　状況から，届いた製品の破損について問い合わせていることを押さえる。順に聞いていくと，If you need ... to report a problem with an item you have already purchased, press three. の部分に該当するので，**3**が正解。

(K) No. 29　解答　4

Good morning, and welcome to Stanley Park. Due to the storm, there has been some damage to trees in the park. Workers are clearing away fallen trees and branches this morning, so please watch your step. The picnic area has been closed for the morning, but will open from noon today. The trail to Ridgeway Golf Course has been cleared, but there is a detour on the section of the trail near the river due to flooding. The detour is clearly marked. If you plan to hike on the circle path around the pond in the park, be advised you should wear rubber boots or hiking boots, as the trail is muddy.

状況：あなたはスタンリー公園からリッジウエー・ゴルフ場までの道をハイキングするつもりである。あなたはスタンリー公園でこのようなアナウンスを聞く。

質問：あなたは何をすべきか。

おはようございます。スタンリー公園へようこそ。嵐のために，当公園内の木々に多少の被害が出ています。午前中は作業員が倒れた木と落ちた枝を片付けていますので，どうぞ足元にご注意願います。ピクニックエリアは午前中閉鎖していますが，本日正午から開放されます。リッジウエー・ゴルフ場までの道は片付いていますが，川の近くの道の部分では氾濫のため迂回路があります。迂回路にははっきりと印が付けてあります。公園内の池を巡る周回路を歩かれる場合は，道がぬかるんでいますので，長靴かハイキング用の靴をお履きになることをお勧めします。

1 長靴かハイキング用の靴を履く。

2 ハイキングを始めるのを正午まで待つ。

3 落ちた枝を踏むときに注意する。

4 道の一部で別のルートを行く。

解説　状況の「リッジウエー・ゴルフ場まで歩く」から，The trail to Ridgeway Golf Course ... 以下の注意事項を聞き取ることがポイント。一部の道では迂回路（detour）があると言っているので，**4**が正解。

Day
6

筆記試験＆リスニングテスト
解答と解説

問題編　p.83〜100

筆記

1

問題	1	2	3	4	5	6	7	8	9	10	11	12	13	14	15	16	17	18
解答	2	4	3	2	2	2	3	4	1	2	1	1	3	2	1	2	1	1

2

問題	19	20	21	22	23	24
解答	1	2	2	2	4	2

3

問題	25	26	27	28	29	30	31
解答	1	3	1	4	3	2	1

4　解説内にある解答例を参照してください。

5　解説内にある解答例を参照してください。

リスニング

Part 1

問題	1	2	3	4	5	6	7	8	9	10	11	12
解答	2	4	1	3	4	2	2	1	2	3	1	1

Part 2

問題	13	14	15	16	17	18	19	20	21	22	23	24
解答	1	3	3	1	1	3	4	2	2	3	1	1

Part 3

問題	25	26	27	28	29
解答	2	3	3	2	3

1

(1)　解答 **2**

「その保険会社は，保険料を引き下げることによって，３年間スピード違反と自動車衝突がないドライバーに報いる」

解説　保険料引き下げのような特典が与えられる優良なドライバーの特質を考えると，スピード違反や自動車の衝突（collisions）がないことである。intrusion「侵入」，temptation「誘惑」，illusion「幻想」

(2)　解答 **4**

「言うまでもなく，半導体の分野でわれわれが主導権を握り続けるためには技術革新が必要不可欠である」

解説　be integral to「〜に必要不可欠である」とすれば意味が通る。intensive「集中的な」，extensive「広範囲な」，overall「全体的な」

(3)　解答 **3**

「症状が続いた場合には，直ちに医者に相談してください」

解説 直ちに医者に相談するのは，symptom「症状」が続いた場合だと推測できる。contrivance「工夫」，menace「脅威」，outcome「結果」

(4) 解答 2

A「こんにちは，メアリー！」

B「何という偶然でしょう！ ここニューヨークであなたにお会いできるとは思いませんでした」

解説 会うと予期していなかった状況から，coincidence「偶然」が適切。benevolence「慈悲」，prosperity「繁栄」，motivation「動機」

(5) 解答 2

A「あなたは本部長のポストに声がかかったのに断ったらしいですね。難しい決断でしたか」

B「まあ，それは魅力的だったのですが，正直に言うと，私は製品開発にもっと直接的に取り組む方が好きなのです」

解説 「本部長のポストは魅力的な（tempting）オファーだったが，製品開発に携わりたいので断った」という流れ。expressive「表現に富む」，obnoxious「不快な」，numbing「まひさせる」

(6) 解答 2

「つづりの間違いは気にしないでください。このコンピューターに入っているソフトが，原稿からほとんどのスペルミスを自動的に取り除いてくれます」

解説 スペルミスを心配しなくてよいのは，ソフトが自動的にeliminate「取り除く」からである。adhere「付着する」，foster「育てる」，relieve「和らげる」

(7) 解答 3

「弁護団は，20年前に殺人犯として有罪を宣告された囚人が無実であることをついに証明した」

解説 be convicted ofは「～の罪を宣告される」という意味。ascribe「原因を帰する」，distill「蒸留する」，corrupt「腐敗させる」

(8) 解答 4

「その若者は今年ウィンブルドンでのテニストーナメントできっと優勝するだろうと言われているが，私は懐疑的である。彼には経験があまりにもなさ過ぎる」

解説 第2文で経験がなさ過ぎると言っているので，勝つだろうという大方の見方にはskeptical「懐疑的」だと推測できる。affirmative「肯定的な」，decisive「決定的な」，faithful「誠実な」

(9) 解答 1

「マークは，今朝目が覚めると風邪をひいていたため，学校に行かなかった。彼は今，喉に痛みがあり，鼻が詰まっている」

解説 風邪の症状として考えられるのは，喉の痛みと「鼻詰まり」である。congestedは「密集した」のほかに「（鼻が）詰まった」の意味がある。dreary「わびしい」，ominous「不吉な」，enviable「うらやましい」

(10) 解答 2

「私はあの政治家を信用していない。彼はよく矛盾したことを言い，みんなにいい顔をしようと不可能な約束をする」

解説 政治家を信用しないのはcontradict oneself「矛盾したことを言う」からと考える。acclaim「称賛する」，embrace「抱く」，interrogate「尋問する」

(11) 解答 1

「そのインタビューの写しは6月3日までにKNTV局に電話かメールをすると手に入れることができる」

解説 後日入手できるものは，インタビューのtranscript「写し」である。transaction「（業務の）処理」，confession「自白」，circumstance「事情」

(12) 解答 1

「その川の近くの住民は，提案されているダムが環境に及ぼす影響を着工前に慎重に評価することを要求している」

解説 住民が環境を心配して要求することは，ダムが及ぼす影響を事前にassess「評価する」こと。invoice「送り状を送付する」，smear「中傷する」，venture「思い切ってする」

(13) 解答 3

「物語を子供たちに読んであげることは読書愛を育む。したがって，すべての親が子供たちに物語を読んであげることが推奨される」

解説 目的語のloveに合う動詞はnurture「育む」。convert「変える」，crumble「崩れる」，preside「取り仕切る」

(14) 解答 2

「ポールはドイツでの生活に適応するのに数カ月かかった。祖国オーストラリアとはあまりにも多くのことが違っていた」

解説 続く living in Germany「ドイツでの生活」に

合うのは，adapt to「～に適応する」。display「示す」，adjourn「延期する」，subsist「残存する」

(15) 解答 1

「ジョシュはかなりの財産を相続した。彼の祖母が亡くなり，彼にかなり大きな遺産を残した」

解説 第2文の left him a sizable inheritance から，ジョシュは財産を「相続した」と考えられる。come into a fortune で「財産を相続する」の意味。hold out「～を差し出す」，drag out「～を長引かせる」，turn out「判明する」

(16) 解答 2

「長引く不況のために，日本の多くの企業は給料を削減する以外に道がなかった」

解説 長引く不況という文脈で，目的語が「給料」なので，cut back on「～を削減する」がふさわしい。catch hold「つかむ」，end up「（～に）終わる」，get

2

全訳
かがり火の夜

　毎年11月5日にイギリス人は夜の冷気をものともせず，公園や広場に立って花火を見て，かがり火として知られる大きな火の周りに集まってくる。これはガイ・フォークスの捕獲を祝うものである。彼は，政治の中心である国会議事堂を爆破しようとした4人の男による陰謀の一味であった。歴史によれば，彼は1605年11月5日にかなりの量の火薬とともに国会の地下室で警備の者によって逮捕された。自白を強要され，彼はこれが国王ジェームズⅠ世を殺害しようとするもっと大きな陰謀の一部であることを明らかにした。

　彼の逮捕から1年後，国会はそれ以降，その日を年1回の公の感謝を表す日にすることを定めた。この祭りの花火の部分は，国会が危うく逃れた運命を表している。しかしながら，かがり火を燃やすことはさらに時をさかのぼり，それが悪霊を撃退する最も効果的な方法であると人々が思っていた時代にまで至る。かがり火は古代の新年の祭りの不可欠な部分だった。時を経て，これらの結び付いた伝統がガイ・フォークスの日として知られる現在の儀式に進化した。

　ガイを燃やさなければ，かがり火の夜は完結しない。これは大きな人形で，元々はガイ・フォークスを表し

away「～を取り除く」

(17) 解答 1

「政府は1800年代に作られた多くの時代遅れの法律を最近廃止した」

解説 目的語が「時代遅れの法律」だから，do away with「～を廃止する」がふさわしい。throw up「～を跳ね上げる」，make up「～を作る」，fall back「（たじろいで）身を引く」

(18) 解答 1

A「ジョン，もう寝る時間よ。11時過ぎよ」
B「うん，わかったよ，お母さん。おやすみなさい」

解説 「もう11時過ぎ」という言葉や，「おやすみなさい」という表現から，turn in「寝る」が適切。hold up「持ちこたえる」，leave out「～を省く」，hand over「～を手渡す」

ていた。しかし，過去百年の間に，あらゆる種類の評判の悪い公人が順番にガイになっていった。

　かがり火の夜を計画する上で，安全は大きな影響を持つ。次第に，人々は私的な祝事ではなく，大掛かりに組織された祝典に参加する方を選んでいったのだ。

(19) 解答 1

解説 空所の後の the fate that Parliament had barely escaped は，国会議事堂が爆破を免れたことを指す。これを祝して祭りを催し花火を上げるのだから，その日は1「公の感謝の表れ」と考えられる。

(20) 解答 2

解説 元々のガイ・フォークスの祭りにあった花火と，別の習慣である悪霊よけのかがり火が結び付いて現在の儀式に進化したとある。よって，2「（これらの）結び付いた伝統」が適切。

(21) 解答 2

解説 大きな人形を燃やすことがかがり火の夜には不可欠で，元々その人形は名前のとおりガイ・フォークスを指したが，それが評判の悪い公人に変わったという文脈である。よって，2「順番にガイになっていっ

た」がふさわしい。

全訳

人口──過去と現在

世界の人口は現在70億人以上となっている。私たちのほとんどは自分のすべきことをする際の日常的な人込みと雑踏に慣れてしまっている。しかし、これまでずっとこうだったわけではない。実際、このような膨大な人口は、人口に関する研究である人口統計学によれば、最近の現象なのである。

人類の歴史の大半を通して、地球上に生存している人の数はどの時点でも数億人にすぎなかったのであり、これは今日いくつかの国が容易に上回ることのできる数である。人口が10億の水準に達したのは、たかだか過去2世紀の間のことなのである。

こうした情報はしばしば「人類の始まり以来、どれだけの数の人間が地球上に生きてきたのだろうか」という疑問を生じさせる。もちろん、その厳密な答えは正確に推測することは難しい。詰まるところ、人類の歴史の過去1％に関してしか記録が残っていないのである。この疑問に興味をそそられて、国連の人口調査官が入手し得る限りの最高のデータと人口増加に関する最近の理論を使い、おおよその答えに至る試みをした。これまでの世代の平均寿命、1人の女性が産んだ子供の数、人類は正確にはいつ出現したと考えられるかなど、ある特定の数値に関するさまざまな仮説や推定をする必要があった。

最も信頼できる科学者によれば、上記のような仮説とその他多くのものを考慮に入れると、総数はおよそ

1,050億人と見積もられている。今度はこれがもう1つのとても興味深い数字、すなわちこれまで生まれたすべての人間の6％が今日生きているという点へとつながる。これは、約5万年と考えられている人類が地上に生存してきた時間の長さを考慮すると、驚くほど大きな数である。しかし、来る日も来る日もラッシュアワーの人込みに巻き込まれていると、地球が現代になっていかに込んでしまったかという事実を避けるわけにはいかないのである。

(22) 解答 **2**

解説 空所の前の it has not always been this way は、ずっと70億もの人がいたわけではないという意味。それに「このような膨大な人口は最近の現象」と続くのだから、前文に情報を補足する **2**「実際」が適切。

(23) 解答 **4**

解説 第3段落冒頭に「人類が誕生してから今までの人口を知りたい」とあるが、空所の次の文には「人類の歴史の過去1％に関してしか人口の記録が残っていない」とある。したがって、人口の総数に関する厳密な答えは **4**「正確に推測することは難しい」と考えられる。

(24) 解答 **2**

解説 5万年かけて1,050億人に達した延べ人数の6％が現在、地球上に住んでいるのだから、それは **2**「驚くほど大きな数」である。

3

全訳

電子レンジはどのように機能するか

マイクロ波は空間を移動する一種の電磁エネルギーである。食物には吸収されるが金属には反射し、ガラス、紙、プラスチック、その他同様の物質を通り抜ける性質があるので、マイクロ波は料理に役立つ。

電子電磁管で生み出されたマイクロ波は、金属性のレンジ内を食物に吸収されるまで跳ね回る。マイクロ波によって、食物中の分子（例えば水分などの非常に効率的なマイクロ波の吸収体）は高速で振動し、これにより食物を調理する熱が発生する。新鮮な野菜のような水分の多い食物がほかの食物に比べて電子レンジ

で速く調理されるのはこうした理由による。マイクロ波で調理された食物には、ほかの方法で調理された食物より多くのビタミンとミネラル類が残っている。マイクロ波による調理は時間が少なくて済み、追加の水分を必要としないからである。しかし、従来どおり調理した料理の方がおいしいことにほとんどの人が同意する。

食品医薬品局の医療機器・放射線保健センターで、テレビ、音響およびマイクロ波製品部門の指揮を執るジョアン・バロンによると、マイクロ波は食物内で直接熱を発生させるが、実際には食物の内部から外側に向かって調理することはない。「ロースト肉のような厚

い食物だとマイクロ波の熱は一般的に表層から1インチくらいの所にしか達しません」と彼女は言う。「熱はそれからゆっくりと内側に伝わりながら調理を行うのです」

食物の水分が多い箇所は，ほかの箇所より速く熱くなる。したがって，例えばゼリーロールを加熱するときは，1，2分調理した後そのまま放置し，熱が全体に行き渡るようにするとよい。むらのない料理ができるように，電子レンジでの調理法には，「料理の途中で食物の向きを変えること」，「調理後そのまま置いておくこと」といった指示が通常含まれている。

今日，電子レンジはアメリカの家庭のほぼ90％で見られるが，みんなが愛好しているわけではない。いくつかの研究によれば，マイクロ波で加熱された分子の高速回転は，実際には隣り合う分子同士を切り離し，食物にダメージを与えるような影響を及ぼすという。ある短期の研究では，ボランティアの人々が異なる方法で調理された同じ食物をさまざまな組み合わせで食べた。マイクロ波で調理された食べ物はボランティアの血液中に不穏な変化を引き起こした。ヘモグロビンの値が減少し，白血球とコレステロールの全体的な値が増えた。1991年，ローザンヌ大学の教授であるハンス・ウルリヒ・ヘルテル博士は論文を発表し，その中でマイクロ波による調理が食品の組成と栄養素に変化を引き起こすとし，それが血液へのがん化の影響を含む，健康への危険を引き起こすかもしれないことを示した。

しかし，ほかの研究ではマイクロ波による調理は安全であるとの結論が出されている。したがって電子レンジを使うかどうかの判断は，消費者に委ねられているのである。

(25) 解答 1

「電子レンジは，〜によって食品を加熱する」
1 水分子を高速で振動させること
2 ガラス，紙，またはプラスチック製の食品容器に吸収されること
3 速い速度で食物分子を通過すること
4 すぐに水分子を水蒸気に変えること
解説 加熱の原理に関しては，第2段落第2文にThey (= microwaves) cause ... water ... to vibrate at high speeds and thus produce heat to cook the food. とある。**1** が正解で，oscillate は「振動する」という意味。

(26) 解答 3

「文章から推測できることは」

1 マイクロ波で調理された食物は，ほかの方法で調理した食品よりも味が良くなることが多い。
2 マイクロ波は最初食物の中に深く吸収されるので，食物を完全に調理する。
3 マイクロ波で調理された食物は，従来の方法で調理した食品よりも多くの栄養素を保つことができる。
4 マイクロ波で調理された食物は，調理された後に放置してはいけない。
解説 第2段落第4文中のretains more vitamins and minerals「より多くのビタミンとミネラル類を保つ」をretain more nutrients「より多くの栄養素を保つ」と言い換えた**3** が正解。

(27) 解答 1

「文章の筆者がほのめかしていることは」
1 マイクロ波で調理された食物に関するさまざまな研究結果は互いに矛盾している。
2 マイクロ波で調理された食物に関する研究の大部分は，それらが食べるには危険であることを示している。
3 いくつかの研究は，マイクロ波で調理された食物ががんを引き起こすことを決定的に示した。
4 証拠が明確になるまで，消費者は電子レンジを使用しないことが奨励される。
解説 マイクロ波による調理について，第5段落の最終文では「健康への危険を引き起こすかもしれない」とする研究，最終段落では「マイクロ波による調理は安全である」とする研究が紹介されている。つまり，研究結果は contradict each other「互いに矛盾している」と言えるので，**1** が正解。

全訳
環境人種差別

気候変動などの環境に関する懸念は，今日われわれが直面している最も差し迫った問題の1つである。これらの問題は突き詰めていくとすべての人間に影響を及ぼすものであるが，一部の集団と地域は偏った影響を受けている。多くの場合，その結果は破壊的であるだけではなく，意図的なものである。この不均衡とその背景にある体系的な虐待が，環境人種差別の問題を生み出した。「環境人種差別」という言葉は1980年代に初めて生まれたが，人種集団をさいなむ環境上の不公平の例は何百年もさかのぼる。

環境人種差別は，しばしば特定のコミュニティーを公害やその他有害な物質にさらす形を取るが，考慮すべき要因はほかにもある。例えば，自然災害に弱い場

所や，利用できる飲料水から遠い所にコミュニティーを設置することなどの行動は，環境人種差別的であると見なされる場合がある。そのほかには，差別的な廃棄物処理プロセスや不公平な天然資源の利用などが含まれ，環境破壊につながっている。戦時下において，特定のコミュニティーの近くに軍事基地と保管設備を設置することも，環境人種差別の行為であると言われている。

　驚くことではないが，環境人種差別の被害者はたいてい少数民族と低所得コミュニティーである。この慣習の歴史上の例は，しばしば植民地化と工業化と結び付いており，それはまだ続いているが，多くの場合ではさらに悪化している。例として，裕福な西洋の政府はしばしば自国の産業から発生する有害な廃棄物を自国内で廃棄することに消極的であり，それ故リスクを受け入れてくれる途上国に輸送する。しかし，現実は国が「受け入れてくれる」というほど単純なものではなく，それは，関連する貿易協定と社会的支援の提供が強制の一種として働いているからである。政府は利益を得るかもしれないが，廃棄物が置かれ，捨てられた地域は，多くの場合ひどい結果に苦しむ。これらの結果は，高い幼児死亡率，がんや心血管系の疾患および身体的異常の発生の大幅な増加などである。

　しかし，環境人種差別とそれがもたらす悪影響は，途上国に限定されるものではない。アメリカなどの国でさえ，最近のいくつかの事例が示すように，それに苦しんでいる。2005年にハリケーンカトリーナによってもたらされた破壊と，政府の反応は，人種隔離政策の結果として少数民族に偏って影響した。もう1つもっと最近の例として，人口の大半がアフリカ系アメリカ人であるミシガン州フリントでは，環境保護庁による「有毒廃棄物」の定義に見合うほどの鉛を含む水を飲んだり入浴に使ったりしていた。支配的な多数集団がさらされている大気汚染と水質汚染のレベルをはるかに超えるレベルの汚染に少数民族がさらされている事例が，先進国においてほかにも多く存在する。

　遺憾なことに，環境人種差別につながるプロセスを制御しているのは，力のある富裕層である場合が多く，しばしば法の裁きを受けさせることが難しい。しかし，それによって環境正義団体と公民権運動が活動の成功を追求するのを阻まれたわけではない。その結果，影響を受けたコミュニティーと社会的周辺に置かれた集団が，居住地の状態を改善するための組織的な運動に成功した。ソーシャルメディアを通じて注目度を高め，国連などの国際組織が関与することで，環境人種差別の事例はうまくいけばいつか過去のものとなるかもしれない。

(28)　解答　4

「環境人種差別について正しいことは何か」

1 ほとんどの環境問題と同様に，環境人種差別は地球上のあらゆる地域に影響を及ぼす。

2 環境人種差別の問題は，1980年代に始まって以来，世界中に広がっている。

3 特定の司法制度による虐待が環境人種差別と誤って捉えられることがよくある。

4 環境人種差別は特定の人種集団の体系的な抑圧に起因している。

解説　環境人種差別の原因について述べた第1段落の It is this imbalance, and the systematic abuse behind it, that has given rise to the problem of environmental racism. の部分と**4**が一致する。

(29)　解答　3

「どんな要因が環境人種差別の事例の発見に役立つ可能性があるか」

1 天然資源や自然災害を扱う政策が考慮されないこと。

2 環境保護機関と政府部門による管理不良。

3 特定の集団が自分たちの環境から特別な危険にさらされることになる状況。

4 国立公園やほかの保護区域の近くに軍事基地を配置すること。

解説　第2段落全体を費やして，公害，自然災害，廃棄物処理，軍事基地の設置などさまざまな危険な状況が，環境人種差別の事例として挙げられている。つまり，特定のコミュニティーがそうした危険な環境に置かれているかどうかが環境人種差別の指標と言える。したがって**3**が正解。

(30)　解答　2

「支配層エリートは，環境人種差別に関連する問題を悪化させるために何をしているのか」

1 彼らは歴史的過ちから学び，罪を償う気があることを証明している。

2 彼らはしばしば自国の問題を無視するか，強制的な戦術を駆使して他国にリスクを負わせる。

3 彼らは国内の問題に対処しない一方で，外国企業が大きな経済的取引を行う手助けをしている。

4 彼らはがんや心血管疾患のような病気を治療するのを助けるのに，得たいかなる利益をも利用しようとしている。

解説　第3段落の Rich western governments, ... の

文から，**2**が正解。Rich western governments が質問文では the ruling elite に，they ship it to developing countries willing to accept the risks を選択肢では force other nations to take risks と表している。

(31) 解答 **1**

「文章によると，環境人種差別の問題はどのように解決され得るか」

1 主要組織やインターネットからの支援を得ることによって。

2 裕福な人々に公民権運動を掌握させることによって。

3 ソーシャルメディア上で裕福で力のある人々の運動を広めることによって。

4 環境正義団体に新しいコミュニティーを構築するよう頼むことによって。

解説 環境による人種差別への対処については第5段落の最後の文から，**1** が正解。social media を選択肢訳では the Internet，また international organizations like the United Nations を major organizations と表している。

問題文の訳

長年にわたり，科学者たちは，石油，石炭，ガスなどの化石燃料が環境に与える影響を懸念してきた。これに伴い，再生可能で経済的で，かつ地球への害がより少ない代替エネルギー源が求められてきた。そのような代替の1つがバイオ燃料で，これは主に植物から生成される燃料である。

バイオ燃料は化石燃料よりもクリーンなエネルギー源だと考えられている。その主な理由の1つは，二酸化炭素排出量がはるかに少ないためである。また，バイオ燃料は生産するのに特別な設備を必要とせず，後で使うために確実に貯蔵しておける。このように，風力発電や太陽光発電システムとは異なり，バイオ燃料の効果は天候の影響を受けない。

バイオ燃料は再生可能かもしれないが，その生成に使用される植物を育てるには虫を殺す有害な化学物質と大量の水が必要で，それは環境に良くない，と主張する批評家もいる。さらに，このタイプの農業は広大な土地を必要とし，費用がかかり得るため，バイオ燃料の経済的利益に影響を与える可能性がある。

解答例

　Biofuels are a renewable energy source that are considered to be a good alternative to fossil fuels. Biofuels are better for the environment partly because they emit much less carbon dioxide. Also, they do not need specialized tools and can be put in storage. Nevertheless, the production of plants used for making biofuels damages the environment, and the land required can also be costly. (64語)

解答例の訳

　バイオ燃料は，化石燃料の優れた代替と考えられている再生可能エネルギー源である。バイオ燃料が（化石燃料）より環境に良い理由の1つは，二酸化炭素の排出量がはるかに少ないからである。また，特別な設備を必要とせず，貯蔵も可能である。それにもかかわらず，バイオ燃料を生成するのに使われる植物の生産は環境を破壊し，さらに必要な土地にもコストがかかり得る。

解説　各段落の要点を1（～2）文でまとめて全体を3～4文で書こう。解答例は，第1文「トピックの導入（バイオ燃料）」（第1段落），第2～3文「利点」（第2段落），第4文「欠点」（第3段落）の4文構成。導入となる第1文では，バイオ燃料について第1段落の内容を1文でまとめている。第2段落ではバイオ燃料が化石燃料よりも環境に良い理由やバイオ燃料の利点が列挙されており，解答例ではA because Bの文とAlso, ... の2文に分けている。複数ある理由の1つを表す表現には，本文のOne main reason ... や解答例のpartly because ... がある。Althoughで始まる第3段落では批評家の主張＝バイオ燃料の欠点が書かれており，解答例ではNeverthelessでつなげている。

要点をまとめるポイントは，①重要な情報を見極め，細かい情報や具体例は省く，②具体的な情報を抽象化する，の2点。例えば，第1段落のlike oil, coal, and gasのような具体的な例や，第2段落のunlike wind or solar power systemsのような補足的な情報は解答に含めない。

そのほかの解答例の言い換えは以下のとおり。less harmful to the planet→better for the environment, much lower carbon dioxide emissions→emit much less carbon dioxide（名詞emission→動詞emit）, special equipment→specialized tools, stored→put in storage（動詞stored→名詞storage）, producing（動詞）→production（名詞）, is not good for the environment→damages the environment, expensive→costly

問題の訳

TOPIC：日本は優れたサービスに対してチップを払う制度を導入すべきか。

POINTS：動機・客にとってのストレス・より低い賃金・より良いサービスの奨励

解答例	解答例の訳

解答例

In many countries staff receive tips for good service in hotels or restaurants. However, I do not think it is a good idea to introduce this system in Japan for two reasons.

First of all, tipping can be stressful for the customer. In Japan there is no custom of tipping staff. Customers might be unsure as to when or how to tip. This will ruin their enjoyment.

Secondly, in countries where tipping is common, base wages tend to be lower. While workers have the potential to earn more, the system is unreliable and many hotel or restaurant workers may end up making less money.

Introducing a system of tipping in Japan does not seem to be beneficial to either customers or workers. Therefore, it is better to leave the present system as it is. （134語）

解答例の訳

　多くの国では，従業員がホテルやレストランの優れたサービスに対してチップを受け取っている。しかし，2つの理由から，日本でこの制度を導入することは良い考えではないと思う。

　第1に，チップを払うことは客にとってストレスとなる可能性がある。日本では従業員にチップを払う習慣がない。客はいつ，どうやってチップを渡すのか確信が持てないかもしれない。これは彼らの楽しみを台無しにするだろう。

　第2に，チップが一般的である国の方が基本賃金が低い傾向がある。労働者がより多く稼ぐ可能性がある一方で，この制度は当てにならず，多くのホテルやレストランの労働者は稼ぎが減ることになるかもしれない。

　日本でチップ制度を導入することは，客と労働者のどちらにとっても有益ではないように思われる。したがって，現行制度のままの方が良い。

解説　「日本は優れたサービスに対してチップを払う制度を導入すべきか」という質問に対し，解答例はNoの立場である。序論では，まず多くの国ではチップ制度があると述べた後，Howeverを用いて，「2つの理由で日本はこの制度を導入すべきでない」と反対の立場を明らかにしている。その後，第2段落ではFirst of all, ... の形でPOINTSのStress for customers，第3段落ではSecondly, ... の形でLower wagesの観点について詳しく述べている。

　Stress for customersの観点である第2段落では，チップになじみのない日本で新たに導入すれば客に負担がかかり，混乱を招くという根拠である。Lower wagesの観点である第3段落では，チップが一般的な他国を引き合いに出し，そういった国の基本賃金が低い傾向にあることを指摘した後，チップ制度導入によって労働者の賃金が減る可能性について述べている。While A, B. 「Aである一方，Bである」の使い方を確認しておくとよい。最終段落では，チップ制度について「日本では客にも労働者にも有益とは思えない」「（チップ制度のない）今のままが良い」と結論付けている。

　POINTSのMotivationとEncouragement of better serviceはYesの立場で使えそうだ。例えば，チップ制度導入の利点として，「労働者の意欲が高まる」「より優れたサービスを労働者に促すことができ，客も満足する」などの意見が考えられるだろう。

Listening Test

No. 1 解答 2

○：Dan, don't you think it's about time we got a new car?

★：Trust me, I'd like to, but it's expensive.

○：I know, but I'm just worried it'll cost more money if we keep fixing the car we have now. We don't have to buy a brand new car.

★：That's true, but to be honest, I don't really trust used car salespeople.

○：Well, could we at least look? We don't have to get a really old or cheap one. We could find a private seller, and then we could get an inspection done before we decide to buy anything.

★：OK, I'd be willing to do that.

Question：What does the man agree to do?

○：ダン，そろそろ新しい車の買い時だと思わない？

★：信じてくれ，僕も買いたいけど，高いんだよ。

○：わかっているけど，今持っている車を修理し続ける方がもっとお金がかかるんじゃないかと心配で。必ずしも新車を買う必要はないわ。

★：そうだね，でも正直言うと，中古車の販売員をあまり信用していないんだ。

○：じゃあ，見るくらいはいい？　すごく古いのや安いのは買う必要ないわ。個人で売りに出している人を見つけて，どれか買うと決める前に点検してもらったらいいわ。

★：そうだね，それくらいならしてもいいよ。

質問：男性は何をすることに同意しているか。

1 自動車販売員に相談する。　　　　　　　　**2** 中古車の購入を検討する。

3 さまざまな新車を点検する。　　　　　　　**4** 自分たちの車を修理する人を探す。

解説　女性は冒頭で don't you think it's about time we got a new car? と言って，車の買い換えを提案している。その後2人は中古車を買う方法について話し合っていることから，**2**が正解。

No. 2 解答 4

☆：Would you like a window seat or an aisle seat, sir?

★：Aisle seat, please.

☆：OK, that's fine. We have 12B for you.

★：Thank you.

☆：The flight is boarding from gate number 23 at 2:30 p.m.

★：OK. Where is the executive lounge?

☆：It's in the departure gate area. Turn left after security. It's opposite gate number 12.

Question：What will the man do next?

☆：窓側の席と通路側の席のどちらがよろしいですか。

★：通路側の席をお願いします。

☆：わかりました，大丈夫です。12B になります。

★：ありがとう。

☆：飛行機への搭乗は23番ゲートから午後2時30分に開始になります。

★：わかりました。エグゼクティブ・ラウンジはどこですか。

☆：出発ゲートのエリアにあります。手荷物検査を受けたら，左に曲がってください。12番ゲートの向かいです。

質問：男性は次に何をするか。

1 飛行機に搭乗する。　　　　　　　　　　　**2** 出発ゲートに行く。

3 どのゲートに行くべきかを調べる。　　　　**4** 手荷物検査を通過する。

解説　女性の Turn left after security. という説明から，男性はまず security check を受け，その後エグゼクティブ・ラウンジに行くと考えられる。よって，男性の次の行動として**4**が正解。

No. 3　解答　**1**

★：That kitten Jen found is adorable.

○：It is cute, but ... Frank, we're not set up to have pets right now. Jen is only five.

★：So was I when I got our first dog.

○：Pets cost a fortune, Frank. Pet hospitals, food, and then you have to train them. Cats tear up furniture and need litterboxes.

★：I say it'll be good practice for Jen, helping take care of a pet. I'll help too.

○：Really? OK, I won't say no, but let me think about it for a few days.

Question：What is one reason the woman is hesitant to keep the kitten?

★：ジェンが見つけたあの子猫，愛くるしいな。

○：かわいいけど…フランク，今はペットを飼う準備ができていないわ。ジェンはまだ5歳よ。

★：僕が最初の犬を飼ったのも5歳だったよ。

○：ペットはすごくお金がかかるのよ，フランク。ペット病院，餌，それからしつけもしないといけない。猫は家具をボロボロに裂くし，砂のトイレも必要だわ。

★：僕が言っているのは，ペットの世話を手伝ったらジェンにとっていい習慣になるだろうってこと。僕も手伝うよ。

○：本当に？　わかった,駄目とは言わないけど，2,3日考えさせて。

質問：女性が子猫を飼うのをためらっている理由の1つは何か。

1 生活空間に損傷を与える。
2 娘を傷つけるかもしれない。
3 男性は手伝わないだろう。
4 男性はこれまでにペットを飼ったことがない。

解説　女性が子猫を飼うのをためらう理由をいくつか挙げている中で，Cats tear up furnitureの部分と**1**が一致する。tear upを選択肢ではdamageと表している。

No. 4　解答　**3**

★：Oh my goodness, are you OK?

☆：I'm fine, don't worry. I just tripped on the stairs and fell.

★：You look exhausted. Why don't you go home early today? We can manage without you.

☆：But I have to finish a presentation slideshow by Monday, for the weekly meeting.

★：Nonsense. If you keep working like that, you'll be in no shape to do that presentation. I'll just change the schedule and have John give the sales report instead. Your work can wait until the following week. Go home early and rest over the weekend.

☆：If you say so. Thanks.

Question：What is one thing the man recommends the woman do?

★：何てことだ，大丈夫かい？

☆：大丈夫よ，心配しないで。階段につまずいて転んだだけよ。

★：すごく疲れているようだね。今日は早く帰宅したらどう？　僕たちは君がいなくても何とかなるよ。

☆：でも，週の定例会議に向けて月曜日までにプレゼンのスライドショーを終わらせないといけないの。

★：ばかげているよ。そんなふうに働き続けたら，そのプレゼンができる状態ではなくなるだろう。僕がスケジュールを変更して，代わりにジョンに売上報告をしてもらうよ。君の仕事は次の週に延ばしても構わない。早く家に帰って週末は休んで。

☆：あなたがそう言うなら。ありがとう。

質問：男性が女性にするよう勧めていることの1つは何か。

1 会議で売上について報告する。
2 彼の代わりにスライドショーを完成させる。
3 プレゼンテーションを延期する。
4 オフィス内で休憩する。

解説　男性が女性の体調を心配している中で，I'll just change the schedule ... Your work can wait until the following week. と言っているので，**3**が正解。

No. 5 解答 4

○：There's so much to see in this new city. I'm glad we moved. Did you check out the shopping arcade down the street?

★：It's mostly a bunch of overpriced boutiques and cafés with nobody in them. There was a little deli on the corner, though. It was packed with people.

○：I bet that's where the locals go. Would you like to go get a sandwich there?

★：Maybe later. This area is a pleasant place to live, but personally I wish there were a few more practical things nearby, like a supermarket.

Question：What does the man notice about the neighborhood?

○：この新しい街には見るべきものがたくさんあるわ。引っ越してきてよかった。通りの先の商店街は見た？

★：ほとんどががらがらの高級なブティックとカフェだ。角に小さなデリがあったけどね。そこは人でいっぱいだった。

○：きっとそこが地元の人たちが行く所なのね。そこにサンドイッチを買いに行かない？

★：また後でね。この地域は住むには快適な場所だけど、個人的には、スーパーみたいなもっと実用的なものが近くにいくつかあるといいな。

質問：男性はこの地区について何に気付いているか。

1 さまざまなブティックとデリが大きな特徴である。

2 食料雑貨品の買い物に便利である。

3 近くに安価なスーパーマーケットがある。

4 ほとんどの商店にお金がかかり過ぎる。

解説　男性は地元の商店街について、It's mostly a bunch of overpriced boutiques and cafés と言っている。**4** が正解で、overpriced を cost too much と言い換えている。**3** は、最後の I wish there were ... と合わない。

No. 6 解答 2

☆：Hello, Steve. This is Helen. I think I'm lost. I can't find your place.

★：I thought you'd have difficulty. The map I gave you is pretty complicated. Where are you now?

☆：I'm standing outside a school near a major intersection.

★：OK. I know where that is. Please wait there for a few minutes. I'll come and get you soon.

Question：What do we learn about Helen?

☆：もしもし、スティーブ。ヘレンよ。道に迷ったみたい。あなたの家が見つからないの。

★：わからないかなとは思ったんだ。僕が君にあげた地図はかなり複雑だからね。今、どこにいるの？

☆：大きな交差点の近くにある学校の外にいるの。

★：うん、その場所ならわかる。そこで2、3分待ってて。すぐに迎えに行くよ。

質問：ヘレンについて何がわかるか。

1 彼女はよく道に迷う。

2 彼女はスティーブの家に行くところである。

3 彼女は地図を持っていない。

4 彼女は学生である。

解説　ヘレンの I think I'm lost. I can't find your place. という発言や、スティーブの I'll come and get you soon. という発言から、ヘレンはスティーブの家に向かう途中で道に迷ったことがわかる。

No. 7 解答 **2**

○：Sweetheart, I know money is tight, but I'd really like us to have a house.

★：You mean build one, right?

○：Or we could find one to move into. I'd really like to have my own yard space for a garden, and also for the kids when they come along.

★：Do you really think we can afford it on my salary right now?

○：Well, it depends on what we look at, I guess. We can start by simply looking. Just see what our options are.

★：OK, I'm open to that.

Question：What does the woman say she wants to do first?

○：ねえ，金銭的に厳しいことはわかっているけど，一軒家が欲しいわ。

★：家を建てるということだよね？

○：それか，引っ越せる家を見つけるのでもいいわ。庭を作るのに自分の芝地が本当に欲しいの，それに子供ができたらその子たちのためのスペースもね。

★：君は今の僕の給料でその余裕があると本当に思っているのかい？

○：うーん，何を見るかにもよると思う。まずはただ見始めるだけでいいわ。どんな物件があるかを見るだけ。

★：わかった，それならいいよ。

質問：女性はまず何がしたいと言っているか。

1 庭を作る場所のために芝地を持つ。　**2** 今どんな家が手に入るかを調べる。

3 家賃がより安い家に引っ越す。　**4** 子供のためのスペースがある新しい家を建てる。

解説　女性がまずしたいことは，We can start by simply looking. Just see what our options are. の部分にある。options は住宅物件のことなので，**2** が正解。**1** と **4** は，女性の要望ではあるが「まずしたいこと」として不適。

No. 8 解答 **1**

★：I'm leaving our Tokyo office, Mary. I've just been transferred to the new office in Los Angeles, where I'll be sales manager.

☆：Oh, that's a great break, Tom. When will you be leaving?

★：Next month. But I'm taking a two-week vacation in the U.S. before starting work.

☆：Well, you deserve it. You've done an outstanding job here.

Question：What does the woman say about the man's transfer?

★：メアリー，僕は東京オフィスを離れることになったよ。たった今，ロサンゼルスの新しいオフィスに異動になって，そこの販売部長をすることになったんだ。

☆：まあ，それは大きなチャンスね，トム。いつ出発するの？

★：来月だよ。でも，仕事を始める前にアメリカで２週間の休暇を取るんだ。

☆：まあ，それくらいしたって構わないわよ。あなたはここで抜群の業績を上げたのだから。

質問：女性は男性の異動について何と言っているか。

1 良い機会である。　**2** 彼は東京に残るべきだ。

3 ロサンゼルスは素晴らしい都市だ。　**4** 悪いタイミングに来る。

解説　男性のロサンゼルスへの異動の話を聞いた女性は，Oh, that's a great break と言っている。この break は口語で「チャンス，機会」という意味で，正解の **1** では opportunity と言い換えている。

No. 9 [解答] 2

○：Hello, Mr. Anderson? This is Dry Spell Cleaners, and I'm calling about a suit you dropped off with us this morning. There appears to be a stain on the left sleeve that we can't guarantee will come out with standard cleaning.

★：I see.

○：If you like, we can try some heavy-duty remover for no extra charge, but that would take extra time.

★：So, it wouldn't be done by Saturday?

○：I'm afraid so. Tuesday at the earliest.

★：OK, well, let's just try the regular cleaning. I have to go to a friend's wedding on Sunday.

Question：What does the woman offer to do?

○：もしもし，アンダーソンさんですか？　こちらドライ・スペル・クリーニング店で，お客さまが今朝当店に預けられたスーツについて電話しています。左の袖に，標準のクリーニングで落ちるかどうか保証しかねる染みがあるようです。

★：そうですか。

○：ご希望なら，追加料金なしで強力洗剤を試すこともできますが，追加で時間がかかります。

★：ということは，土曜日までに仕上がらないですよね？

○：あいにくですが，そうです。早くて火曜日になります。

★：わかりました，じゃあ，通常のクリーニングで試してください。日曜日に友達の結婚式に行かなければならないのです。

質問：女性は何をすると申し出ているか。

1 クリーニングの代金を返金する。　　　　**2** 追加サービスを提供する。
3 男性のスーツを早めに返却する。　　　　**4** 日曜日までに作業を終える。

[解説]　クリーニング店の女性スタッフはスーツの汚れについて，we can try some heavy-duty remover ... の部分で追加料金なしで強力洗剤を試すことを提案している。これをadditional serviceと表した**2**が正解。

No. 10 [解答] 3

○：Good morning. U.K. Travel Services. Can I help you?

★：Good morning. This is Terry Rogers, concierge of the London East Piccadilly Hotel.

○：Hello, Mr. Rogers.

★：I'd like to book one open round-trip flight for one of our guests, Ms. Tanaka, from London to Narita, please?

○：Yes, sir. When does she want to depart?

★：On August 29th.

○：There are two British Airways flights from London on August 29th. At 10:30 a.m. and at 2:30 p.m.

★：The afternoon would be fine.

Question：What is Mr. Rogers doing?

○：おはようございます。U.K.トラベルサービスです。ご用件をどうぞ。

★：おはようございます。ロンドン・イースト・ピカデリー・ホテル接客係のテリー・ロジャーズと申します。

○：ロジャーズさまですね。

★：当ホテルのお客さまのお１人であるタナカさまのために，ロンドンから成田まで往復のオープンチケットを１枚予約したいのですが。

○：かしこまりました。お客さまはいつのご出発をご希望ですか。

★：８月29日です。

○：８月29日ロンドン発ですと，ブリティッシュ・エアウェイズの便が２便ございます。午前10時30分と午後２時30分です。

★：午後の便で結構です。

質問：ロジャーズさんは何をしているのか。

1 ホテルの部屋を予約している。　　　　**2** 自分の飛行機をキャンセルしている。
3 飛行機を予約している。　　　　　　　**4** お客に連絡を取っている。

[解説]　旅行会社のスタッフとホテルのスタッフとの電話の会話。ロジャーズさんはI'd like to book one open round-trip flight for one of our guests ... と言って，宿泊客のために飛行機の予約をしているので，**3**が正解。

No. 11　解答　1

☆：Congratulations on your promotion, Stan.

★：Well, thanks, but I'm not so sure I'm ready for this.

☆：Oh come on, you're perfect for the senior marketing position! Everyone wanted you to get the job.

★：Everyone except me, maybe.

☆：I don't get it. You're moving up, and you're unhappy?

★：Not unhappy. Just nervous, I guess. I'll be happy to lead the team, but it comes with a lot of pressure and responsibility. Plus I won't get to work with you guys every day like before.

Question：What does the man say about his new position?

☆：昇進おめでとう，スタン。

★：えー，ありがとう。でも，準備ができているか自信がないよ。

☆：あら，大丈夫よ，あなたはマーケティングの上級職に最適よ。みんなあなたがその職に就くことを望んでいたわ。

★：僕以外のみんながかもね。

☆：どういうこと？　出世しているのに不満なの？

★：不満じゃないよ。神経質になっているだけだと思う。喜んでチームを率いるけど，相当なプレッシャーと責任が伴うからね。それに，これまでのように毎日君たちと仕事ができなくなる。

質問：男性は新しい役職について何と言っているか。

1 きつい仕事になりそうである。	**2** 彼は望んだ仕事を得られなかった。
3 彼は同僚がいなくなる。	**4** 彼のチームによって選ばれたのではない。

解説　男性は新しい職について神経質になっている理由として，..., but it comes with a lot of pressure and responsibility と言っており，これを demanding「(仕事などが) きつい，骨の折れる」と表した**1**が正解。

No. 12　解答　1

☆：What did you think of the exams, Robert? I thought they were really easy.

★：Maybe they were for you, but they were a nightmare for me.

☆：Oh, I'm sure you did better than you think.

★：No, I'm pretty certain I failed politics and history and I'll be lucky to get a passing grade in German.

☆：Come on. You say that after all your exams, and then it always turns out better than you think.

Question：What does the woman imply?

☆：ロバート，試験をどう思った？ 私はすごく簡単だったと思ったけど。

★：君にはそうかもしれないけど，僕には悪夢だったよ。

☆：あら，自分で思うよりよくできているはずよ。

★：いや，確実に政治学と歴史は落としたね。それにドイツ語は合格点をもらえたらもうけものだよ。

☆：大丈夫よ。あなたは試験が終わるたびにそう言って，結局いつも思ってるよりいい結果になるじゃない。

質問：女性は何をほのめかしているか。

1 男性は過度に悲観的になっている。	**2** 男性は彼女より良い結果を出した。
3 彼女は試験が難しいと思った。	**4** 彼女は男性が次回もっと良い結果を出すよう手伝う。

解説　女性は試験の結果について，I'm sure you did better than you think や it always turns out better than you think などと言って，男性の悲観的な発言を繰り返し否定している。

(A)

Giraffes' Sleep

Sleep is an essential part of life for all animals. However, how much sleep each species of animal needs is different. Generally, plant-eating species sleep less than meat-eaters. This is because the amount of calories they can get from their food is small. Plant-eaters, therefore, need to eat a lot more than meat-eaters, and so in order to get enough energy, they take longer to eat. This is particularly true for giraffes, which are one of the largest mammals on land.

Giraffes are rarely seen sleeping in the wild. Until the 1950s, researchers believed that giraffes did not sleep at all. Scientists later found that adult giraffes often rest standing up, in a state of half-sleep. In the 1970s, it was discovered that giraffes only slept about 30 minutes a day in total, with each sleep cycle being as short as a few minutes. When giraffes lie down to sleep, it is difficult for them to get up again. Their minimized sleep helps giraffes survive attacks from lions and other predators.

Questions

No.13 Why do plant-eating animals sleep less?

No.14 What is one thing researchers found out recently?

キリンの睡眠

睡眠はあらゆる動物にとって生活の本質的な部分である。しかし，どれくらいの睡眠を必要とするかは動物の種によって異なる。一般に，草食動物は肉食動物よりも睡眠が短い。これは，食べ物から得られるカロリー量が少ないためである。したがって，草食動物は肉食動物よりもはるかにたくさん食べる必要があるので，十分なエネルギーを得るためには草食動物は食べるのにより多くの時間がかかる。これは特に，陸上で最も大きい哺乳類の1つであるキリンに当てはまる。

キリンが野生で眠っているのはめったに見られない。1950年代まで，研究者たちは，キリンはまったく眠らないものだと信じていた。科学者たちは後に，大人のキリンがしばしば半睡眠の状態で立ったまま休むことを発見した。1970年代になると，キリンは1日に合計30分ほどしか眠らず，それぞれの睡眠サイクルはたった数分であることがわかった。キリンは眠るために横になると，再び起き上がるのが困難である。睡眠が最小限に抑えられていることが，キリンがライオンやほかの捕食者からの攻撃を生き延びる助けになっている。

No. 13 解答 1

「なぜ草食動物はあまり眠らないのか」

1 食べるのにより多くの時間が必要である。

2 肉食動物よりもよくカロリーを処理する。

3 キリンの例に倣っている。

4 目が覚めている状態よりも眠っている状態の方がより多くのエネルギーを使う。

解説 草食動物について，Plant-eaters, therefore, need to eat a lot more ... they take longer to eat.「草食動物は十分なエネルギーを得るために食べるのにより多くの時間がかかる」と言っていることから，**1**が正解。

No. 14 解答 3

「最近研究者たちが知ったことの1つは何か」

1 キリンはまったく睡眠を必要としない。　　**2** キリンは立ったままでしか眠れない。

3 キリンは1日30分ほどしか眠らない。　　**4** キリンは攻撃を逃れるために素早く起き上がれる。

解説 科学者の発見に関する内容の中で，giraffes only slept about 30 minutes a day in total の部分と**3**が一致する。30 minutes を選択肢では half an hour に言い換えている。

(B)

Go-Karts Going Strong

Go-karts are often seen as child's play, but karting is fast becoming the proving grounds for race car professionals. The current leaders in Formula One drivers' championships, Lewis Hamilton and Fernando Alonso, started out racing go-karts, as did the great majority of today's Formula One racers. Thus, karting has become a must for youngsters aspiring to become professional racers.

Furthermore, as race drivers have become national heroes, karting has caught on in a big way in their respective countries. When Germany's Michael Schumacher won the first of his seven Formula One championship titles in 1994, karting in Germany became very popular. Also, in Spain, Fernando Alonso boosted karting by winning his world championships. The karts themselves have evolved into highly efficient machines, vastly different from the primitive karts with lawn mower engines in the 1950s and 60s. Karts for 12-year-old racers now reach speeds of 80 kilometers an hour. And joining a national championship karting season can cost over $30,000, which is certainly not kid's money.

Questions

No.15 What does the speaker say about karting?

No.16 What has helped to stimulate interest in karting in some countries?

ゴーカート，強力になる

ゴーカートはしばしば子供の遊びと見られるが，ゴーカート競走はプロのカーレーサーの能力を試す場に急速になりつつある。現在F1ドライバーの優勝争いをリードするルイス・ハミルトンとフェルナンド・アロンソは，今日の F1 レーサーの大部分がそうであったように，ゴーカートのレースからスタートした。こうして，ゴーカートはプロのレーサーになることを熱望する若者にとって不可欠のものとなった。

さらに，レース・ドライバーが国民的なヒーローになるにつれ，ゴーカートもそれぞれの国で大いに人気となっている。ドイツのミハエル・シューマッハーが 7 回獲得した F1優勝タイトルの最初の1つを1994年に取ったとき，ドイツではゴーカート競走がとても人気となった。またスペインでは，フェルナンド・アロンソが世界チャンピオンになることで，ゴーカート競走を盛り上げた。カートそのものも高性能なマシンに進化しており，1950年代と60年代の，芝刈り機のエンジンを付けた原始的なカートとはほとんど別物である。12歳のレーサー用のゴーカートは今や時速80キロに達する。そしてカートの全国選手権シーズンに参戦するには 3 万ドル以上の費用がかかるが，これは間違いなく子供の出せる金額ではない。

No. 15 解答 **3**

「話者はゴーカート競走について何と言っているか」

1 子供にとって危険になり過ぎた。　　**2** 長い間あまり変わっていない。

3 将来のプロレーサーにとって非常に重要である。　　**4** できる国があまりに少ない。

解説 karting has become a must for youngsters aspiring to become professional racers と言っているので正解は**3**。a must「必要不可欠なもの」を選択肢では vital と表している。

No. 16 解答 **1**

「いくつかの国でゴーカート競走への関心を高めるのに役立ったものは何か」

1 国民的ヒーローになるプロレーサー。　　**2** 大金を稼ぐゴーカート競争の優勝者たち。

3 手頃な価格になりつつあるカート。　　**4** プロスポーツになりつつあるゴーカート競争。

解説 後半に as race drivers have become national heroes, karting has caught on in a big way in their respective countries とあり，続けてヒーローの例としてドイツのシューマッハーやスペインのアロンソが紹介されている。**1**が正解で，caught on in a big way を質問文では stimulate interest と表している。

(C)

Origin of Flea Markets

A flea market is a type of bazaar where ordinary people gather and sell their goods. How did flea markets start? A number of historians believe it came from an early market in Paris, France, called *marché aux puces*, which means "market of fleas" in English. This market was first opened in 1885. It is said that people back then thought that the clothes and furniture put out for sale on the street had fleas, a type of insect that feeds on blood.

This *marché aux puces* in Paris still continues today as the Saint-Ouen flea market. The flea market is the largest of its kind in the world, with more than a dozen smaller markets in an area of 7 hectares. More than 1,700 merchants open their shops that sell antiques, second-hand products, and other interesting finds. It is not only a place for buying items out of the ordinary, but a fun attraction for both tourists and locals.

Questions

No.17　What is one theory about the beginning of flea markets?

No.18　What do we learn about the Saint-Ouen flea market?

のみの市の起源

　のみの市は，一般の人々が集まって品物を売る一種のバザーである。のみの市はどのように始まったのだろうか。多くの歴史家は，それは，英語で「ノミの市場」を意味するマルシェ・オ・プースと呼ばれるフランスのパリの初期の市場に由来すると信じている。この市場は1885年に最初に開かれた。当時，人々は路上で売られていた衣服と家具に，血を吸う種類の虫であるノミがいたと思っていたと言われている。

　このパリのマルシェ・オ・プースは今日でもサン・トゥアンののみの市として続いている。このののみの市は，7ヘクタールの敷地に12を超える小規模市場があり，同種のもので世界最大である。骨董品{こっとう}や中古品，その他の興味深い掘り出し物を売る1,700以上の業者が店舗を出す。それは一風変わった品物を買うための場所であるだけでなく，観光客と地元民の両方にとって楽しいアトラクションである。

No. 17　解答　**1**

「のみの市の始まりに関する1つの説は何か」

1 人々が路上の市場の品物にはノミがいると思っていた。

2 特定の売り手が市場でノミを売り始めた。

3 売り手は「ノミ」という名前の街で品物を売り始めた。

4 人々がノミから血を採取した市場に由来する。

解説　people back then thought that the clothes and furniture put out for sale on the street had fleas の部分から，**1** が適切。clothes and furniture を抽象的に items と表している。

No. 18　解答　**3**

「サン・トゥアンののみの市について何がわかるか」

1 フランスの骨董品を特徴とする。　　**2** 当初の市場よりも小さい。

3 多数の小規模市場から成る。　　**4** 主に裕福な人々を対象としている。

解説　サン・トゥアンののみの市について with more than a dozen smaller markets in an area of 7 hectares と説明している。**3** が正解で，more than a dozen を multiple に言い換えている。

(D)

The Mere Exposure Effect

Scientists have long known the effect of exposure on how much you like something called "the mere exposure effect." For example, when you listen to a new song for the first time, you may think it's just OK, but after listening to it a couple of times, you may come to like it more. The more you are exposed to something, the more you tend to like it.

This has been effectively used in businesses. Big brands rarely change their logos and many video games have been developed based on popular movies or other famous themes. Furthermore, many experiments have found that familiarity attracts people and makes customers choose something that is familiar to them over something new. However, this effect was found to have a limit in a recent study by psychologist Robert Bornstein. He discovered that after a certain number of exposures to a certain thing, people can get "sick" of seeing it.

Questions

No.19 Based on the mere exposure effect, how do people come to like a new song?

No.20 What is one example of the use of the mere exposure effect in business?

単純接触効果

科学者は以前から，「単純接触効果」と呼ばれる，ものがどれだけ好きかに関する接触効果を知っていた。例えば，初めて新しい歌を聞いたときはその歌をまあまあだと思うかもしれないが，数回聞いた後はもっと好きになるかもしれない。何かにさらされるほど，それが好きになる傾向がある。

これはビジネスにおいて効果的に利用されている。有名ブランドがロゴを変えることはめったになく，多くのビデオゲームは人気のある映画やほかの有名なテーマに基づいて開発されている。さらに，多くの実験によると，なじみのあることが人々を引き付け，客にとって新しいものよりもなじみのあるものを選ばせることがわかった。しかし，心理学者のロバート・ボーンスタインによる最近の研究では，この効果には限界があることがわかった。彼は，特定のものに一定の回数さらされた後，人々はそれを見ることに「うんざり」する可能性があることを発見した。

No. 19 解答 4

「単純接触効果に基づくと，人々はどのようにして新しい歌を好きになるか」

1 ほかの似たような歌を聞くことによって。　　**2** しばらくの間それを聞かないことによって。

3 それが好きだとほかの人に言うことによって。　　**4** それを何回か聞くことによって。

解説　新しい歌について，after listening to it a couple of times, you may come to like it more と言っている。このit は new song のことなので，**4**が正解。

No. 20 解答 2

「ビジネスにおける単純接触効果の利用の一例は何か」

1 企業は広告の効果を最大化するためにロゴを変更することがよくある。

2 よく知られているテーマが製品に組み込まれる。

3 ほとんどの企業は有名人が薦める製品を売る。

4 店が客を心地よくするためにさまざまな種類の音楽をかける。

解説　ビジネスでの使われ方については，... many video games have been developed based on ... other famous themes の部分から，**2**が正解。video games を選択肢では抽象的に products と表している。

(E)

Tschäggättä

In the valley of Lötschental in Switzerland, fearful creatures covered in fur roam the streets on a winter night every year. These creatures, which are actually humans wearing scary, wooden masks and dressed in animal furs, are called *Tschäggättä*. How the tradition of *Tschäggättä* came to be is still a mystery. Some believe that it started out as a ritual to chase winter away. Others suspect that *Tschäggättä* masks were made and used to disguise poor robbers when they stole from the rich. Anthropologist Thomas Antonietti explains that young unmarried men became *Tschäggättä* to meet young women.

Today, both men and women, married or unmarried, and even children, participate in the *Tschäggättä* carnival. The carnival became more regulated as it attracted more tourists. Now there are parades, parties, and contests for *Tschäggättä* costumes. *Tschäggättä* still try to scare onlookers. Despite the changes *Tschäggättä* have gone through in recent decades, the tradition still lives on.

Questions

No.21　What is one thing we learn about *Tschäggättä*?

No.22　What characterizes modern *Tschäggättä* events?

チェゲッテ

　スイスのレッチェンタールの谷では，毎年冬の夜，毛皮で覆われた恐ろしい生き物が通りを歩き回る。この生き物は，実際には恐ろしい木製の面を着け，動物の毛皮に身を包んだ人間で，チェゲッテと呼ばれている。チェゲッテの伝統がどのように始まったかはいまだに謎である。冬を追い払う儀式として始まったと信じる人もいる。チェゲッテの面は，貧しい強盗が金持ちから物を盗むときの変装用に作られ使用されたのだろうと見る人もいる。人類学者のトーマス・アントニエッティは，未婚の若い男性が若い女性と出会うためにチェゲッテになったと説明する。

　今日，男女とも，既婚であれ未婚であれ，そして子供でさえも，チェゲッテのカーニバルに参加する。カーニバルは，より多くの観光客を引き付けるにつれ，より規制されるようになった。今では，チェゲッテの衣装のパレード，パーティー，そしてコンテストもある。チェゲッテは今でも見物人を怖がらせようとする。チェゲッテが過去数十年で変化してきたにもかかわらず，その伝統は今もなお続いている。

No. 21　解答　**2**

「チェゲッテについてわかることの1つは何か」

1 それは谷に住む神話上の生き物である。

2 それは面と動物の毛皮を身に着けた人である。

3 それは金持ちから物を盗む強盗グループである。

4 それは子供を怖がらせることしかしない若い男である。

解説　チェゲッテの説明の中で，..., which are actually humans wearing scary, wooden masks and dressed in animal furs の部分から，**2** が正解。チェゲッテは伝統（tradition）であって神話ではないので **1** は不適。

No. 22　解答　**3**

「現代のチェゲッテのイベントにはどんな特徴があるか」

1 夫婦だけが参加できる。　　　　**2** スイスの誕生を祝う。

3 参加者が伝統的な衣装を着て楽しむ。　　**4** 衣装はもはや怖いものではない。

解説　チェゲッテのカーニバルについて「チェゲッテの衣装のパレード，パーティー，そしてコンテストもある」と言っており，これを抽象的に have fun in the traditional costume と表した **3** が正解。traditional costume はチェゲッテの衣装のこと。

(F)

The Stress in Our Lives

We all feel stressed at certain times of our lives, and generally stress has received a bad name. However, stress is natural to humans and has acted as a survival tool to help us deal with new and even dangerous situations. It increases our alertness, effectiveness, and speed of response, such as when we rapidly step on the brakes of our cars to avoid hitting another car. Stress is actually good for us if it is temporary, infrequent and if we have time to recover from it.

However, it becomes damaging when it lasts for a long time, causing our bodies to "burn out." People who experience large amounts of stress over extended periods are often not aware of its symptoms, so they do not know if they are experiencing normal or unhealthy levels of it. Many who are stressed are reluctant to admit they are suffering from it, because there is a common but wrong assumption in modern society that strong people should be able to put up with large amounts of stress.

Questions

No.23　What does the speaker say about stress?

No.24　What is one characteristic of people mentioned who suffer from high levels of stress for a long time?

生活の中のストレス

われわれは皆，生活の何らかのときにストレスを感じる。そして，ストレスは一般に悪評を受けてきた。しかし，ストレスは人間にとって生まれつきのものであり，われわれが新たな状況や危険な状況にすら対処するのを助けてくれる，生き残るための道具としての役割を果たしてきた。ストレスは，例えばほかの車との衝突を避けるために車のブレーキを素早く踏むときのように，われわれの警戒心，有効性，反応の速度を増してくれる。ストレスは実際のところ，一時的でめったに起こらず，回復する時間があるならば，われわれにとって良いものである。

しかし，それが長い間続くと有害なものとなり，われわれの体を「燃え尽き」させる原因となる。長期にわたり大きなストレスを経験する人はしばしばその兆候に気が付かないので，自分が通常レベルのストレスを経験しているのか，それとも不健康なレベルのストレスを経験しているのかわからない。ストレスを受けている人の多くは自分がそれに苦しんでいることを認めたがらないが，それは，強い人間は大量のストレスに耐えられるはずであるという一般的な，しかし誤った考えが現代社会にあるからである。

No. 23　解答　**1**

「話者はストレスについて何と言っているか」

1 少しのストレスは実際は健康的である。　　**2** ストレスは自然に有害になる。

3 強い人はより多くのストレスに対処できる。　**4** ストレスは人間の体の自然な部分ではない。

解説　放送の中ほどで Stress is actually good for us if it is temporary, infrequent ... と言っている。**1** が正解で，if 以下の内容を a little stress，good を healthy と言い換えている。

No. 24　解答　**1**

「ここで言及されている，高いレベルのストレスを長い間受ける人の特徴の1つは何か」

1 彼らはストレスの兆候を認識し損なうことが多い。

2 彼らは頻繁にそれについてほかの人に不満を言う。

3 彼らは実際，ストレス中毒になることがある。

4 彼らはより効率良くストレスに対応するようになるかもしれない。

解説　高いレベルのストレスを長い間受けている人については，後半で People who experience large amounts of stress over extended periods are often not aware of its symptoms と言っている。**1** が正解で，are often not aware of its symptoms を often fail to recognize signs と言い換えている。

(G) No. 25 解答 **2**

> This area has quite a few coffee shops. For example, Mark's Café down on Portner Road. Young folks love it because it has a little stage area, with famous DJs and live music by local bands. Or there's O'Toole's Coffee in the business district. Executives occasionally bring their laptops and work there over their Wi-Fi system, so it's pretty quiet and relaxed. On Eleanor Avenue there's Margaret's Café, which has become a popular spot for young people to hang out. It's right next to the library, which has free Internet access and would be perfect for taking a break, but both will be closing in 30 minutes.

状況：あなたは休暇中で，にぎやかな観光地を散策している。あなたはインターネットにアクセスでき，騒がし過ぎない場所で数時間休憩を取りたいと思っている。あなたは案内所に立ち寄り，助言を求める。

質問：あなたはどの場所を選ぶべきか。

この地域にはかなりたくさんのコーヒー店があります。例えば，ポートナー通りのマークズ・カフェです。小さなステージがあり，有名なDJがいて地元のバンドによるライブ演奏もあるので，若者たちはそこが大好きです。もしくは，ビジネス地区にオトゥールズ・コーヒーがあります。会社の重役たちが時々自分のノートパソコンを持ち込み，そこでWi-Fiシステムを介して仕事をしているので，とても静かでくつろげます。エレノア通りにはマーガレット・カフェがあり，若者が集まる人気スポットとなっています。そこは図書館のすぐ隣ですが，図書館には無料のインターネットアクセスがあり，休憩には最適でしょうが，どちらも30分後に閉まります。

1 ポートナー通りのマークズ・カフェ。　　**2** ビジネス地区のオトゥールズ・コーヒー。
3 エレノア通りのマーガレット・カフェ。　　**4** エレノア通りの図書館。

解説 「インターネットが使える」「騒がし過ぎない」「数時間」のすべての条件を満たすのは，ビジネス地区にあるO'Toole's Coffeeである。Mark's Caféは音楽でにぎやかな場所だと推測されるので不適。Margaret's Caféと図書館は30分後に閉まるので不適。

(H) No. 26 解答 **3**

> Welcome students. To register for spring semester classes, please follow these procedures. First, go to the Registration Office on the second floor of the Administration Building and hand in your Course Selection Form. Next, proceed to the Finance Office on the third floor and pay your fees. All fees must be paid in full at the time of registration. Finally, proceed to Steinbeck Library, which is just across the road. Go first to the photograph area to have your photograph taken for your Student Identification Card. Then, apply for a library card at the main desk. You may pick up your Student ID Card tomorrow at Hancock Student Union.

状況：あなたは大学のオリエンテーションに参加している。あなたは次の指示を聞く。

質問：写真を撮ってもらうにはあなたはどこへ行くべきか。

学生の皆さん，ようこそ。春学期の履修登録をするには，以下の手続きに従ってください。最初に，管理棟2階の登録課まで行き，履修科目選択用紙を提出してください。次に，3階の会計課に行って授業料を支払います。授業料はすべて登録時に全額納入されなければなりません。最後に，道路を隔てて真向かいにあるスタインベック図書館に行ってください。最初に写真コーナーに行き，学生証用の写真を撮ってください。それから事務カウンターで図書カードを申請してください。学生証は明日，ハンコック学生会館で受け取れます。

1 管理棟へ。　　　　　　　　　**2** ハンコック学生会館へ。
3 スタインベック図書館へ。　　**4** 登録課へ。

解説 写真を撮る場所については，Finally, proceed to Steinbeck Libraryの後，Go first to the photograph area to have your photograph takenと説明している。よって，行くべき場所として**3**が正解。

Day 7

(I) *No. 27* 解答 **3**

Hello, this is Frank Markowski at Heaver Vacuum. Just to let you know, the vacuum we'd talked about on the phone last week arrived here today, along with its unlimited warranty certificate. We've inspected it, and because it's a slightly older model, we'll need to send it to another of our repair centers, which will take around one month. If you'd prefer we not repair it, please give us a call within the next three days, and we'll send it back to you free of charge, or we can dispose of it for you. Otherwise, we'll send it to be repaired at our other center.

状況：あなたは修理のために掃除機を送った。2週間以内に修理できない場合は処分したいと思っている。あなたはメーカーからボイスメールを受け取る。

質問：あなたは何をすべきか。

もしもし，ヒーバー・バキューム社のフランク・マルコフスキです。お客さまにお知らせですが，先週電話でお話しした掃除機が，無制限保証書と一緒に本日こちらに届きました。弊社で検査しましたが，少々古いモデルのため，別の修理センターに送る必要があり，およそ1カ月かかります。もし弊社での修理を望まれない場合，3日以内にお電話くだされば，無料でお客さまに返送するか，お客さまに代わって処分することもできます。お電話がなければ，修理のためほかのセンターに送ります。

1 保証書を送る。   **2** 工場へ製品を取りに行く。
3 3日以内にメーカーに電話する。   **4** 修理が終わるのを待つ。

解説　状況に「2週間以内に修理できない場合は処分したい」とあり，別の修理センターに送ると1カ月かかるため，それを避ける必要がある。If you'd prefer we not repair it, please give us a call within the next three days から，**3**が正解。

(J) *No. 28* 解答 **2**

Thank you for calling our service desk. At Zossley Bank, our goal is to make every transaction a plus. To help direct your call, please choose from the following options. For information on an existing account, or to open a new account, press one. For questions regarding your current balance or about your monthly balance statements, press two. To learn more about credit options, or for questions about home loans, car loans, student loans, or other loans, press three. To hear these options again, press four. Or, stay on the line and the next available customer service representative will assist you.

状況：あなたは銀行口座の月次明細書に50ドルのサービス料が記載されていることに気付く。あなたはそれが何に対するものかわからない。あなたは銀行の顧客サービスホットラインに電話をする。

質問：あなたは何番を押すべきか。

サービスデスクにお電話いただきありがとうございます。ゾスリー銀行では，すべての取引をプラスに変えることを目標としています。頂いたお電話を転送するため，次のオプションから選択してください。既存の口座に関する情報，または新しい口座の開設には，1を押してください。お客さまの現在の残高や毎月の残高明細書に関する質問については，2を押してください。クレジットのオプションの詳細について知りたい場合，あるいは住宅ローン，自動車ローン，学生ローン，その他のローンに関するご質問については，3を押してください。これらのオプションをもう一度お聞きになりたい場合は，4を押してください。もしくは，電話を切らずにお待ちいただくと，次に空いた顧客サービス担当者が対応いたします。

1 1番。   **2** 2番。   **3** 3番。   **4** 4番。

解説　状況から，銀行口座の明細書に不明な項目があることを押さえる。順に聞いていくと，For questions ... about your monthly balance statements, press two. の部分に該当するので，**2**が正解。

(K) No. 29 解答 3

Your teeth are in fairly good shape. I'm glad to hear that you've been brushing regularly and flossing your teeth. However, the x-rays show that you have a slight cavity in one of your molars, so we'll need to fill that during your next appointment. I see some scarring on your gums, which shows that you vigorously brush your teeth with a hard-bristle toothbrush. You'll want to purchase a softer brush and use that for the next few weeks, and let me see if the scarring goes away by your next appointment, which is on May 17th. I'll see you then.

状況：あなたは健診を受けるために歯科医院にいる。健診の後，あなたは歯科医の説明を聞いている。

質問：あなたは次の予約の前に何をすべきか。

歯はかなり良い状態です。規則正しく歯磨きとフロスをしてきたと伺って私もうれしいですよ。しかし，レントゲンで見ると，臼歯の1本に小さな穴があるので，次の予約の際にそこを詰める必要があります。歯茎に少し傷跡が見えますが，硬い毛の歯ブラシで強く歯磨きをしているからですね。もう少し柔らかい歯ブラシを買って数週間使っていただき，次の予約の5月17日までに傷が消えているかどうか見せてください。では，また。

1 歯をもっとしっかりと磨く。　　　　　　　　　**2** デンタルフロスを購入する。

3 より柔らかい歯ブラシを買う。　　　　　　　　**4** 歯のレントゲンを撮る。

解説　予約前にすべきことは，後半の You'll want to purchase a softer brush ... by your next appointment, ... の部分にヒントがある。You'll want to ... は「…してください」という遠回しな指示。

Day 7

MEMO

MEMO

MEMO

MEMO